PLATS DU JOUR

the girl & the fig's
Journey Through the Seasons
in Wine Country

Sondra Bernstein

Recipe Development
by John Toulze

Photography by
Steven Krause

Styling & Production by
**Lauren Benward Krause
Brooklyn Studio West**

with
Laura Holmes Haddad

With love, really big hugs, and gratitude to my family. They are always there with their unconditional love, support, and friendship; it means more than words can express.

Also from Sondra Bernstein
the girl & the fig Cookbook
More than 100 Recipes from the Acclaimed California Wine Country Restaurant

the girl & the fig, LLC
110 West Spain Street
Sonoma, California 95476
www.thegirlandthefig.com

Text copyright © 2011 by Sondra Bernstein
All photographs copyright © 2011 Steven Krause/Brooklyn Studio West
     with the exception of author photograph (flap) copyright © 2010 In Her Image Photography, www.inherimagephoto.com
     and group shot (front and back inside cover) copyright © 2011 Chris Berggren, Custom Image Sonoma
All rights reserved, including the right of reproduction in whole or in part in any form.

For information about special discounts for bulk purchases, please contact Special Sales
at 1-866-420-3447 x 7 or figstore@thegirlandthefig.com.

Book Design by Sondra Bernstein
Printed in China through Four Colour Print Group, Louisville, Kentucky

First printed in 2011
10 9 8 7 6 5 4 3 2 1

Library of Congress Cataloging-in-Publication Data is available.
Bernstein, Sondra.
Plats du Jour: the girl & the fig's Journey Through the Seasons in Wine Country/Sondra Bernstein;
Recipe Development by John Toulze.

Library of Congress Control Number: 2011934599

ISBN-13   978-0-615-51364-5
ISBN-10   0-6155-1364-6

a thank you note

My gratitude runs deep to those who have been a part of the girl & the fig, past and present. Running a restaurant is never about just one person. There are hundreds, even thousands, of people that touch the girl & the fig on a regular basis. Every single one of them has contributed to our success.

I often compare my life to that of a spider web (no, I am not all tangled up). I am connected by fine lines that intersect, stop and grow. I am the spider in the middle, and with one line I connect with the staff, another with the guest, another with our delivery drivers, our farmers, our trash men, our winemakers, our gardeners, and on and on. Our success demands that we are all connected together, and when one strand breaks and disconnects from the rest, it needs to be woven back together.

Our staff is incredible, each of them with their special talents and their own abilities to make their own connections with their guests, their co-workers, the products and the atmosphere. I find that I learn from each and every one of them everyday. There are some real outstanding members on the team who are like sparks that ignite the night sky. They are the ones that you want to stay forever, to watch succeed, to be inspired by and see them inspire others. They are the ones who are kind and charitable and they make a difference every day. One of those special people is, of course, my business partner, John. That he still puts up with me after 17+ years is a miracle. With John, I have come to understand the following about us in business: he is black & white while I am shades of grey, but blended together we are a work of art. He is about getting it done, and I am dreaming of the next idea. Somehow, it works for us.

Our guests are world class! They are our extended family. They visit us regularly, tell us when we are doing a good job, and give us a nudge when we need to do better. They are willing to try our experiments and like to call our staff by their names. Though they don't all speak English, we do share the language of FOOD, WINE and SONOMA. Because of this, we understand them.

I took a completely different approach to this book compared to the first. When we found ourselves without a publisher, we were still determined to make this book happen. Over the past few years, self-publishing has become a viable option for any author, and we thought it would create other opportunities that we did not have the first time (creating our own design, selecting paper stock, colors ...).

When writing the first book, I labored over every single word, to be edited and then edited again. This time around, my dear friend and author in her own right and talent, Laura Holmes Haddad assisted me as my Collaborator and was able to put my thoughts to words. She transcribed our long detailed conversations and added her own very special expertise to the book. Our history from the

previous book and a friendship that goes beyond words created magic. With Laura on board, I knew that she would understand my heart and commitment to what I do everyday and help me translate it to you.

Without a publishing house in tow, John reached out to one of his longtime friends Matt, who is in the book publishing business with Unicorn Books & Crafts in Petaluma. Matt has been a gracious, giving and an amazing resource that has been by our side for duration of the process. He certainly gave us the encouragement to make this happen.

Luckily, Lauren and Steven came as a package deal. Their company, Brooklyn Studio West is a full service photography studio. Steven is an incredible photographer as you will see on the pages that follow, and Lauren is a talented stylist and production coordinator. We were barely acquaintances a few years ago when they had requested to photograph some of our food for their growing portfolio. The resulting images were a constant reminder of the hope that someday we would be able to work together on a project like this. Over a year of photographing the seasons, our recipes, raw ingredients, the people, and, of course, our beautiful Sonoma, we have become friends and have worked diligently together to create this incredible book. A year ago, they were just newly engaged, now as we move forward to the printing press they are husband and wife, and we, the girl & the fig CATERS!, had the extreme honor of being able to create their wedding feast at Lauren's beautiful family property, Beltane Ranch.

In the first book, we were armed with binders of recipes that had been written over the years, but this time around John has taken the recipe concepts and reworked them with our new respect for the artisanal methods and farming that we have been learning and practicing. Oh yes, I can't forget the recipe testing, we started our search on Facebook, embracing the technology to gather our team of testers. The Internet truly brings us all together as our recipe testers came from as far as Anchorage, Alaska to Concord, Massachusetts and many places in between. They did a great job, and it was not an easy one, since they were working with the very rough first drafts. Thank you to Lynn, Krista, Lorrie, Diane, Liz, Monica, Serena, Seana, Gillian, Cara, Ron, Jennifer, Susan, Lee, Kristin, Renee, Jane, Karen, Jody, Rick, Susy, Maureen, Rebecah, Elizabeth, Helen and Nancy.

Merrilee - thank you for what seemed as the craziest recipe testing marathon of all time. I really appreciate your efforts, your time and suggestions, especially as busy as you were. I hope you didn't gain too much weight!

A special thank you goes out to my personal assistant, Kimberly, who probably had no idea what she was getting into when she took the job as my assistant. I threw her so many different parts of

the project, and she never gave it a second thought. Kim kept up with all the recipes going out to the testers and made sure they came back on time. She translated the notes, and got them ready to retest - not an easy task for over 25 testers. In between, she worked on fact checking, sourcing, communicated with the proofreaders and the indexer and way too many other things to mention here. Thanks, Kim, but the hard part has yet to come!

Jennifer, our very detail-oriented and very busy HR Director, took the time to give it a thorough once-over, which will guarantee that the grammar will be correct! Thank you Bear!

I can only imagine that the restaurant and catering chefs are happy to see the book completed, knowing that their long days of recipe testing, ordering and recording product, and early morning photo shoots have ended. They were a huge help and definitely made the process a bit easier.

I would be remiss if I didn't thank my whole management and administrative team for keeping everything together while I checked out for this project. Not that I doubted their ability in any way, but I am further convinced that they are all ROCK STARS!

To Stephanie, the cheeriest and best dog walker ever - Sophie, Lucie and I thank you for their walks and gopher-chasing time!

We happen to take our special dining experiences for granted, and in many ways I believe we should. We dine in restaurants for many reasons: to take a break from our routine, to reunite with friends, to tend to business, sometimes for romance, often for hunger, the longing for new experiences and discoveries, and to nourish our soul. Nourishing the soul is probably the trickiest of all. How do we do it? One of the methods to achieving any of the above is to make the little details in the operations seem effortless and almost invisible. You can only achieve that by surrounding yourself with people that want to excel and, especially in the restaurant business, people who are anxious to please.

I really do hope you enjoy this book as much as we all enjoyed making it, but these recipes and a peek at our Sonoma are not a substitute for dining in our restaurants. When guests ask us what the secret ingredient is, the one that makes our food taste so good, my standard response, with feeling, is that we cook with love.

Thank You, Merci & Gracias!

Sondra

contents

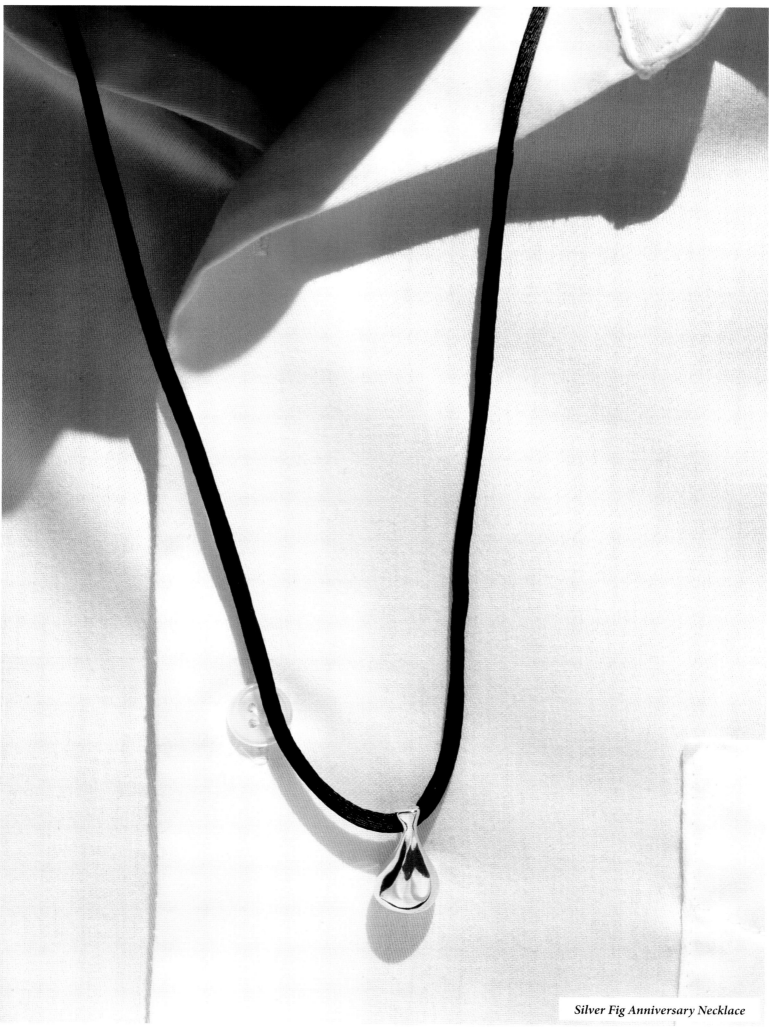

Silver Fig Anniversary Necklace

introduction

On the chalkboard:

PLAT DU JOUR

3 COURSES $34

⬥ ENTRÉE:
salt cod
croquettes

⬥ plat:
chicken paillard

⬥ dessert or fromage

buttermilk
panna cotta
OR
Blue de Basque
& Cyprus grove
Midnight moon

wine flight paired
with the menu
- add $10

ENTRANCE

INTRODUCTION

Change, as they say, is the only absolute, and nothing could be more true in the food and restaurant world. So much has changed for us since our first cookbook was published eight years ago. We've opened two additional restaurants—the fig café & winebar and ESTATE—as well as a catering company. We've started growing our own produce on a local farm, added several new products to our FIGfood line, and we are now pressing our own olive oil and making our own salumi. Our guests have changed, too: diners are more sophisticated than they once were, and the access to ingredients is unparalleled.

Because of this, we are always trying to keep the restaurants fresh and new, and I like to think that we are evolving with the times and the community. We are not reinventing ourselves every year; rather, we're making small adjustments to keep the restaurants current. But the more things change, the more they stay the same, so while we've created dozens of new recipes we've also remained true to the original girl & the fig philosophy and included a few favorites that our regulars go back to again and again. (We could never take the Fig & Arugula Salad, Pernod Steamed Mussels, or Duck Confit off the menu!)

One of the changes we've introduced is the concept of Plats du Jour, a set weekly menu that includes a starter, main course, and dessert or cheese course. We began the Plats du Jour concept as an innovative way to offer our guests a great value utilizing the best of the season. The plat du jour (literally, "plate of the day") is a traditional concept in France dating back to the 1800s, when restaurants served only one meal each day. Each year, we work to create 52 new, three-course seasonal menus to show off the best of what's available in Sonoma County at that time. In the girl & the fig's *Plats du Jour* we've distilled those down to a more manageable 28 menus for the home cook.

As I often say, the Plats du Jour menus are a tour of ingredients through the year. The 28 three-course menus are arranged by season and include a cheese pairing for each menu. Though the menus we've created are set, there is plenty of opportunity for creativity. The menus simply give you a chance to plan ahead for a dinner party or family gathering, and you can mix and match the recipes from various menus according to your taste. All of the recipes serve six people, allowing for a weekend dinner party or a weekday dinner with a day or two of delicious leftovers. This stays true to my philosophy that friends and family should gather as often as possible over a great meal!

While we're devoted to the ingredients and wine from Sonoma, California, the restaurants' recipes and wine lists are influenced by regions around the world. Our travels to Spain, Italy, and France educate and inspire us and bring a global perspective to the restaurants and our approach to food. I like to say that though the girl & the fig is located in Sonoma, it would work just as easily in any wine region in the world. The devotion to seasonality and the respect for the land are universal and reflect the spirit of wine country. The plethora of farmers and year-round access to local produce allow us to create seasonally inspired recipes that embrace casual yet sophisticated wine country cooking. Every dish is a celebration of the local abundance.

Our approach is seasonal wine country eating, which can be adapted to any location with just a few tweaks. Thanks to the resurgence of small family farms and eating locally, virtually everyone has the ability to create their own personal wine country experience using local ingredients. We've worked hard to translate this approach to food for any location to show you that a visit to wine country can continue even after you leave the region. We may use spring strawberries in our strawberry tart but if you have access to crisp local apples, substitute those instead. Substitutions and minor adjustments—swapping walnuts for chestnuts, for example—can produce just as good a meal, and one that allows you to express your individual style and locale.

Eating seasonally may seem restrictive to some people but I think it's the opposite: you get the chance to cook with—and eat—the best fruits and vegetables available. This book reflects my passion for seasonal, country cuisine; "country food with a French passion," has been our guiding principle since the beginning. These are not intimidating restaurant recipes; they use widely available ingredients and are appropriate for both the beginner and more seasoned home cook. Some recipes will be relatively familiar and comfortable while others will challenge and inspire you.

Cheese is an integral part of the girl & the fig experience. In addition to the recipes, each chapter includes further information on seasonal cheeses and cheese pairings. One-third of our restaurant menu is devoted to cheese and we maintain a list of special cheeses. The seasonal cheese menu changes every three weeks and incorporates new finds that we've discovered. We are so passionate about cheese that we built a custom Salon du Fromage in the girl & the fig in 2006. Customers can walk up to the cheese bar and taste a cheese or a FIGfood product (compote, jam, mostarda); I love to see the interaction and the education at these tastings.

Wine lovers won't be disappointed: we are still committed to our award-winning "Rhône-Alone" wine list that features Rhône varietals from around the world. For this book, I have selected an assortment of some of my favorite wines and producers that I have had the pleasure of tasting and would be happy to drink them again and again. I have chosen specific wines for each recipe, but they are only suggestions and ideas for varietal pairing. We've also started making our own wine, Très Bonnes Années, with Jeff Cohn of JC Cellars in Northern California, which has deepened our appreciation for both the grape-growing and winemaking processes.

In the Nibbles section that kicks off each chapter, you'll find small bites that are perfect party starters that could make a light meal when served together. Inspired by the tradition of tapas in Spain, antipasti in Italy, and hors d'oeuvres in France, these small bites are meant to be eaten with friends over a glass of wine. These are favorites from our catering menu, so we know they are party-friendly!

Infused cocktails that utilize seasonal fresh fruits and herbs have become a signature item at both the girl & the fig and ESTATE, and each season includes four specialty cocktail recipes incorporating seasonal fruits, vegetables, and herbs. A detailed sidebar gives you the tips and tricks behind these tempting libations.

What keeps our tables full night after night? We really want you to be here! We welcome you into our house when you come to our restaurants. We are constantly striving to make sure people get the best experience, and I hope this book is a reflection of that. I want to give you a taste of the land, take you through the seasons, and celebrate the food, wine, and people in our corner of wine country.

Sondra Bernstein

The Artisanal Larder

Any good cook knows that great food starts with the basics, and a well-stocked pantry is the foundation of any meal. This chapter is devoted to the five groups of ingredients that are an integral part of any wine country table: salumi, bread, olive oil, vinegar, and FIGfood—our own line of vinaigrettes, vinegars, and condiments.

We start off with a primer on salumi, the Italian term for cured meat and what the French call charcuterie. (See page 263 for more details on MANO FORMATE, our housemade salumi production.) No meal is complete without a loaf of bread, and that is certainly true in our restaurant. Here we share the basics of bread baking (including information on the various types of flour), which should convince any home cook to give it a try. Next, we'll walk you through the basics of olive oil, the quintessential wine country ingredient. Olive oil has always been an important component in our dishes, and in 2009 we began making our own oil with a local olive oil company. Vinegar is another favorite ingredient, and last year John began making his own red wine vinegar. You'll be amazed how just a few drops of vinegar can completely transform a dish. Finally, we share the story of our FIGfood, a line of vinaigrettes, vinegars, salts, sauces, jams, compotes, and mostardas that we use in a variety of dishes.

Salumi

One of our newest projects at the restaurant is MANO FORMATE, meaning "hand formed," our housemade salumi. We've served charcuterie on our menu since we first opened and now we are making our own salumi. When we opened ESTATE in 2008, we expanded the cured meat component of our menu concept. With the success and quality of the few items we started to do, we realized that we could produce all of our cured meats for the company. Now we make our own pancetta, prosciutto, sausage, salame, and bacon.

Salumi is a meat product that is air-dried, salted, cooked, smoked, or a combination of all four methods. It's an Italian tradition that dates back thousands of years and was used to preserve meat before the invention of refrigeration. We primarily use pork and beef and we've even tried lamb. We view salumi as a pantry staple simply because of its versatility. You can serve it alongside cheese as an appetizer (or even a meal!) or make it the star ingredient of a sandwich. Salumi adds depth to soups and salads, and a pizza without salumi is really not a pizza at all!

One of the most versatile types of salumi is lonzino, a spice-rubbed cured pork loin we use for sandwiches or on a pizza. If you're passionate about salumi and can commit the time and space at home, you can easily make your own. (For more detailed information on salumi making, see page 263.)

Bread

It's hard to imagine a meal without bread. We love to savor a piece of freshly baked bread slathered with butter or dipped in olive oil, and of course it's the foundation of any memorable sandwich or pizza. We have always served baskets of fresh bread, made by the Basque Boulangerie in Sonoma, at all of our restaurants, but when we opened ESTATE we had the space in our kitchen to finally make some of the bread ourselves. We installed a wood-fired pizza oven that assists in creating a wonderful texture to the crust of our bread.

While it takes only three ingredients to bake a loaf of bread—flour, yeast, and water—baking at home can seem intimidating. But if you measure carefully and practice, you'll be making your own bread at home in no time. (John got plenty of practice making pizza dough with the opening of ESTATE.)

The secrets of great bread are flour and gentle kneading. Flour in particular makes a significant difference in the texture of both bread and pizza dough. Here's a quick primer on flour to help you understand why we are so particular about it:

Flour is made up of proteins, carbohydrates, and in whole-wheat flour, a small amount of fat. Proteins are what bakers care about most. The proteins in wheat are called gluten-forming proteins, and the quantity and quality of these proteins determines how a flour will react in dough forming and baking. A high protein content makes a harder flour, while lower proteins mean a softer flour. In the U.S., the protein content in flour ranges from 5 to 15 percent. Hard flours have protein contents of 12 to 15 percent.

We use different flours for different recipes, based on what works best for us. We find that Italian and Italian-style flours work best for our pizza, so we use "00" unbleached flour from Italy to make our pizza dough. Companies such as Molino Caputo and Molino Pasini have been milling flours in Naples, Italy, for more than 100 years. The "00" designation is an Italian classification—flours are "1", "0", or "00", classified according to how finely ground the flour is and how much of the bran and germ have been removed.

Pasini "00" is used throughout Italy and is considered one of the best "00" flours available. It's milled from winter wheat and has a lower ash content, so it has less bran and wheat germ, etc., which results in a silkier, "whiter" flour that feels almost like talcum powder. This results in a more supple mouthfeel in the pizza.

For our bread, we use a combination of Giusto's flour. Giusto's is a family-owned company in San Francisco that has been milling flour for 70 years. (These flours are available online from various stores; see Sources, page 318.)

Olive Oil

Olive oil is an essential part of our cooking and something we can't live without. It is truly a wine country ingredient and a reflection of the region it is made in, with silvery-green olive trees flourishing throughout the Mediterranean climate of Northern California. Olive oil can be used in a myriad of ways. Sautéing, frying, and even baking are all enhanced by this fragrant oil, and just a drizzle of a high-quality, extra-virgin olive oil can transform a dish.

California has a long history with the olive; trees were planted by the Spanish missionaries at each of the 21 missions they built from San Diego to Sonoma in the late 1700s. By 1885 there was a healthy olive oil industry in the state, but it was put out of business by the less expensive, subsidized European oils. The industry rebounded in the 1970s, and today there are about 25,000 acres of olive trees planted in the state, which in 2009 produced 870,000 gallons of olive oil. A variety of olive trees are planted, including Missions, Manzanillos, and Picholine, but the most common is the Arbequina, a native of Spain. (Several California olive oil producers, including Nan McEvoy of McEvoy Ranch, have imported trees from Tuscany.) Growing olive trees takes patience; the trees don't bear fruit for five to seven years, and each tree produces only about three or four quarts of oil.

We became so enamored with olive oil that we started pressing our own olives for our ESTATE extra-virgin olive oil. For the first few years, Deborah Rogers, owner of The Olive Press in Sonoma, guided us through the process, from making sure our trees were healthy to advising us when to hand-harvest the 25 or so trees on the property. Our first attempt resulted in 6.5 gallons of extra-virgin olive oil from about 750 pounds of olives. Though we aren't able to identify the type of olives on the ESTATE property, we do know that they produce a lovely oil that tastes very green, has a slight minerality, and is velvety smooth.

Living in Sonoma, it's impossible to miss the signs of the olive harvest. Every year the town holds a three-month festival of events called Sonoma Valley Olive Season. The celebration runs December through February, and dozens of local businesses work to promote the olive—and the town—through classes, dinners, and tours and tastings of local olive mills. (There are hotel packages, too!) It's a wonderful time to visit the valley; it's the low season for tourists, and it's a chance to interact with the local producers (chefs, olive oil producers, and winemakers) while enjoying the crisp winter days.

In Northern California, the olive harvest begins in mid-November, with both weather and ripeness determining the exact date. Though some types of olives ripen more quickly than others, the harvesting process is the same around the world. First, the olives are harvested by hand. Nets or tarps are often spread on the ground at the base of the trees to catch the olives, although bruised fruit is not ideal since it can affect the taste and quality of the oil. Machines can also be used to pick the olives, but usually are used only by the large bulk producers. Some California producers pick their olives at two different times and release early and late-harvest oils. The early-harvest oil comes from green, underripe olives, while the late-harvest oils come from sweet, very ripe olives. The difference may be only three or four weeks (mid-November versus mid-December), but the flavor changes drastically.

The harvested olives are washed, deleafed, and crushed. Like wine grapes, it's best to press the olives the same day they are harvested; as the olives sit they can warm up and start to ferment, so 24 hours is the maximum time between picking and pressing.

Next, the olives are crushed into a paste, which is then mixed to allow the oil to seep out of the fruit. There are several methods used to extract the oil from the olive, some artisanal and others that are used by the bigger producers. The most common method is with a high-speed centrifuge, while some smaller, artisan producers still use a stone press. (We make our house olive oil using the commercial method.) Oil from the first pressing of the olives is the best: it has the most flavor and the most health benefits.

Once the oil is collected, it's bottled and ready to use (often called olio nuovo, "new oil") or it is transferred to a stainless steel tank to rest for a couple of months before bottling.

Deborah Rogers - The Olive Press

That's another reason we love local oils; you can buy them within days of pressing, rather than waiting for them to be packed and shipped from overseas.

While extra-virgin olive oil is what most food lovers are familiar with, there are several types of oil. Olive oil is graded according to the process, flavor, and acidity level. Extra-virgin is the highest grade, most sought after oil, and also the most expensive oil. This is the oil to drizzle over dishes or add to salads; the flavors are destroyed if you try to cook with it. In our kitchens, we use a blend of oil, (referred to as "blended oil" throughout our recipes), a combination of three parts canola oil and one part extra-virgin olive oil. You get the flavor of extra-virgin olive oil but the canola oil stands up to high heat.

The flavor and color of olive oil are determined by two factors: the type of olive pressed and the age of the olive. Just like wine, extra-virgin olive oil has many flavor profiles, including peppery, grassy, buttery, bold, and fruity. The color of olive oil can range from a bright green to a deep, buttery yellow. Generally, the green oils have been pressed from olives early in the season, and the yellow oils indicate a pressing later in the season. Acidity levels also determine the flavor and quality of olive oil; the best oils have low acidity levels.

The best way to determine what type of extra-virgin olive oil you prefer is by sipping them straight, just like wine tasting. It may sound strange, but it's a very effective way of understanding the differences. Pour a few tablespoons of olive oil into small glasses or cups, swirl it around, and drink it. You'll soon discover which ones appeal to you. Try a wide variety of oils from different locations, too; it's fun to taste an olive oil from France and notice how different it is from a Tuscan olive oil or one from Greece or California. (For our favorite California producers, see Sources, page 318 to 320.)

Because olive oil labels are often confusing, here is an explanation of the grades as used in Europe.

Extra-virgin olive oil: Extra-virgin oils must be made from the mechanical extraction of olives, be cold pressed, and have no more than 1 percent acidity. They also must have a "perfect taste," a standard determined by the International Olive Oil Council. Though there is no official standard for the state, the California Olive Oil Council was established in 1992 to provide guidelines and education, and they also certify California extra-virgin olive oils.

Virgin olive oil: This is an oil whose acidity level is above the 1 percent mark but is still under 2 percent. It also means that the oil was pressed without any chemicals.

Olive oil: This classification is usually a blend of refined and virgin olive oils.

Storing olive oil: To keep your olive oil fresh, avoid heat, air, light, and age. Bottles shouldn't be older than eighteen months (check the label; there is always a "use by" date or a harvest date), and store it in a dark, cool cupboard. (Do not keep it next to the stove! The heat will destroy the delicate oil.)

Vinegar

Red wine vinegar is another staple in our kitchen. While we love our semi-sweet Fig Balsamic Vinegar, red wine vinegar adds a different kind of tang. We use it for braising, in salads, and as a flavor enhancer. In keeping with our goal to make as much as possible in-house, we began making our own vinegar in 2010. Since we always end up with leftover red wine, John decided to experiment. He bought a used wine barrel from a local winery and a "mother," or starter, online. (The chemical reaction between the mother and the wine produces vinegar.) John added the mother and then began adding leftover wine from the restaurants to the barrel for five months. After letting it sit and age for three months, we decanted about half of it into bottles. Our process now is to add wine for three months and then let it sit for one month, decant, and repeat.

As John notes, because we use high-end, high-quality wine, we end up with a high-quality product. This is a simple way for us to reduce waste while producing something delicious.

Balsamic Vinegar

Balsamic vinegar is another essential ingredient in our restaurants. John and I saw the original balsamic process in Emilia-Romagna, Italy, and it was a life-changing experience. Much like wine, the tradition of making balsamic is very complex and historic. So much tradition, time and labor go into that bottle that sits in the kitchen cupboard. It's incredible that a liquid can be sweet and sour, with hints of vanilla, currants and a bit of oak, and a syrupy texture that coats the palate.

True balsamic vinegar is traditionally made in the districts of Modena and Reggio Emilia in Italy. (You'll see this on the label: "MO" stands for Modena, "RE" for Reggio Emilia.) Only authentic balsamic can carry the label "Aceto Balsamico Tradizionale." while the mass market version is called "Industriale." Each region has its own packaging; balsamic from Modena comes in short, thick glass bottles on a square base, while the Reggio bottle is thinner and taller. Balsamic vinegar has always been a prized condiment in Italy. It has been crafted and enjoyed by nobility, and there is even evidence that balsamic was graded even in the 16th century. It was passed down from generations in families and even given as wedding gifts, but no one sold it until the late 1970s.

Balsamic vinegar starts with must, the fresh juice of local grapes. Trebbiano is the most widely used grape, but a handful of other local varieties are allowed as well. The grapes are crushed and the juice is poured into copper or stainless steel kettles. It's then carefully cooked down over a wood fire until it's reduced to a thick consistency. The cooking time varies according to the flavors the producer is looking for; it can range from 12 to 36 hours. The reduced must is transferred to large wooden barrels where fermentation and acetification begin. Some producers allow the must to remain in these barrels for months, others from two to four years.

When the producer is ready, the must is transferred to the *batteria*, a series of used wooden barrels where the balsamic will age further. Some old vinegar is mixed with the must, and the mixture is transferred to the largest barrel in the series to continue aging. The aging room for balsamic vinegar is called the *acetaia*, and contains barrels of all sizes and ages. Strict guidelines regulate type of wood barrels that are allowed to be used (oak, ash, locust, and mulberry are among the approved woods). The barrels are seasoned before use, and a five- to six-inch hole is cut in each one to allow oxygen to flow into the barrel, which is crucial for the acetification process. The vinegar is transferred to a series of barrels during the aging process, from the largest to the next size down and so on, ending with the smallest barrels (known as the *regina*, or queen). There is no recipe for great balsamic; producers are constantly tasting, blending, and tweaking. The final balsamic is a blend and is usually made in winter because bacteria are less active in the cold weather and the vinegar is at its clearest.

A sample of the final blend is taken to the Consorzio Produttori Aceto Balsamico Tradizionale di Modena to be tasted and scored. A vinegar must score at least 229 out of a total 400 points to be allowed to be sold, and those that do not make the grade are returned to the producer so that they can let the vinegar develop further.

If a producer sells the rejected batch, it is labeled *condimento*. The vinegar that is allowed to be bottled is done so not by the producer but by the Consorzio, and the bottle is then sealed and stamped with the official registration number.

There are different grades of balsamic depending on the region: in Reggio, the first level is "Red Label," while in Modena it is "Vecchio." This means the balsamic has been aged a minimum of 12 years. The second level, "Gold Label" in Reggio and "Extra Vecchio" in Modena, means the balsamic has been aged at least 25 years. In Reggio, balsamic aged a minimum of 18 years is designated "Silver Label." Aged balsamic is well worth the fuss (and expense). The kick of the younger balsamic vinegar is replaced by a syrupy-smooth liquid with deep, intense flavors. There's a reason why aged balsamic can cost $50 an ounce; it's an elixir unlike any other.

If you don't feel like paying $60 or more for a bottle of balsamic, you will be perfectly happy with a bottle labeled *condimento*. Many well-respected Italian producers release delicious balsamic that didn't make the grade. You'll pay between $15 and $50 for a good *condimento*. (Cavalli, Giusti, and Leonardi are labels to look for.) When balsamic vinegar is used in a cooked dish, it should be added just before the dish is removed from the stove so that it has the right amount of time to flavor the food without losing its aroma. However, real balsamic should be treated like the star ingredient it is: we like to drizzle balsamic over platters of vegetables, over certain cheeses, and even ice cream.

Olives

Who would have thought the American palate would make the leap from the mild, boring canned black olive to the green, yellow, and brown cured varieties available today? My love for olives developed in France, nibbling on little green Picholine olives or spearing a fat, black Niçoise in my Tuna Niçoise. Dinner guests at the girl & the fig are welcomed with a small bowl of mixed French olives: Lucques, Picholine, Niçoise, and Nyons. We purchase these in huge tubs and then toss them with lemons, olive oil, and fresh thyme. You will almost always see olives on our cheese platters, as well as in an occasional salad or pizza at ESTATE.

Today, California produces 95 percent of America's olive crop and grows a huge array of olive varieties such as Manzanillo, Mission, Sevillano, Ascolano, and Barouni, among others. Olives can be harvested in early fall when the fruit is green-ripe and contain more oleuropein. Though it is non-toxic, oleuropein a bitter compound that leaves an unpleasant taste in the mouth which in

makes the olives inedible when raw. Left to ripen on the tree into November and December, the olives turn darker and the bitterness decreases, developing a mellow flavor.

Cured olives have become the ubiquitous nibble among American foodies. The key to curing olives is to eliminate the bitterness while preserving their other flavors.

There are four curing methods used: water, brine, dry salt, and lye.

Water curing has the least impact on the flavor of the olive; the olives are soaked for a few weeks and then drained.

Brine curing allows the olives to naturally ferment in a salt solution for several months.

Dry salt curing involves packing olives in salt to draw out the water and oleuropein.

Lye curing means the olives are soaked in an alkali solution and then rinsed in several water baths, cleaned, and finally brined; it's the fastest method and results in mild, buttery olives. This is the method used for the most common black olive, known as the Lindsay olive, as well as for the French Lucques, Italian Cerignola, and Spanish Manzanilla.

One word of caution for those of you who want to cure at home: working with lye can be hazardous—it's a poison if not used properly.

FIGfood

We started our line of girl & the fig food products—what we call FIGfood—in 1999. It was a natural extension of the restaurant, a chance to showcase figs in products that our guests could take home with them to enhance their meals. The compotes, jams, chutney, and mostardas became essential as we started to serve more charcuterie and salumi at ESTATE. (The contrast of sweet jam or chutney and salty cured meat is something no one can resist!) The products complement the Plats du Jour concept, as well. When people stop by your house for a drink (expected or not!), it's nice to have things on hand to accompany a plate of cheese and meat. What could be easier than pulling a jar from the pantry?

Our products reflect the same commitment to food that we have in our restaurant, always using all-natural ingredients and using local ingredients when possible. We started with our Fig & Port Vinaigrette, made with port, Black Mission figs, olive oil, red wine vinegar, and shallots, and a Fig Balsamic Vinegar made from Black Mission figs and balsamic vinegar.

To diversify our fig condiments, we took some liberties with the "preserve" terminology (jam, compotes, chutneys, confit, and mostardas) and created a variety that would complement our charcuterie and salumi platters. Traditionally, the difference between a jam and a compote is that a jam is fruit cooked with sugar with no chunks of fruit and a compote is fruit cooked in syrup, usually with large fruit chunks. A chutney is a spiced condiment that can be made from fruit or vegetables, vinegar, and spices, and a mostarda is a classic Northern Italian condiment that combines fruit and mustard and is served with boiled meat. We started with the original concepts but added our own touches. In reality, all of our products work with a huge variety of recipes and menu items.

Jams are a must for any slice of bread or cheese plate, and our Black Mission Fig Jam is a jar of luscious fig goodness (and is also amazing on a peanut butter and jelly sandwich). Our Apricot Fig Chutney is made with apricots, Calimyrna figs, ginger, and dried cherries. For our Dried Fig Compote, we blended both Black Mission and Calimyrna figs with apricots and dried cherries and the result is a chunky, thick condiment that can be spooned on its own or served on a sandwich or with a salumi plate. For our Red Onion Confit, we slow cook the onions down until they are soft and concentrated to reveal the sweet red onion flavor. The confit can be spooned over roasted meats and also makes a great topping for a burger or grilled cheese sandwich.

Our newest additions to the FIGfood line are two mostardas: Golden Raisin & Dried Fig Mostarda and Gravenstein Apple, Raisin & Fig Mostarda. Our Golden Raisin Mostarda is a tempting blend of golden raisins, Black Mission figs, and mustard seeds that result in a sweet and slightly tangy condiment which would add a nice sweetness to a sandwich or a piece of cheese.

Our Gravenstein Apple Mostarda is made with organic apples from a local producer, Nana Mae's Organics, and contains subtle flavors of rosemary, cinnamon, coriander, and ginger that add depth and create a nice balance. This second mostarda is a collaboration between the girl & the fig and Nana Mae's Organics in Sebastopol, California. Nana Mae's Organics, owned by Kendra and Paul Kolling, has been committed to creating the best possible product with their 300+ acres of organic Gravenstein apples. Their lineup includes apple juice, pear juice, applesauce, apple cider vinegar, and honey. (For more on Nana Mae, see page 193.)

During the Gravenstein Apple Project a few years ago, Kendra and I brainstormed to create a new and different product that would highlight the Gravenstein as well as the fig. We share a tremendous passion for Sonoma County and wanted to embrace wine country living and a healthy lifestyle. I'm thrilled with the result: a delicious mostarda with a unique flavor combination of sweet apple and tangy mustard. (For ordering information, see Sources, page 320.)

the girl & her cheese

In case you hadn't noticed, we are crazy about cheese. Each of our restaurants (and our catering company) has a stellar cheese menu, with more than a dozen cheeses available on a daily basis.

Over the years, we've developed strong relationships with our cheese purveyors. They delight us with new findings, special limited editions, and when we're lucky, some of their wonderful secrets. We purchase cheese from some of the cheese makers directly, as well as from purveyors that represent a group of cheese makers.

We are fortunate to work with some specialists, including a company that specializes in Italian cheese. They have shown us cheeses that you would never stumble upon in an American market, but would find at an early morning farmers market in Sicily or in a quaint Italian wine shop that offers little bites of cheese to taste with their wine.

A few years ago, we had the pleasure of being introduced to Pascal Beillevaire, one of the finest Maître Fromager/Affineurs in France. This relationship allowed us to taste cheeses from small producers that were in limited supply, traditionally crafted, and aged to perfection. We are thrilled when we can pass along these pleasures to our guests.

Our bank of cheese knowledge is constantly growing and the information available is increasingly at our fingertips. Our chefs take time to select the best cheeses to create a cheese menu that is well balanced and varied in texture, milk, and flavor. We love cheese that tells a story about a place, the people that produce it, or an artisanal tradition that is kept alive through the cheese. (For more specifics on seasonal cheeses, see pages 23, 34, 108, 176, and 246 and serving and pairing tips, pages 24, and 25.)

Cheese Curds

Burrata with Extra Virgin Olive Oil

Seasonal Cheese

Besides wine, bread, and olive oil, nothing says wine country more than cheese. Artisanal cheesemaking seems to exist wherever wine grapes grow, and it's always been an important part of our restaurants. We've recently started to focus on the seasonal aspect of cheese, serving and buying cheeses that fit with the seasons.

The word seasonal is often used with vegetables and fruits but rarely with cheese. Traditionally, however, cheese was a very seasonal product, made only when the milk was available. (Production adjustments have been made that allow year-round access to certain cheeses.)

The availability of milk is tied to the birth and weaning of babies. Most cows, goats, and sheep produce milk for their young in the autumn, and only after they have weaned can the mothers be milked through spring, summer, and early autumn. The end of autumn means the beginning of the breeding cycle and no milk is available. The level of fat and casein (milk protein) present in the milk is also seasonal. Milk is richest in fat directly after birthing and at the end of the lactation cycle, so cheesemakers try to take advantage of that. The change in feed from season to season also affects both the fat and flavor of the milk. When the animals graze on rich green grass in the spring their milk is completely different from their winter diet of feed. The animals' diet depends on the location of the dairy and this in turn affects the decision about when the cheese is made.

Redwood Hill Farm Camellia with Mostarda

Seasonal cheesemaking continues even today. Roquefort, a sheep's milk blue cheese from France, is made only seven months out of the year. Quite a few American cheesemakers also follow a "natural" calendar with their cheesemaking. Shelburne Farms in Vermont, who make outstanding Cheddar, lets their Brown Swiss cows go dry in the winter. Uplands Cheese Company in Wisconsin only makes their Pleasant Ridge Reserve cow's milk cheese from spring through autumn, and they sell their milk in winter rather than make cheese with it.

Cheese is also seasonal in regard to aging. Weather, particularly dampness or extreme heat, affect mold and bacteria growth and also influence how a cheese ages. Traditionally, cheesemakers in warmer climates made fresher cheeses because the cheese wouldn't keep in the hot weather. Colder climates called for harder cheeses that would keep through the winter. In modern times, this isn't necessarily the case but it does explain the reasoning behind traditional, regional European cheesemaking techniques and types. And certain cheeses taste better at particular times of the year. There's a reason why ripe summer tomatoes and fragrant basil are paired with mozzarella, while a creamy triple-cream Brie is served with Champagne in the winter. While each cheesemaking region has its own seasonal rhythms, it's helpful to understand the seasonal aspects of cheese when pairing it with food.

I suggest that you purchase your cheese selections from a reputable cheesemonger or at least someone that is passionate about their goods. The finer cheese departments or stores will often allow you to taste a cheese before you buy it. The folks behind the counter who love cheese will usually engage you in cheese lore,

share their knowledge, and give you the opportunity to start a relationship with cheese. These are the people whom you can trust to let you taste something wonderful, whether something just discovered or one of your favorites at its peak.

Cheese is a living, breathing product that changes drastically with time, air, light, and especially poor packaging. Because cheese can get very pricey, particularly those that have been set away to age, they should be handled with care. I would stay away from sloppy cheese counters and those that lack imagination.

How to serve cheese, and what to serve it with, are matters of personal taste but there are tried-and-true pairings that will always work and new pairings we've created over the years that we're happy to share with you. We love the traditional French cheese course, served after the main meal. This lusciously transitions diners from savory to sweet and often replaces dessert.

Our cheese plates contain between two and six cheeses and two to three accompaniments served as an appetizer. If a guest selects cheese instead of dessert, they will enjoy a small plate of two cheeses with two or three condiments, or accompaniments, served after the main course. When you're serving cheese at home we suggest one cheese for each menu to keep it simple. There are no exact substitutions for each cheese so you should feel free to try different cheeses and create your own pairings using the cheeses available to you.

Cheese Tasting

Cheese Pairings

A few basic serving tips will get you started:

Serve cheese at room temperature. The true flavor and texture of cheeses are expressed at room temperature. Remove the cheese from the refrigerator about one hour before serving.

For an intimate dinner party, select one or two cheeses for a cheese plate. For a larger group, up to five cheeses make an ideal cheese board.

Serve cheeses with varied shapes, sizes, colors, and flavors.

Serves cheeses that reflect the season. Rather than serving a heavy blue cheese on a hot summer's day, try a fresh goat's cheese, fromage blanc, or mozzarella.

Try to eat the mildest cheese first and end with the strongest-flavored cheese.

Themed cheese plates are a fun idea. Try three or four goat's cheeses from various regions, or a plate of four cheeses from France or four from Italy. A plate of five American farmstead cheeses is also wonderful, particularly if you can find several from your region.

Buy small quantities of the best cheese. It's better to spend more on one amazing cheese than buy three that are just mediocre.

We love to serve cheese with a wide range of accompaniments. The accompaniment should accentuate the cheese rather than detract from it. Toasted bread and/or crackers is a classic, but depending on the cheese we'll also add cornichons and other pickled vegetables; slices of fresh, seasonal fruit; fruit jam, compote, or mostarda; toasted or candied nuts; honey; and, of course, our FIGfood. Cheese and fruit are a natural pairing, and the earthiness of the cheese plays nicely off the juicy, sweet fruit.

We offer a cheese course as part of our Plats du Jour menus, serving two different cheeses with accompaniments. Throughout the book you will find pairing suggestions with each cheese. Many of these condiments have an information link in the Source section at the back of the book. These condiments are from small artisanal companies that make their products seasonally, so not everything will always be available.

Pairing cheese and wine is another passion of ours. It can be a subjective task, with personal taste playing a big role, but there are some pairings that work wonderfully every time.

Wine and cheese are a natural duo and have been enjoyed together for thousands of years. A successful pairing has much to do with terroir. Because cheese so often comes from a region that makes wine, the wine and cheese from the region will make a perfect match. A few classic examples: Sauvignon Blanc or Chenin Blanc from the Loire Valley in France paired with a Loire Valley goat's cheese; Roquefort cheese with Sauternes; and red Burgundy with Epoisse, a creamy cow's milk cheese from the same region. Some of our other favorite combinations are Viognier with aged cow's or goat's milk cheeses, sparkling wine with blue cheese, and Manchego (a Spanish sheep's milk cheese) with Rioja. Remember, the wine and cheese should enhance each other, not detract from either product.

Cheese & Wine Pairings

Here are a few basic wine and cheese pairing tips to get you started. Though I respect the many philosophies about pairing cheese and wine, I always go back to my tried and true law that says if you like the way a combination tastes, then that is the perfect pairing. Don't be afraid to experiment. Sometimes the condiment that you serve with the cheese will throw the "perfect pairing" out the window.

Pair salty cheeses with sweet wines. Blue cheese works very well with sweet wines, particularly Port.

Tangy cheeses need a dry, crisp wine to balance them.

In general, white wines work better with cheese than reds, due to the tannins in red wine.

Consider the body of the cheese and wine when creating a pairing. Just as with the main course, a lighter cheese calls for a lighter wine.

Rich, creamy cheeses can pair with powerful red wines such as Syrah.

Most hard aged cheeses such as Parmigiano-Reggiano and Cheddar work well with big red wines.

Sparkling wine and Champagne work wonderfully with rich, creamy cheeses, including blue cheeses.

Fresh cheeses call for light wines that won't overpower them.

In 2008, we started experimenting with making fresh cheese. It started as most of our projects do: to see if we could do it. After several attempts we realized that it isn't difficult and the results were more delicious than what we were able to purchase. While home cheesemaking may seem daunting, it's actually quite simple once you get the hang of it and the flavor of freshly made fromage blanc and ricotta compared to store-bought is far superior.

We use these cheeses in various ways at the restaurants, including adding ricotta to our meatballs, in fromage blanc ice cream, and for a perfect, light ricotta cheesecake. For simple nibbles, you can spread either of these fresh cheeses on a crostini with a condiment from your fridge or some freshly chopped herbs.

Unlike many other cheeses, which should be brought to room temperature before eating, ricotta and fromage blanc should be kept cold until you are ready to use them.

Très Bonnes Années
2009 sonoma county syrah

Rhône–Alone
the girl & the fig wine list

A great meal isn't complete without a great glass of wine. From the day we opened the girl & the fig we've offered a Rhône-Alone wine list, serving varietals from the Rhône Valley in France and Rhône-styled California wines. (At ESTATE restaurant, we've strayed from this idea, serving wines from California and Italy, which fits with that particular restaurant concept.)

We chose these varietals for several reasons, but primarily for their compatibility with our food. We also saw an opportunity to educate guests about varietals they might not have heard of or experienced. That's what inspired our wine flight program, where guests can taste three different wines from the same varietal, or five different varietals. Guests love to compare and contrast the wines and it gives them a chance to try wines they might not be familiar with. We also love to suggest wine pairings with our dishes, and offer wine pairings with our Plats du Jour menus.

Since we first placed Rhône varietals on our wine list, we've become very active in the Rhône community, particularly with Hospice du Rhône, a California-based nonprofit dedicated to promoting Rhône varietals. We've traveled to France a handful of times and met and cooked for many winemakers in the Rhône Valley. We've also been fortunate enough to attend the Rhône Découvertes, a week-long wine tasting held every other year. We became so enamored with Rhône wines that we started bottling our own!

Très Bonnes Années was created to celebrate our ten years in business; the name translates to "very good years." It's a toast and tribute to the talented winemakers, farmers, friends, family, and purveyors who work with us and support us. Working with the talented Jeff Cohn of JC Cellars (more on Jeff on page 282), each year we make 50 cases (2 barrels) of Très Bonnes Années. The first vintage was a blend of Syrah grapes from four different vineyards but each year the wine has been different. So far, we have mainly worked with Syrah, but that could change, too. The next three vintages used only Syrah grapes from the Rockpile Vineyard in Sonoma County. In 2008, the blend had a smattering of Viognier in it but the 2009 Très Bonnes Années, our fifth vintage, is a blend of two Sonoma County Syrah vineyards.

Our latest wine project was a white Rhône blend that combines Roussanne and Marsanne from Saralee's Vineyard in Sonoma County and Viognier from Catie's Corner Vineyard. We produced 50 cases (2 barrels) at CrushPad in Napa (now located in Sonoma), a custom crush facility. It also has the Très Bonnes Années label and our trademark Julie Higgins "fig art" label. The staff was very involved in this project; some of them visited CrushPad, took a sensory evaluation class, and got an in-depth look at the winemaking process.

We've listed profiles of the Rhône grape varietals here to give you brief introductions to the wines we feel allow the truest expression of our food. Throughout the book, I have given you specific wine suggestions for each recipe. These are only some of my favorite producers, there are way too many to include here, but I encourage you to taste the wines one by one.

white

Grenache Blanc

This is an emerging category of white wine in the U.S. While Grenache Blanc is widely used as a blending grape in the Rhône region of France (it's the fourth-most planted white grape in France) and in Spain, it's just starting to emerge in California. It makes a full-bodied, high-alcohol wine with nice acidity, orange and peach notes on the nose, and flavors of green apple, citrus, and anise. Grenache Blanc needs heat to grow and flourishes only in Mediterranean climates. The yields need to be low to allow the true expression of the grape to come through. In California there are great examples from Beckman Vineyards in Los Olivos, Sans Liege Wines, and Bonny Doon Vineyard.

Even though you may typically pair this wine with spicy Japanese or Thai food, Grenache Blanc is a full-flavored wine that will go nicely with grilled fish or salad entrées on a warm day.

Marsanne

I like to think of Marsanne as a cross between Chardonnay and Sauvignon Blanc. Not a lot of Marsanne is made in California, but we like the examples from JC Cellars, Qupé Vineyards, and Krupp Brothers. We also are quite fond of La Diligence, which is a wonderful collaboration among our friends Dave Miner and Gary Brookman from Miner Family Vineyards, and French winemaker François Villard. They have combined their very talented passions and blended fruit from the Napa Valley with François French winemaking techniques.

Marsanne is a crisp, dry, medium-bodied wine that is very food-friendly. While Marsanne from France tends to be more delicate and a bit steelier in flavor and body than California examples, it generally has flavors of pears, melons, orange rind, peaches, and vanilla. It's wonderful with poultry and seafood.

Roussanne

This is an elegant, crisp white that isn't widely made in California. You'll more often see Roussanne-Marsanne blends, however we are happy to see more winemakers producing Roussanne wines since the publication of our last book. The Roussanne from Truchard Vineyards in Napa is a favorite with our guests and is simply the perfect choice to pair with our Pastis-Scented Steamed Mussels or as an aperitif with our heirloom radishes. Copain Wine Cellars in Healdsburg makes an incredible Roussanne from the famous James Berry Vineyard in Paso Robles. We also love offering the Wellington Vineyards Roussanne from our longtime neighbors in Glen Ellen who share the Rhône passion.

Roussanne has a fragrant aroma of melons and honeysuckle and this medium-bodied white stands up well to high-acid and herb-based sauces. It is another perfect pairing for seafood, salads, and vegetable dishes.

Viognier

Of the white Rhône grapes grown in the U.S., Viognier is the most widely planted. It does well in the warmer microclimates, but it only produces good wine when the grapes are allowed to ripen fully. French Viognier has flavors of apricots with a glycerin-like texture, while American Viognier tends to be fuller-bodied and slightly less nuanced. Viognier from Alban Vineyards, Imagery Estate Winery, Kunde Family Estate, and Stags Leap Winery are just a handful that we love to share with our guests.

This full-bodied white wine has flavors of apricots, figs, and peaches with a slightly floral nose. It's a perfect match for heavier foods like crab cakes, braised chicken or rabbit, mushrooms, and creamy vegetable dishes.

Late Harvest Viognier

This is our dessert wine of choice. What I like to call "nectar of the wine gods" is a luscious dessert wine made from Viognier grapes that are picked when their sugars are at their highest level and aged between 15 weeks and 1 year. The wine explodes with flavors of apricots, orange zest, apricot jam, and orange marmalade. It goes beautifully with any tart or butter-based cake as well as our famous Lavender Crème Brûlée. A small glass of this sweet wine goes a long way! Look for bottles from Cambria Winery & Vineyards, Anaba Wines and Salamandre Wine Cellars.

red

Grenache

I am particularly fond of wines made with the Grenache grape, because they pair perfectly with my favorite foods. The biggest change on our wine list from the last book is the number of Grenache-based wines that have been added to our list. More and more I am reminded of why I like the Grenache grape so much. The approachable flavors and mouthfeel create such a nice addition to so many meals. We've also included a lovely Garnacha from Spain and a few special wines from Châteauneuf-du-Pape and Vacqueyras that round off the category nicely.

Grenache is used in many white and red wines throughout the world, including the famed rosé from Provence and the explosive reds from Gigondas. On its own it makes a lush and rich wine bursting with blackberry and herbal flavors. In California, we look to producers such as Quivira Vineyards and Winery, newcomer Leojami Wines, Mounts Family Winery, Skylark Wine Company, and Prospect 772 Wine Company. In Sonoma, our dear friend Peter Mathis makes a Grenache that our staff is just bowled over by. They sell it like crazy and love to tell his story of being a one-man operation, with his small Grenache vineyard right in our backyard.

Pull out the big dishes for Grenache; it is the perfect accompaniment to roasted and grilled meats, charcuterie, or even a great burger!

Cinsault

Cinsault is probably the least known of the Rhône varietals. It's often blended with other red varietals to add flavor and structure but true Cinsaults are a pleasure, if you can find them. In California, Frick Winery and Black Sheep Winery consistently produce tasty examples. This is a light-bodied wine that boasts flavors of strawberry, spice, and earth. The light-bodied, low tannin Cinsault pairs wonderfully with a wide range of dishes from poultry and soups to pastas and main courses like duck confit.

Carignane

This red varietal makes big red wines with concentrated fruit, deep color, and high tannins and alcohol. This wine boasts flavors of clove, chocolate, spice, and earthy fruit. Some of my favorite Carignanes comes from the Priorat region of Spain, especially when they are blended with Grenache to produce lovely, multidimensional wines. Carignane has made some interesting leaps over the past few years. More California producers are highlighting this varietal on its own, and it is proving to be a complex, earthy wine that could easily be mistaken for French wine.

Carignane from Baxter Winery, Ranchero Cellars, and Preston Vineyards are all great options. Our friend and extremely talented winemaker Chris Brockaway makes a delightful version under his Broc Cellars label with grapes from the Alexander Valley. Another unique Carignane comes from the folks at Lioco using Mendocino County grapes.

This is the wine to serve with hearty, wintery meat dishes like braised or grilled meats and roasted vegetables.

Mourvèdre

Mourvèdre is one of my favorite red varietals, as I find its spicy, peppery and seductive character interesting and thought-provoking. There are a handful of California winemakers that are focusing on the varietal and are creating some amazing wines.

Cline Cellars Mourvèdre has always been a benchmark on our wine list. Their "Ancient Vines" is a consistent wine, each vintage showing the true character of the varietal. We are flattered and thrilled to have one of our recipes on the back of their Mourvèdre labels for the past few vintages. Villa Creek, our friends in Paso Robles, California, also understand this grape extremely well. They make a Mourvèdre with layers of complex flavors, a wine that's moody and sexy, their "Damas Noir" is exquisite. Our other favorite California producers include Spann Vineyards and Broc Cellars.

Our wine list is not complete without the most famous Mourvèdre of all, Domaine Tempier from Bandol, France. We treasure having this on our list and are disappointed each year when it sells out and we must wait for the next release.

Mourvèdre is a robust, inky wine that's full of flavor. This full-bodied red should be served with a hearty meal and savored with dishes like seared, grilled, or braised meats and even with dark chocolate.

Syrah

Syrah came into my life in 1997, about the same time it came into its own in California. Syrah has become increasingly popular, but in the early 1990s few American wine drinkers were familiar with this complex, earthy varietal. Once California winemakers realized that our climate was perfect for the hardy Syrah grape, we've been extremely successful in replicating Syrah from the Rhône and Provençal areas of France. Syrah from France, particularly the famed region of Côte-Rôtie, is a lean, rugged, earthy wine. California Syrah tends to be slightly fuller-bodied with a bit more oak and vanilla than its French counterpart.

We're particularly fond of Syrah from Loxton Vineyards, Nicholson Ranch, Benziger Family Winery, Tallulah Wines, Deerfield Ranch Winey, Audelssa, Scribe Winery, Paul Lato Wines, and Wind Gap.

This grape produces robust wines with smoke, spice, and tar elements on the nose and earthy, spicy, black pepper, and black raspberry fruit on the palate. Serve Syrah with anything grilled, seared, or smoked; it's also lovely with blue cheese.

Red Blends

Red blends play an important role in the Rhône Valley, where winemakers carefully blend the varietals to bring out the best in each one. The most famous red blend combines Grenache, Syrah, and Mourvèdre. Blends from the Southern Rhône generally use Grenache as the dominant grape, while the Northern Rhône uses Syrah as their primary grape. We feature many red blends on our list and we're particularly fond of "Le Cigare Volant," a red blend from Randall Grahm, founder of Bonny Doon Vineyard, a genius, pioneer, and friend. This is Randall's flagship wine and though the blend changes every year, it usually includes Grenache, Syrah, Mourvèdre, Carignane, and Cinsault.

We also like some of the newcomers, like the Syrah-Grenache from Grey Stack Cellars. Grey Stack makes cool climate French varieties in Sonoma County's Bennett Valley. "Veracity," the Grenache, Mourvèdre, and Syrah blend from Epoch Estate Wines in Paso Robles, is also out of this world. We're also wild about Margerum Wine Company's "M5," a blend of five varietals in the style of Châteauneuf-du-Pape. The blend is comprised of Syrah, Grenache, Mourvèdre, Counoise, and Cinsault, all from Santa Barbara County.

We couldn't forget the wines from our friends at Arrowood Vineyards & Winery, "Cotes de Lune Rouge" and the Lasseter Family's "Chemin de Fer" as great examples of "GSM" red blends that combine Grenache, Syrah, and Mourvèdre.

Red blends are wonderful food wines, pairing with everything from hearty entrées like beef, lamb, and game to cheese courses and chocolate desserts.

John Toulze

Most of you know Executive Chef John Toulze as the culinary face of the girl & the fig. We've worked together for more than 15 years now, and he has become one of my closest friends as well as my business partner. As the restaurant has evolved, so has John, taking on new responsibilities and learning new techniques while remaining committed to maintaining the integrity of local ingredients.

John's role has evolved since the last cookbook. He opened ESTATE restaurant in Sonoma, paying homage to rustic Italian food, and John is now in charge of all restaurant operations, which means less time in the kitchen. It's been nothing but positive for our restaurants, as we have created projects that satisfy his culinary curiosity and add substance and further authenticity to our diners' experience, including making salumi, bread, and vinegar in-house and creating **the farm project**. (More on those on pages 16, 19, and 56.) "These projects I have taken on become group projects. I love the opportunity to teach the chefs other techniques and watch them learn and excel with them."

As our business has grown, "I had to work on my other skill sets, including my ability to manage people," says John. Working within our philosophies of being a teaching kitchen and restaurant, John has mentored and trained many of our ground-level prep cooks to become excellent line cooks and chefs. "I am now teaching chefs and managers how to train their staff members and have been able to give our lead chefs the ability to write their own menus, make purchasing decisions, and have input in hiring their staff," says John. They are the team that helps execute his vision and handle the daily kitchen operations. John also hits the road for restaurant events both at home and abroad, gaining inspiration from the chefs and the regions he visits, whether it's an ingredient, a wine, or a dish he's tried.

John's background is what has allowed him to explore his passions. During John's college years, he came to the wine and restaurant business as a way to make money. He was as surprised as anyone to find that it was a comfortable fit and that he had the natural ability to become a self-taught chef. Growing up in a French family, his passion for local ingredients and regionality are paramount. He loves the food of Italy, Southern France, and Spain; what he calls "ingredient driven Mediterranean food." He loves the idea of letting the ingredients speak for themselves. "I think of it as the minimalist approach to transporting food to a plate," notes John.

John is dedicated to making as many of our items from scratch as possible. For a culinary event in San Francisco, he made corn bread topped with crème fraîche and chorizo—all of it made in-house. "The dish was simple and delicious, but for the consumer it was the fact that I made each ingredient, and so there was a story behind each ingredient," says John. "People want to eat real food, food that was handmade, not perfect. They want simpler food that is honest. Maybe that's what we want right now in our culture— honesty and transparency."

The menus John creates are now heavily influenced by **the farm project** and our focus on house-made ingredients; salumi platters and sausage-topped pizzas are the norm, and the Plats du Jour menus have allowed a constant infusion of seasonal produce from the farm. The ingredient sources have changed since our last book. Since 2003, we only we only offer fish that are approved on the Monterey Bay Aquarium Seafood Watch list. We rarely offer salmon on our menus, we don't use monkfish or sea bass anymore, and we serve only domestic caviar. Ray, the salmon fisherman we profiled in our first book, fishes for both salmon and halibut since the collapse of the California salmon population. "It's forced us to be more creative," says John. "The fish that are overfished are the easiest to prepare." The seafood restrictions also led John to study up on sustainable seafood. "I've become more educated about what is farmed positively and negatively," he says. "Most people assume all farmed seafood is bad, but shellfish is farmed, and most of that is farmed sustainably." John points to Laughing Bird Shrimp, our shrimp supplier. "We use Laughing Bird because it's farmed sustainably off the coast of Belize in saltwater and hand-peeled." Most fish, however, are not farmed sustainably, and as John notes, there are no rules for fish farms and no oversight or regulation. "It's harder than ever to make a menu that people want and sticks to the sustainable guidelines, and the price of fish is up," says John.

With John's passion for food and natural curiosity and drive, I'm always surprised by what he will think of next. Despite his quest for knowledge, learning new techniques, and seeking out new ingredients he remains true to the girl & the fig roots. "You'll never see us do a sharp rise," says John. "We will do our business slow and steady, and in ten years we'll still be here and authentic."

Spring in Sonoma unfolds slowly after the heavy February and early March rains. Wild yellow mustard fills the hillsides; cows, goats, and sheep roam on fields bursting with fresh tender grass; gnarled gray grapevines stand bare, not yet showing their first green budbreak. The sun rises a bit earlier, sets a bit later, and the winter chill has eased ever so slightly.

We feel the subtle seasonal shift in the kitchen, too. After a few months of root vegetables it's a joy to see the first boxes of bright green asparagus arrive from the Delta region, a couple of hours away. The crates of spring onions, broccoli, artichokes, and arugula demand a new restaurant menu. Local mushroom foragers appear on the restaurant doorstep with bags of wild morels, which we quickly incorporate into the menu. Strawberries burst on the scene, almost embarrassingly early given that most of the country is still digging out from snowstorms. Dark yellow Meyer lemons—a cross between a lemon and an orange—bring a cheeriness and an intoxicating scent to the kitchen. Their season is winter through early spring, so we add their sweet flavor to any dish we can think of: vinaigrettes, sauces, and especially desserts.

The real sign of spring in Sonoma is the day the Tuesday night farmer's market opens in downtown Sonoma. The market is held on Friday mornings year-round, but from April through October a larger nighttime market is added. Local farmers park their trucks, set up their stalls, and ready themselves for the crowds of shoppers. Anne Teller's 700-acre Oak Hill Farm brings baskets of arugula, fresh herbs, and spring specialties like red stem dandelions, fava beans, and Easter radishes. Hector Alvarez, a third generation beekeeper, owns Hector's Honey and sells jars of local honey, beeswax candles, honey sticks, and some of the best eggs in the valley. Arrowsmith Farms is a great source for lavender honey, a local specialty. A taste of creamy cow's milk cheeses like cheddar, jack, and feta from Spring Hill Cheese Company is a must, followed by a stop at The Bejkr. Owner Mike Zakowski stack loaves of his unique artisan wood-fired bread, and a line always forms for his amazing pretzels and flatbread. It's a festive atmosphere, and everyone is eager to be outside, enjoying the chilly night air after months of cold, rainy evenings.

On market night, the girl & the fig bar is bustling with locals who've stopped in for a glass of wine before heading out to shop. Others sit on the patio, heavy bags overflowing, and relax over a meal. It's my favorite season here; the vibrant green hills are almost blinding as you drive through Sonoma Valley. It's the time before the heat of summer settles in and imbues the landscape with a golden hue, the color of wheat, and the tourists begin to arrive. It's a welcome break after the short winter days and a glimpse of the long, leisurely summer days to come.

spring cheese

As we adjust the restaurant menu with each new season, the cheese menu changes as well. Most people don't realize that cheese is a seasonal product. Flavors and textures of cheese change throughout the year due to aging and storage, as well as what the animals are eating in any given month. With a similar climate and food culture, Sonoma Valley is often compared to the region of Tuscany, Italy; the Rhône Valley and Provence regions of France; and the Priorat region of Spain. The European influence is strong in the foods and products available in Sonoma, especially cheese.

The spring cheese season is like the beginning of a new year—an awakening of flavors, particularly in young, fresh cheeses. When the rains subside and the pastures grow thick with luscious green grass, wildflowers, dandelions, and miner's lettuce the dairy animals are in for a feast. The first milk of the year is less acidic and slightly lower in fat during this period of time. The addition of wildflowers to their diet produces milk with a fuller, richer flavor. Another influence that will change the flavor of the milk is the proximity of the pasture to the ocean. The saltwater air that permeates the pasture will end up in the animals' milk, giving it a slightly briny flavor that naturally brings out other flavors, just as salt does in cooking. Similarly, pastures next to thick forests of pines or eucalyptus will impart those flavors as well. This is Mother Nature at her most magical. (For more on seasonal influences on cheeses see pages 23, 108, 176, 246.) It tickles me to drive through the rural areas of Sonoma and watch the frolicking baby cows and goats nursing their mothers or tumbling with their siblings. To me, it is the perfect picture of "joie de vivre" in wine country.

I am excited to share some tidbits of information with you about the seasonal aspects of cheese throughout the book. However, it does not preclude me from saying that no matter what the season may be if a cheese looks interesting and tempting you should try it.

Taking into account factors such as flavor and texture, the cheeses listed here were selected to pair with each menu in a way that would complement the rest of the menu.

(Clockwise from top left; Jean de Brie, Epoisses, Bellwether Farms Pepato, Nicasio Square, Bohemian Creamery Bo Peep)

SPRING ANTIDOTE
MAKES 2 COCKTAILS

1 TABLESPOON LOCAL BEE POLLEN (SEE SOURCES, PAGE 320)
1 TABLESPOON SUGAR
2 PINCHES CHOPPED FRESH ROSEMARY
JUICE OF 1 LEMON
1 OUNCE WHITE PEACH PURÉE
2 OUNCES WHITE CRANBERRY JUICE
1 OUNCE LOCAL RUNNY HONEY (SEE BELOW)
2½ OUNCES SQUARE ONE ORGANIC VODKA

MIX THE BEE POLLEN AND SUGAR TOGETHER AND RIM THE MARTINI
GLASSES WITH THE MIXTURE. MUDDLE THE ROSEMARY WITH THE
LEMON JUICE IN THE BOTTOM OF A MIXING GLASS. FILL THE MIXING
GLASS WITH ICE. ADD THE WHITE PEACH PURÉE, WHITE CRANBERRY
JUICE, HONEY, AND VODKA. SHAKE THE INGREDIENTS VIGOROUSLY.
STRAIN INTO THE MARTINI GLASSES AND SERVE.

RUNNY HONEY
THIN HONEY WITH A SMALL AMOUNT OF BOILING WATER UNTIL
THE HONEY BECOMES POURABLE. LET COOL BEFORE USING.

ESTATE'S FELLINI
MAKES 2 COCKTAILS

2½ OUNCES LIMONCELLO
2 OUNCES BLOOD ORANGE PURÉE
SPARKLING WINE
ORANGE WEDGES OR SLICES, FOR GARNISH

IN A MIXING GLASS FILLED WITH ICE, COMBINE THE
LIMONCELLO AND BLOOD ORANGE PURÉE. MIX TO CHILL.
STRAIN THE MIXTURE INTO TWO CHAMPAGNE FLUTES,
DIVIDING EQUALLY. TOP WITH WELL-CHILLED SPARKLING
WINE AND GARNISH WITH AN ORANGE WEDGE OR A SLICE.

MEYER LEMON DROP
MAKES 2 COCKTAILS

4 OUNCES VODKA
JUICE OF 2 MEYER LEMONS
1½ OUNCES SIMPLE SYRUP (PAGE 36)
LEMON TWISTS, FOR GARNISH

CHILL THE MARTINI GLASSES.
IN A COCKTAIL SHAKER FILLED WITH ICE, COMBINE THE VODKA, MEYER LEMON JUICE, AND SIMPLE SYRUP. SHAKE WELL AND STRAIN INTO THE MARTINI GLASSES. GARNISH EACH COCKTAIL WITH A LEMON TWIST.

Simple Syrup

Simple syrup is the base for many cocktails and takes only a few minutes to make at home. Just combine equal parts sugar and water and bring to a boil. Lower the heat and simmer until the sugar is completely dissolved (about 3 minutes). Let cool before using. You can store simple syrup in a glass jar in the refrigerator for up to 1 month.

Lavender

This fragrant flower with gray-green stalks can be found all over Sonoma County and is actually a member of the mint family. While it's considered a French ingredient—lavender blooms throughout southwest France—it didn't gain a true following until the early 1970s, when it was introduced as an ingredient in the famous herb blend Herbes de Provence. But lavender has been used for centuries, with a history that traces back to the Egyptians.

We've used lavender in many ways over the years, including our Lavender Crème Brûlée, Lavender Sea Salt, and Lavender Mojito. Blended with other herbs, it makes an intriguing spice rub for meat and fish. Lavender is as easy to use as any other herb—the flowers and leaves can be used fresh, while the stems and buds can be used dried.

The sweet-tasting English lavender and a hybrid called "Provence" are the two types most commonly used in cooking but there are dozens of varieties to try, whether English, Spanish, or French. Culinary lavender is available at specialty stores (see Sources, page 318).

When using lavender in any of our recipes, be mindful of the strength of the flower you are using. It's easy to add more, but very difficult to remove the aggressive flavor when steeped too long. Using too much lavender will make a dish taste like perfume and very bitter at the same time. If you're using fresh lavender, be sure to get flowers from a plant that has not been treated with pesticides; certified organic is ideal.

LAVENDER SIMPLE SYRUP

1 CUP SUGAR
3 TABLESPOONS CULINARY LAVENDER

IN A SAUCEPOT, BRING 1 CUP OF WATER, SUGAR, AND LAVENDER TO A BOIL. SIMMER UNTIL THE SUGAR HAS COMPLETELY DISSOLVED. TURN OFF THE HEAT AND LET SIT UNTIL COOL. STRAIN THE MIXTURE THROUGH A FINE-MESH STRAINER AND DISCARD THE LAVENDER. STORE THE LAVENDER SIMPLE SYRUP IN THE REFRIGERATOR FOR UP TO 1 MONTH.

NOTE: ADJUST THE AMOUNT OF LAVENDER AND THE STEEPING TIME BASED ON THE STRENGTH OF THE LAVENDER AND YOUR PERSONAL TASTE.

LAVENDER MOJITO
MAKES 2 COCKTAILS

4 OUNCES LIGHT RUM
16–20 FRESH MINT LEAVES
JUICE OF 2 LIMES
2 OUNCES LAVENDER SIMPLE SYRUP (SEE BELOW LEFT)
CLUB SODA
LAVENDER SPRIGS, FOR GARNISH

MUDDLE THE MINT LEAVES IN THE BOTTOM OF A PINT GLASS. ADD THE RUM, LIME JUICE, AND LAVENDER SIMPLE SYRUP AND MUDDLE A BIT MORE. ADD THE ICE, STIR, AND TOP WITH A SPLASH OF CLUB SODA. GARNISH WITH A LIME WEDGE, MINT LEAVES OR A LAVENDER SPRIG.

SWEET CORN MADELEINES, CRÈME FRAÎCHE & CAVIAR

When making these buttery bites, select a coarse cornmeal to add more texture to the madeleines. Either homemade crème fraîche or store-bought will work nicely. The caviar or fish roe adds a salty pop but can be substituted with crispy prosciutto or fresh corn kernels with a sprinkling of sea salt.

2 ears fresh corn, roasted and kernels removed
½ cup whole milk
2 large eggs
1 teaspoon sugar
½ cup fine yellow cornmeal
4 tablespoons all-purpose flour, sifted
¼ teaspoon baking powder
¼ teaspoon salt
1 teaspoon melted unsalted butter
3 tablespoons very cold crème fraîche
1 ounce American caviar

Preheat the oven to 375°F. Brush a mini-madeleine mold with softened butter and dust it with flour.

In a blender, purée the corn kernels with the milk. In a mixer fitted with a paddle attachment mix the eggs and sugar on low to medium speed until the mixture is white and creamy, about 3 minutes. Add the cornmeal, puréed corn, flour, baking powder, and salt. Once the flour is incorporated into the batter, slowly add the melted butter.

Fill the molds three quarters full with the batter. Tap the molds lightly to remove any air bubbles from the batter and to prevent holes from forming in the madeleines. Bake the madeleines for 8 to 10 minutes, or until lightly golden brown. Remove the madeleines from the oven, immediately unmold them, and let them cool on a rack.

Place the madeleines on a platter and top with a tiny dollop of crème fraîche and a few grains of caviar. Serve immediately.

Makes about 36 nibbles

Crème Fraîche

Creamy, tangy crème fraîche is a staple in our kitchens, essentially the French version of sour cream. We use it as garnish and in dozens of sweet and savory dishes. crème fraîche is particularly suited to sauces because it will thicken without curdling. Made from cow's milk, a lactic bacteria is added to the milk to thicken it and give it a subtle sharpness. We love crème fraîche from Bellwether Farms in Sonoma, but there are several good brands available nationally. (If you want to make your own, you'll find the recipe on page 311.)

GOAT CHEESE & LAVENDER-HONEY TOASTS

It's hard to believe that this is one of the most popular small bites in our catering department. It is true that sometimes less is more. This combination of spring flavors makes the perfect bite to pair with a glass of bubbly or rosé. Look for a fresh goat cheese; we prefer Laura Chenel's Chevre for this recipe for its slightly tart, creamy, and fresh flavors.

½ cup honey
1 tablespoon culinary lavender (save a pinch for
    garnish)
1 cup fresh goat cheese
¼ cup heavy cream

Place the honey and lavender in a medium saucepot over medium heat. Let the lavender steep in the honey until you have reached the desired intensity. Strain the lavender and set aside.

Place the goat cheese and cream in a mixer fitted with a whisk attachment. Add the lavender honey to taste (about 5 tablespoons). Whisk until the mixture is light.

Place the goat cheese mixture on a toasted baguette or cracker of your choice. Drizzle with the honey and garnish with the reserved lavender.

Makes about 50 nibbles

PARMESAN CROQUETTES, PEA MINT PESTO

These cheesy croquettes are a perfect bite-size morsel for a cocktail party. They're relatively simple to prepare and, as usual, there's room for variation and substitutions. Even though we love the pea mint pesto you can substitute ready-made condiments such as pesto, chutney, or spicy tomato sauce.

For the croquettes:
2 tablespoons unsalted butter
2 -3 cups hot Chicken Stock, (page
    313; vegetable stock or chicken
    broth can be substituted)
½ cup diced onion
1 garlic clove, minced
1 cup Carnaroli rice (see page 318)
¼ cup dry white wine
½ cup grated Parmesan cheese
2 large eggs
½ cup bread crumbs
¼ cup all-purpose flour

For the pesto:
¼ cup peas, blanched
12 fresh mint leaves
¼ cup plus 2 tablespoons olive oil
3 tablespoons toasted pine nuts
3 tablespoons Parmesan cheese

To prepare the croquettes:
Melt the butter in a medium saucepan over medium heat. Add the onion and garlic and sauté for 5 minutes or until translucent. Add the rice and cook for 1 minute until the rice is well coated in the butter. Add the white wine and stir until the rice has absorbed all the liquid. Season lightly with salt. Add ⅓ cup of hot stock and stir until the liquid has absorbed.

Repeat this step until you have used all the stock and the rice is cooked al dente about 15 minutes. Add the ½ cup cheese, taste, and season as needed. Set aside and let the risotto cool slightly.

In a bowl, whisk the egg with 1 tablespoon water. In a separate bowl mix the flour and the bread crumbs together.

Set a deep fryer to 375°F (a deep saucepan filled with canola oil will work as well as a deep fryer). Roll the rice into 18 to 24 balls. Coat each croquette with the egg and then the flour mixture. Fry the croquettes until golden brown, about 4 to 6 minutes.

To prepare the pesto:
Place the peas, mint, olive oil, and a pinch of salt in a food processor and pulse briefly until the ingredients have been roughly puréed. Add the pine nuts and 3 tablespoons cheese and process again until all the ingredients are well combined.

Serve the croquettes with a dollop of pesto or a bowl of pesto on the side for dipping.

Makes about 18 to 24 nibbles

Smoked & Cured Salmon

We adore smoked salmon for its deep flavor and silky texture and we use it in brunch, lunch, and dinner dishes. The chefs prefer either cold-smoked or cured wild salmon. Smoking salmon began as a way to preserve the fish when refrigeration was limited. The United Kingdom is famous for their Scottish salmon but in North America Alaskan wild salmon is the most common.

There is much debate about wild versus farmed salmon and farmed will almost always be less expensive but there is a definite flavor difference: wild salmon is meatier with a more robust flavor, while the farmed salmon has a flabby texture. Whichever type you choose, serve it at room temperature to maximize the flavor. (For more on farmed versus wild fish, see page 126.)

The labels on smoked salmon can be confusing so here's a brief guide to help you choose:

Cold smoking: *Most smoked salmon is cold-smoked, typically at 99°F. The cold smoking does not cook the fish, resulting in a delicate texture. The exposure to smoke from oak chips is what gives it a smoky flavor.*

Hot smoking: *Hot smoking "cooks" the fish, making it less moist with a less delicate flavor. It may be eaten like cold-smoked salmon or mixed with salads or pasta. This method is commonly used for both trout and salmon.*

Cured salmon: *Although often confused with smoked salmon, Scandinavian gravlax is not smoked but cured. Gravlax is cold-cured using sugar, salt, and dill.*

APRICOT-CURED SALMON, CRÈME FRAÎCHE, BRIOCHE TOASTS

Most people don't take the time to cure or smoke their own salmon. It seems like a difficult task but this recipe will change your mind. Make sure to purchase a perfectly fresh side or two of salmon from your fishmonger. The addition of the dried apricots adds a level of sweetness to the velvety fish once it is cured. If you need a quick nibble and you don't have the time to prepare the salmon, use a presliced smoked or cured salmon from your local market. I prefer Ducktrap River Fish Farm (see Sources, page 318).

6 slices brioche, ½-inch thick (about ¼ loaf)
4 tablespoons unsalted butter
½ pound thinly sliced Apricot-Cured Salmon (page 316)
¼ cup crème fraîche
1 ounce American caviar
1 bunch chives, diced

Preheat the oven to 375°F.
Cut each slice of bread in 4 triangles. Melt the butter in a small pan. Add the brioche toasts to the pan to coat. Place the toasts on a sheet pan and bake for 5 to 7 minutes or until the toasts are golden around the edges.

Top each brioche toast with a piece of salmon, a dollop of crème fraîche, a touch of caviar and a pinch of chives.

Makes about 24 nibbles

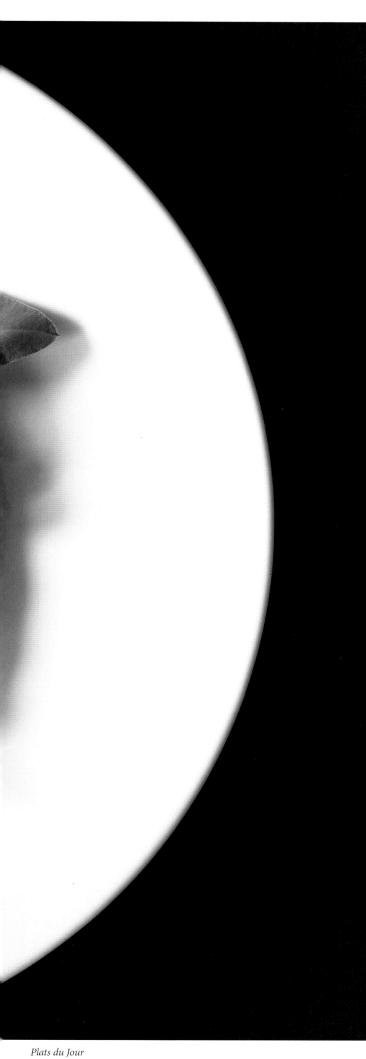

spring menus

Entrée
Dungeness Crab & Avocado Salad

Plat
Pan-Seared Pacific Snapper,
Meyer Lemon Beurre Blanc

Dessert
Strawberry & Kumquat Crisp,
Crème Chèvre

Fromage
Ossau-Iraty

Dungeness Crab & Avocado Salad

Wellington Vineyards Roussanne, Sonoma County, California
Kamen Estate Wines Viognier, Sonoma Valley California

Crab is almost impossible to resist on our menu. Though we don't serve it often, whenever we do it's an instant hit. Folks from the East Coast are often surprised to see the enormous size of the Dungeness Crab, being more familiar with the smaller varieties like the Blue Crabs from the Chesapeake Bay. This salad is quite simple to prepare and is beautiful on the plate. Just try not to eat all the crab before you plate the dishes!

For the aioli:
1 large egg yolk
1½ teaspoons fresh lemon juice
½ teaspoon fennel seed, toasted and ground
Pinch of salt
½ cup blended oil

For the salad:
2 avocados
1½ teaspoons fresh lemon juice
6 orange segments
6 ruby grapefruit segments
9 ounces Dungeness crabmeat
Zest of 1 lemon
Zest of 1 orange
1 teaspoon fennel pollen (see Sources, page 318)
½ cup whole parsley leaves
Salt and white pepper to taste

To prepare the aioli:
Place the egg yolk, lemon juice, fennel seed, and a pinch of salt in a stainless-steel bowl. Slowly drizzle the blended oil into the bowl, whisking rapidly until all the oil is incorporated and the mixture is thick. If the mixture becomes too thick, add a few teaspoons of water if needed. Season with salt and pepper to taste. Refrigerate and set aside.

To prepare the salad:
Dice the avocados into ½-inch pieces and toss them with the lemon juice and season with salt and white pepper to taste.

Place a 2½-inch ring mold or cookie cutter on a plate and distribute the avocado equally among the ring molds. Cover the avocado with the grapefruit and orange segments and top with 3 tablespoons of the crabmeat. Repeat with the remaining plates.

Garnish each plate with the fennel aioli, citrus zest, fennel pollen, and parsley leaves. Serve immediately.

Serves 6

Citrus

Citrus fruit plays a key role in our food—it accents a dish or can be the star ingredient. Our mild winters allow citrus to flourish in California, providing us with a steady stream of colors, scents, and tastes through the winter and spring seasons. Clementine mandarins are available through February and Satsumas throughout the winter. Oranges, grapefruit, pomelos, and kumquats are harvested into spring. Blood orange and tangelo harvests begin in winter and continue into March or even later.

At ESTATE, we were lucky enough to inherit a citrus tree that has been grafted. Each year we discover a new fruit—last year we harvested a Buddha's hand, lemons, limes, grapefruit, and possibly some yuzu. We use the juice and zest of the fruits in salads, sauces, and desserts as well as in cocktails.

Blood oranges are one of my favorite citrus fruits. (For my other favorite, Meyer Lemons, see page 128.) We use them in salad dressings, desserts, sauces, and cocktails. These oranges reveal a deep purple-red interior and ruby-red, sweet, intense juice that's less acidic than other orange varieties.

The Italians are wild for blood oranges. Fresh blood orange juice is available all over, and it is used in various dessert creations. The most common varieties that are available are Moro and Tarocco, in season December through May. While blood oranges will last for two days on the countertop, they stay fresh for up to two weeks in the refrigerator.

One prep tip: one pound of blood oranges equals about three medium oranges and yields one cup of juice.

Pan-Seared Pacific Snapper, Meyer Lemon Beurre Blanc

Miner Family Vineyards Viognier, Simpson Vineyard, California
Stag's Leap Winery Viognier, Napa Valley, California

Yellowtail Snapper is a delicately flavored fish that is easy to cook and pairs with a wide range of spring ingredients. We recommend using the Meyer Beurre Blanc because both the acidity from the citrus as well as the creaminess of the butter are wonderful complementary flavors. Other sauces that would work are Spring Onion Vinaigrette (page 50) or Warm Bacon Vinaigrette (page 134).

For the vegetables:

3 bunches baby carrots, peeled and blanched

1 bunch asparagus, trimmed

8 baby artichokes, trimmed, blanched, and cut in half

2 tablespoons unsalted butter

For the beurre blanc:

16 tablespoons (2 sticks) plus 1 tablespoon cold unsalted butter, diced

1 shallot, minced

¼ cup dry white wine

1 sprig fresh thyme

3 Meyer lemons, zested and juiced (fresh lemon juice can be substituted)

Salt and white pepper to taste

For the snapper:

6 snapper filets (6 ounces each, skin-on, scaled and cleaned)

Salt and white pepper to taste

¼ cup blended oil

¼ cup lemon segments (from about 2 lemons), for garnish

To prepare the vegetables:

In a medium sauté pan combine the baby carrots, asparagus, artichokes, and butter with ¼ cup water. On medium heat cook until the vegetables are heated through, about 3 to 5 minutes. Season with salt and pepper to taste.

To prepare the beurre blanc:

Melt 1 tablespoon of butter in a small saucepan over low heat and add the shallots. Sauté the shallots until soft, about 3 minutes. Add the white wine and thyme, increase the heat to high, and reduce the liquid until almost dry. Remove the pan from the heat and add the lemon juice and zest. Put the pan back over very low heat and while whisking, slowly add a few squares of cold butter one at a time, making sure all of the butter is emulsified before adding more butter. Repeat until all the butter has been absorbed into the sauce. Strain the sauce through a fine-mesh sieve. Season with salt and white pepper to taste. Keep warm.

To prepare the snapper:

Season the snapper filets with salt and white pepper. Heat a large sauté pan over medium-high heat. Add the blended oil to the hot pan and place the filets skin-side down in the oil. (Be careful when placing the fish in the hot pan, as the oil can splash.) Sauté the filets until the skin is well browned, about 3 to 5 minutes. Turn the fish over and continue to sauté the flesh side until browned. (The fish should be cooked through at this point.) Remove the fish from the pan and set aside on paper towels.

To serve:

Warm the plates. Carefully remove the vegetables with a slotted spoon and place them in the center of each plate. Drizzle the beurre blanc around the vegetables and place a piece of snapper on top. Garnish with the lemon segments.

Serves 6

Strawberry & Kumquat Crisp, Crème Chèvre

Holly's Hill Vineyards Late Harvest Roussanne, El Dorado, California
Cambria Winery & Vineyard Late Harvest Viognier, Tepusquet Vineyard, Santa Maria, California

Even though supermarkets offer a plethora of fruit almost any time of year, fresh local fruit really does vary according to season. Depending on how our spring weather is, the local strawberries that arrive mid to late spring sometimes overlap with the kumquats that arrive in winter to early spring. These two fruits are an unusual combination but work nicely together. The addition of goat cheese in the garnish adds another tart flavor. If you don't have kumquats in your local store you can order them online (see Sources, page 318).

For the filling:
1 pound kumquats, sliced
2 pints strawberries, sliced
½ cup sugar
2 tablespoons cornstarch
1 tablespoon chopped lemon zest
2 tablespoons Grand Marnier

For the topping:
4 ounces (1 stick) unsalted butter
1 cup all-purpose flour
½ cup rolled oats
¼ cup toasted pecans
⅔ cup firmly packed brown sugar
1½ teaspoons baking powder
Pinch of salt

For the Crème Chèvre:
½ cup crème fraîche
½ cup fresh chèvre, crumbled
3 tablespoons sugar
2 teaspoons pure vanilla extract

Preheat the oven to 375°F.

In a large bowl, mix together the kumquats, strawberries, sugar, cornstarch, lemon zest, and Grand Marnier. Place the fruit mixture in an 8x8-inch baking pan.

Cube the butter into ½-inch cubes and place them in a food processor with the flour. Pulse the mixture until it becomes granulated. Add the oats, pecans, sugar, baking powder, and salt and pulse until the mixture just comes together.

Place the crème fraîche and 4 tablespoons of chèvre in a bowl, add the sugar, and whisk until soft peaks form. Add the vanilla and whisk until soft peaks form.

Scatter the crisp topping equally over the fruit and bake for 25 minutes or until the filling is bubbling and the topping has browned. Remove the crisp from the oven and sprinkle with the remaining crumbled chèvre. Let the crisp cool slightly before serving.

To serve:
Place a large dollop of the Crème Chèvre on top of each portion and serve.

Serves 6

OSSAU-IRATY

REGION:	Midi-Pyrénées, France
MILK:	sheep
PROCESS:	raw
PRODUCTION:	uncooked, lightly pressed, semi-hard, natural rind
AFFINAGE:	at least 3 months
FLAVOR:	spicy, tangy, salty, robust, grassy, fruity
AROMA:	sour, wine-like, barnyard
TEXTURE:	supple, smooth, slightly oily
SIMILAR CHEESES:	Abbaye de Belloc, Petit Agour, Pecorino
PAIRINGS:	the girl & the fig Apricot Fig Chutney Queener Fruit Farm Black Cherry Jam Hector's Honeycomb fresh fruit Marcona almonds
NOTES:	There are only about 100 farmhouse producers that still make Ossau Iraty. They continue to maintain an unchanged traditional cheesemaking process for over 4,000 years.

spring
Nº 2

Entrée
Heirloom Radish & Mâche Salad,
Spring Onion Vinaigrette

Plat
Spring Lamb Leg,
Chickpea, Cucumber & Feta Salad

Dessert
Strawberry Tartine

Fromage
Jean de Brie

Heirloom Radish & Mâche Salad, Spring Onion Vinaigrette

Arrowood Vineyards & Winery "Côte de Lune Blanc," Saralee's Vineyard, Russian River Valley, California
Booker Vineyard White Blend, Paso Robles, California

There is something so simple and refreshing about a plate of radishes. I love the texture of radishes, from the crunch and the freshness they bring to the surprisingly peppery bite some radishes deliver. This is a simple dish to prepare and is easily customized; feel free to substitute different salad greens and your favorite vinaigrette.

For the vinaigrette:

4 spring onions, cleaned and cut into 1-inch pieces
¼ cup champagne vinegar
Juice from ½ lemon
¾ cup canola oil
Salt and white pepper to taste

For the salad:

4 bunches radishes (such as Easter Egg, Icicle, Flambo,
    Watermelon, or Black Spanish), tops removed, cleaned, and
    quartered or sliced
6 bunches mâche (watercress or arugula can be substituted)
6 to 12 white anchovies (optional)
Sea salt to taste

To prepare the vinaigrette:

Bring a pot of salted water to a boil and blanch the onions until tender, about 3 minutes. Remove the onions and place them in ice water until cool. Transfer the onions to a blender and add the champagne vinegar and lemon juice. Purée on high speed. Slowly drizzle the oil into the onion mixture until the oil is emulsified. Season with salt and pepper to taste and refrigerate.

To serve:

Arrange the cut radishes among 6 plates. Generously sauce the radishes with the vinaigrette and garnish with the mâche, white anchovies, and sea salt.

Serves 6

Heirloom Radishes

Most people only know radishes as the white-and-red garnish on salads, but heirloom radishes have become more widely available, bringing an array of texture and color to the plate. One of our popular starter plates is a very French way to serve radishes: thinly sliced radishes served with anchovy butter and sea salt.

Radishes are members of the mustard family and have mild, sweet, slightly bitter or peppery flavors depending on the variety. They come in all shapes and sizes, from red and white to even black. The most common is the Cherry Belle variety, a round, bright red radish with a white interior and a mild, slightly sweet flavor. The Watermelon variety has a vivid purple-pink interior, while the long, tubular French Breakfast radish has a pale red exterior and white interior with a mild, slightly sweet flavor.

The Sparkler White Tip is a round, bright red radish with white tips and a mild flavor, while the White Icicle is a long, thin variety with a milky white color and a rich, spicy flavor. You'll find a wide range of radishes at your local farmers market and at good specialty grocery stores; try a few different varieties and discover your favorites.

If you have a green thumb, radishes are one of the easiest crops to grow in the garden and will be among the first to emerge in the spring. Choose radishes with unblemished skin that are firm to the touch and remove the green tops before storing in the refrigerator. Radishes will be extra crispy if you soak them in ice water for a few hours before serving.

Spring Lamb Leg, Chickpea, Cucumber & Feta Salad

Frick Winery Cinsaut, Dry Creek Valley, California
Les Jamelles Cinsault Rosé, France

The sheep at Benziger Winery are raised to become eco-friendly weed whackers for the vineyards. Each spring we've been lucky enough to purchase the newborns that are raised organically and result in tender, delicately flavored meat. If you have the opportunity to buy lamb from a local source, give it a try; you'll notice a textural and flavor difference from the lamb found in a supermarket. Here, the flavors of spring highlight the earthy, flavorful leg meat.

For the marinade:

1 cup extra-virgin olive oil

1 tablespoon chopped fresh thyme

1 tablespoon chopped fresh rosemary

1 tablespoon chopped fresh sage

1 tablespoon chopped fresh flat-leaf parsley

4 garlic cloves, crushed

2 bay leaves

10 whole black peppercorns, crushed

6 top round lamb steaks (7 ounces each)

For the vinaigrette:

¼ cup champagne vinegar

¾ cup blended oil

½ cup fresh lemon juice (from about 4 lemons)

Salt and white pepper to taste

For the vegetables:

2 cups chickpeas, cooked (see Note)

1 small red onion, julienned

2 English cucumbers, seeded and sliced into
¼-inch half moons

1 cup fresh mint leaves, chiffonade

8 ounces feta cheese (preferably French sheep's
milk feta)

½ cup Lemon Vinaigrette (see above)

Extra-virgin olive oil

¼ cup Balsamic Reduction (page 311; optional,
for garnish)

Salt and pepper to taste

⅓ cup blended oil

To prepare the marinade:

Combine the olive oil, herbs, garlic, and peppercorns in a bowl. Pour the marinade over the lamb steaks and refrigerate for at least 24 hours and up to 3 days.

To prepare the vinaigrette:

Whisk the vinegar, oil, lemon juice, salt and pepper together. Refrigerate for up to 1 day ahead.

To prepare the vegetables:

Combine the chickpeas, onion, cucumbers, mint, and feta with the vinaigrette. Toss gently, season with salt and pepper, and refrigerate for 30 minutes. Remove the vegetables from the refrigerator about 30 minutes before serving.

Preheat the oven to 400°F.

Remove the lamb from the marinade and discard any excess marinade. Season the lamb with salt and black pepper. In an ovenproof pan over medium-high heat, heat the blended oil and sear the lamb on all sides. Place the pan in the oven and roast until the desired temperature is reached, about 7 minutes for medium-rare. Let the lamb rest for at least 10 minutes before serving.

To serve:

Divide the chickpea salad among 6 plates. Slice the lamb steak into 4 pieces and fan them out next to the salad. Garnish each plate with a drizzle of extra-virgin olive oil and Balsamic Reduction. Season with salt and pepper to taste.

Note:

If possible, use fresh garbanzo beans. They are in season from approximately June to September in Northern California. If you can't find fresh garbanzos, try Rancho Gordo classic garbanzo beans (see Sources, page 319). Both of these options will have a much brighter, earthier flavor than canned beans.

Serves 6

Chickpeas

The chickpea is one of the most historical ingredients we eat! These little beans have a history dating back to the Iliad, where they were referred to as erabinthos. (Chickpeas are also known as garbanzo beans; "garbanzo" comes from the Basque garbantzu, meaning "dry seed.") It thrives in the hot, dry Mediterranean climate and is a staple in Middle Eastern cuisine (celebrated in hummus, a dish of puréed chickpeas, tahini, lemon juice, and olive oil).

This legume is so versatile—in soups, stews, salads, or simply fried and spiced, as we serve them at ESTATE. They're available canned, dried, and fresh.

Strawberry Tartine

JC Cellars Late Harvest Viognier, Ripkin Vineyards, Lodi, California
Domaine Fontanel Rivesaltes Ambre, France

A tartine is not just for sandwich ingredients; it can be a dessert, too! Sometimes dessert just needs to be one small, perfect sweet bite to let you know that the meal is coming to an end. This not-too-sweet strawberry tartine is one of those desserts for me. The luscious, juicy strawberries that appear in early spring hit the spot. Make this tartine only when the strawberries are at their peak—it's really all about the strawberries.

For the crust:

1 cup pine nuts

3 tablespoons sugar

1½ cups all-purpose flour

8 tablespoons (1 stick) unsalted butter at room
    temperature

1 large egg yolk

½ teaspoon pure vanilla extract

For the filling:

2 cups mascarpone cheese

½ cup heavy cream

Zest of 1 orange

1 tablespoon Grand Marnier

¼ cup sugar

For the topping:

14 medium strawberries, tops removed, sliced
    into ¼-inch pieces

1 tablespoon sugar

Pinch of salt

1 tablespoon Grand Marnier

6 fresh mint leaves, cut in chiffonade, for garnish

To prepare the crust:

In a food processor pulse the pine nuts, sugar, and flour together a few times to break up the pine nuts. Transfer the mixture to a mixer fitted with a paddle attachment and add the butter, egg yolk, and vanilla. On low speed, mix until the dough just comes together. Form the dough into a ball, wrap it in plastic wrap, and chill for 1 hour or overnight.

Preheat the oven to 350°F. Line a baking sheet with parchment paper or a Silpat baking mat.

On a lightly floured surface, roll the dough out to a ¼-inch thickness. Cut the dough into six 4x2-inch pieces. Place the pieces on the baking sheet and bake for 9 to 11 minutes or until dough just begins to brown on the edges.

To prepare the filling:

In a mixer fitted with a whisk, combine the mascarpone and heavy cream and whip until incorporated. Add the orange zest, Grand Marnier, and sugar and whisk until the mixture holds a soft peak. Place the mixture in a pastry bag fitted with a ½-inch tip.

To prepare the topping:

Place the strawberries, sugar, salt, and Grand Marnier in a bowl and toss together. Allow the fruit to macerate for 10 minutes. Strain the liquid from the fruit and set aside.

To serve:

Place one crust on each plate. Pipe the mascarpone filling over the crust and cover with the strawberries and mint. Drizzle the reserved strawberry liquid around each tartine.

Serves 6

JEAN DE BRIE

REGION:	Île-de-France, France
MILK:	cow
PROCESS:	raw and pasteurized
PRODUCTION:	uncooked, unpressed, soft, washed rind, sometimes natural mold
AFFINAGE:	45 days
FLAVOR:	trace of sweetness, grassy, fruity, buttery
AROMA:	not overpowering, pungent
TEXTURE:	soft, supple
SIMILAR CHEESES:	Pierre-Robert, Camembert, Saint André
PAIRINGS:	Loulou's Garden Rose Petal Jam
	Happy Girl Kitchen Co. Pickled Beets
	Inna Jam Seascape Strawberry Jam
	Rustic Bakery Kalamata Olive Flatbread
	Jimtown Store Chopped Olive Spread
NOTES:	Even though it is called a brie, it really is a triple cream cheese with 80% butterfat.

the farm project
Sonoma, California

Starting **the farm project** was one of the most interesting collaborative experiences we've had yet. In 2010, we found an amazing plot of land and a family who believes in local produce and is committed to the effort. The Benziger family owns Imagery Estate Winery, a 20-acre property in Glen Ellen and a short drive from the restaurants. Wine grapes are planted on 7 acres and vegetables, herbs, and fruit orchards fill about 12 acres. In addition to the land at Imagery, we have a half-acre plot adjacent to the girl & the fig restaurant and several raised beds next to ESTATE, about 2 acres total.

The goals of **the farm project** are to see how farming our own produce will affect our business and in what ways—that's why I call it a project. So far, the year has shown that it adds a lot of "feel-good" product diversity, major amounts of manpower, and a lot of aspirin for the back pain!

There is an amazing feeling watching food grow, a process that we often take for granted—from when a seedling is first placed in the earth right through the magnificent cycle that brings it to its full flavor and beauty. Working under "the biodynamic and organic" philosophies that the Benzigers are committed to adds another level of pride and satisfaction. In this scenario, we really know where our food comes from, how it has been farmed, what critters have visited, and when it was harvested.

For John, **the farm project** is a natural extension of our philosophy at the restaurants, serving wonderful food that reflects a sense of place.

We were also committed to the idea of reducing waste, both in the kitchen and our own waste output. One of the hardest things to control in a restaurant kitchen is food wastage. We strive to train our employees not to take shortcuts in the prep kitchen. There are valuable scraps that can go into stock, soup, or other dishes. What is sometimes seen as waste is actually perfectly good product for another use.

We asked the sous chefs to help plant, weed, and harvest, giving them a true appreciation for product and hopefully reducing waste. Involving the prep and line cooks in the farm duties has given them a new perspective on how much effort it takes to farm and our wastage conversations are no longer ignored. We've also reduced waste through composting. The kitchen scraps go into the compost pile at the Imagery farm, which is then used to fertilize the crops and as mulch. Not only is composting better for the environment but it's made a difference in our bottom line as well. When we started composting, we took a trash day away from our delivery, and we've saved a lot of money by reducing what we pay the trash company; John notes that we've cut our trash bill by 33 percent. By next year we will have our own compost and we won't have to buy any.

On the Imagery farm the orchards are brimming with an amazing assortment of produce, often several varieties of one crop. For example, there are five types of peaches (Babcock, Elberta, O'Henry, Indian Free, and Frost), three types of apricots (Blenheim, Tilton, and Tom Cot), and three types of Pluots (Flavor Queen, Flavor King, and Dapple Dandy).

We planted two types of cucumbers (Armenian and Lemon), three types of squash (zucchini, Green Tint patty pan, and a yellow variety), and five types of beans (Tricolor, Cold Rush, Bluelake, Haricots Verts, and Romano). Sometimes this bounty keeps us menu-planning well into the night. The variety of produce gives us so many wonderful options to work with, inspiring menu changes and new dishes. Each type is suited to a specific dish; some peaches are better for baking, while others are better for canning and preserving, for example.

Rows of herbs flourish alongside the vegetables, both familiar (Italian parsley, chives, tarragon, rosemary, and thyme) and the more unusual (lemon verbena, Opal basil, nettles, and marjoram). All of the produce from the farm ends up on our menu while some of it is devoted to our Sonoma Valley Sharecropping project (more on that on page 61).

Through farming, which is the epitome of the seasonal experience, we've gained an even deeper appreciation of the word "seasonal". "We're experiencing micro seasonality," as John puts it. He remembers the summer of 2010 in particular, which had very unusual weather for Sonoma, staying cool for a month longer than usual, delaying the tomato crop. "At one point, we had tomatoes everywhere, because when the tomatoes ripened they all came in at once," notes John. "So we had cases and cases of tomatoes. We made sun-dried tomatoes but we had to think, what else can we do with a tomato?" With the abundance of green and red tomatoes we were forced to get creative and John made cases of green tomato jam. "Normally we would have just bought San Marzano tomatoes and never made green tomato jam," says John. "We're forced to deal with the reality of the season, not the idea of the season. It made us plan our menus from a less macro to a more micro seasonal perspective."

Viewing farming from a macro perspective also means the seasons overlap a bit. Who would think you could have Delicata squash and cucumbers appearing on a menu at the same time, harvested from the same farm? You cook what the farm provides and you make adjustments and get creative. "the farm project sharpened our appreciation for seasonal," says John. "You stop thinking fall versus summer but start to think of what is ripe. It has made us better produce buyers and better farmers."

Eating seasonally is good for the planet and for your taste buds and it also makes financial sense for a restaurant. "It's common sense to be seasonal. If we have to have tomatoes year-round and tomatoes taste better in summer, why not put them up when they are at their peak to be enjoyed in winter?" John explains. "You want to pay the least amount when they taste best. It's common sense for the restaurant."

Even with the amazing amount of food we're growing (2,000 pounds in October 2010 alone), we're not able to supply the restaurants with all that we need. September 2010 was our biggest harvest to date, yet only 8 percent of our total produce purchases were from the farm. That's because we're not professional farmers yet—as we learn, we'll increase our yield and one day hopefully be able to grow all of our own food.

John oversees **the farm project** and has become a devoted farmer himself. When he's not overseeing the kitchen or working with the staff, he's reviewing crop plans, researching organic ways to eliminate pests (like the dreaded gopher), or harvesting crops. "I'm just fascinated by the entire process," attests John. "I want to understand the kitchen side of it but as time has gone by I want to understand the entire circle, from growing it to cooking it."

One way we've tried to bring the farm to the table—literally—is through themed farm dinners at ESTATE. Not only did the farm dinners help pay for the farm, but our customers got a chance to experience local and seasonal to the utmost degree. "It's a way to tell a story about the farm through a dinner," says John. The dinner begins with a conversation among the landowner-rancher, Chris Benziger; the head farmer, Colby; and the chef, John. Each describes his role in the farm and the inspiration that the others attribute to their own success.

Recently we had two wildly successful farm dinners, the first being a Small Plate Tomato Dinner, in which every course featured tomatoes using different cooking methods, and an Heirloom Apple Dinner that we collaborated on with Kendra and Paul from Nana Mae's Organics, which highlighted at least ten of the apples from their orchards.

Many of our guests share our passion for the farm and some have participated in one way or another. We have had extra hands helping with harvest; I have been the recipient of gifts from their own farms (including the most amazing blood red peaches); and we have shared stories and conversation through our social media activities.

As with most of our projects, we're always looking for ways to improve and explore new things. In 2010, most of our crops were transplants but we built a greenhouse so we can start certain crops from seed from local seed companies. Next year the goal is to pull our own seeds out. (See page 318 for seed and transplant contacts.) In farming there's always something else to do, to tweak, to improve on, and we're dedicated to making **the farm project** a long-term part of our restaurants.

Rafael & Jaime at the farm project

Rafael & Jaime at the farm project

Sonoma Valley Sharecroppers
Sonoma, California

Sonoma Valley Sharecropper—our line of pickled and canned fruits, preserves, vegetables, and tomato sauce—started with **the farm project**. When we agreed to farm the land at Imagery we consented to give the Benziger Family part of the harvest, and how we were going to do that was part of the question. They could come down and grab whatever they wanted from the fields, but Chris Benziger wondered if we could can the produce instead. This kick-started the Sharecropper idea.

Sharecropping is an agricultural system where the tenant farms the land in exchange for giving the landowner a share of the crop. The term fit perfectly, and Sonoma Valley Sharecropper Project was born. We had made the Bread & Butter Pickles in the restaurant for years so we were familiar with canning and pickling processes, and John also developed new recipes. Pickling and canning aren't difficult, but they are time-consuming. I decided to create a Sharecropper label for the glass jars and found some old farming photographs from the 1930's that depict actual farmers from that time.

The seasons determine the product lineup, so whenever we're harvesting, we're also pickling or canning. Once we knew we would be canning, we planted accordingly. For instance, we planted more cucumbers to make the pickles, Mother Nature doesn't always cooperate, last spring we planted more tomatoes in order to make tomato sauce, but we didn't get the last ripening of tomatoes, which led to a bumper crop of green tomatoes. We learned that we have to can while we can, with what we have!

The 2010 harvest rewarded us with beautiful produce that became Bread & Butter Pickles, Pickled Peppers, Dilly Beans, Lemon Verbena Poached Apricots, Brandied Plums (made with a dash of Domaine de Canton Ginger Liqueur), Sweet & Sour Squash, Sun-Dried Tomatoes, Pickled Jalapeños, Chili Flakes, Strawberry & Black Pepper Jam, San Marzano Tomato Sauce, Pickled Garden Salsa Peppers, Pickled Green Tomatoes, and Green Tomato Jam. Both green tomato products were made when the tomato season went cold, and we had a ton of green tomatoes; I love the acidic zing of the Green Tomato Jam on a slice of bread or on top of scrambled eggs. We use the Sharecropper products on our charcuterie platter, on sandwiches, and on cheese plates, and we're not the only ones who think they're delicious; the Sweet & Sour Squash was a finalist in the 2010 Good Food Awards.

In winter, we're pickling cauliflower, carrots, and fennel; in spring we might pickle spring onions, ramps, leeks, fava beans, and more carrots. We make a limited quantity, sometimes only 13 or 14 jars of one product. (The most we made was 143 jars of pickled peppers due to a stellar pepper season.) Though it's hard work, the project has underscored the idea of seasonal cooking and working with what you have. To be able to open a jar of San Marzano Tomato Sauce on a cold winter's day and taste summer on a spoon is an unparalleled experience.

Rafael making way for new crop

Entrée
Braised Leeks, Crème Fraîche & Truffles

Plat
Sweetbreads with Spring Vegetables

Dessert
Espresso & Brown Sugar Crème Brûlée

Fromage
Bellwether Farms Pepato

Braised Leeks, Crème Fraîche & Truffles

Tablas Creek Vineyard "Côte du Tablas Blanc," Paso Robles, California
Très Bonnes Années "the girl & the fig" Blanc, Russian River Valley, California

Watching leeks grow in the garden is magical—they look like tall soldiers standing at attention. It's amazing that these seemingly tough stalks can cook down to tender strands of herbal goodness. When properly cooked, leeks are delicate and have a base flavor that easily combines with other ingredients to create perfect harmony.

1 teaspoon minced garlic
1 teaspoon chopped fresh flat-leaf parsley
1 teaspoon chopped fresh thyme
½ cup dry white wine
2 cups Chicken Stock (page 313)
Salt and pepper to taste plus 1 teaspoon sea salt
9 leeks, trimmed and cleaned
¼ cup crème fraîche
1 tablespoon chopped black truffle shavings
2 hard-boiled egg yolks, passed through a fine-mesh sieve
2 tablespoons plain bread crumbs
1 teaspoon chopped chives
2 tablespoons diced red onion

In a large skillet or baking pan, bring the garlic, herbs, white wine, and chicken stock to a boil and season to taste. Add the leeks, reduce to a simmer, and cover. Cook for about 20 minutes until the leeks pierce easily with a fork. Remove from the heat and cool to room temperature.

Remove the leeks from the braising liquid. Slice 6 of the leeks in half lengthwise and 3 of the leeks into ¼-inch coin shapes.

In a small bowl, whisk together the crème fraîche and truffles. Divide the crème fraîche equally among six plates and place 2 leek halves on each plate. Divide the leek coins equally among the plates and garnish each serving with a sprinkle of the egg yolks, bread crumbs, chives, onion, and a pinch of sea salt.

Serves 6

Leeks

Leeks belong to the onion family but have a milder flavor than most onions. The thick stalks are dark green on top with a white base and they're very popular in Europe, particularly France. Leeks range in size from very large to fairly petite; smaller leeks are more tender than larger ones.

Leeks are extremely versatile, and the flavor seems to come to life when braised in stock or baked with potatoes in a gratin. They also make a delicious tart or savory pie and add tremendous flavor to soups, stocks, and sauces.

Leeks are available year-round. Look for leeks that have no yellow leaves. Store them in the refrigerator but not in a plastic bag. Before using, trim off the top tough green tops and cut them lengthwise to wash them thoroughly. Layers of dirt accumulate in the middle of the layers, which requires several changes of water.

Sweetbreads with Spring Vegetables

Shane Wine Cellars "Ma Fille" Rosé, Sonoma County, California
Bedrock Wine Company "Ode to Lulu" Rosé of Mourvèdre, Sonoma Valley, California
Domaine de Nizas Rosé, Coteaux du Languedoc, Languedoc-Roussillon, France

Most people don't even consider sweetbreads on a restaurant menu, but sweetbread devotees order them every time we feature them. (Sweetbreads are the thymus gland of veal, lamb, or pork.) When properly cooked the texture of sweetbreads is very satisfying, offering a firm bite with a gentle chew. This dish is the sum of its parts; the delicate flavors of early spring vegetables contrasts nicely with the earthy flavor of the sweetbreads.

For the sweetbreads:
2 pounds sweetbreads
6 cups whole milk
5 cups extra-virgin olive oil
3 sprigs fresh thyme
1 garlic clove, smashed
2 teaspoons salt
1 cup all-purpose flour
2 tablespoons cornmeal
½ cup blended oil

For the sauce:
2 tablespoons chopped shallots
1 sprig fresh thyme
1 bay leaf
1 teaspoon whole peppercorns
1 cup dry white wine
½ pound (2 sticks) plus 1 tablespoon unsalted butter, cubed
18 baby carrots, blanched (about 3 bunches)
1 cup spring peas, blanched
Salt and pepper to taste

Spring Peas

My mom loves peas and every spring she would fill bags with fresh pods to be snacked on through the week. I loved popping open the pods and getting a whiff of spring. Raw peas have a nice crunch and are great on their own or in salads. Cooked, they are perfect in ragouts, risotto, or puréed into a fresh spring sauce for fish.

Fresh peas are a fantastic spring and summer treat. Crunchy and sweet, they are delicious simply boiled and served with melted butter and even better with a spoonful or two of chopped fresh mint leaves. Pea soup is an easy way to celebrate their fresh flavor.

Spring peas are at their peak from March through May. Look for fresh pea pods that are plump and brilliant green in color. They will keep in the refrigerator for up to 3 days. A helpful prep tip: 1½ pounds of fresh pea pods yields about 1½ cups of fresh peas.

To prepare the sweetbreads:
Place the sweetbreads in a container, cover with 3 cups of milk, and soak for 3 hours. Strain the milk, cover the sweetbreads with the remaining milk, and soak them overnight. Remove the sweetbreads from the milk and pat dry.

In a non-reactive pan place the sweetbreads, olive oil, thyme, garlic, and salt and cook over low heat for 40 minutes. Remove the pan from the heat and let the sweetbreads cool to room temperature.

Place the sweetbreads in a loaf pan, cover with plastic wrap, and add a weight on top (such as cans, bricks, or rocks). Refrigerate overnight. The next day remove the sweetbreads from the pan and cut them into 1½-inch cubes. Set aside.

To prepare the sauce:
Place a small saucepan over low heat and add the shallots, thyme, bay leaf, peppercorns, and white wine and cook slowly until the wine has evaporated. Slowly whisk in the butter, being careful to hold the emulsion and not break the sauce. Strain the sauce and place it in a warm (not hot) spot.

To prepare the vegetables:
Heat the carrots and peas together in a saucepan with 2 tablespoons of water and 1 tablespoon of butter over medium heat.

To finish the sweetbreads:
In a large bowl, mix the flour and cornmeal together and season with salt and pepper. Toss the sweetbreads in the flour mixture to coat. Heat the blended oil in a large skillet over medium heat, add the sweetbreads, and cook on all sides until golden brown, about 3 to 5 minutes per side.

Add the warm carrots and peas to the butter sauce and gently stir.

To serve:
Divide the vegetables equally among 6 plates, top each portion with sweetbreads, and drizzle with any additional sauce.

Serves 6

Sweetbreads

Technically, sweetbreads are the thymus gland of beef, lamb, and pork, although other cuts of meat are sometimes called sweetbreads as well. There are two glands in the animal connected by a tube, resulting in two "types" of sweetbreads. The gland near the heart is the more popular type of sweetbread, known for its delicate flavor and smooth texture. Depending on the type and age of the animal, the flavor of sweetbreads can range from sweet and mild to very strong.

Preparing sweetbreads at home is easier than you think if you take just a few steps. Traditionally they must be soaked in several changes of acidulated water (water with lemon or vinegar) and the outer membrane must be removed.

Alternatively, you can soak the sweetbreads in milk, but cooking them in olive oil eliminates the need to peel the outer membrane. Sweetbreads can be poached, sautéed, braised, or even fried. When buying sweetbreads at a butcher shop, look for those that are milky-white in color and plump. They're very perishable so cook them within 24 hours of purchase.

Espresso & Brown Sugar Crème Brûlée

Firelit Liqueur, California

One year I ordered crème brûlée or crème caramel every time I went out to dinner. I was on a hunt for the very best version. Truth be told, I tasted many dismal examples: some had a gritty, grainy texture, some were overcooked, and some were too runny. A beautifully cooked crème brûlée should be a textural experience. Cracking through the delicate layer of burnt sugar to get to the creamy silky custard is a treat as the cream lingers on the palate. Although we're known for our Lavender Crème Brûlée, this version uses two complementary flavor elements—coffee and brown sugar.

4 cups heavy cream

1 vanilla bean, scraped and reserved

2 tablespoons instant espresso powder

2 tablespoons coarsely ground espresso beans

6 large egg yolks

½ cup sugar

½ cup turbinado brown sugar

½ cup whipped cream, for garnish

3 tablespoons chocolate covered espresso beans,
   optional, for garnish

Preheat the oven to 300°F.

In a medium saucepan, heat the cream, vanilla (pods and seeds), espresso powder, and espresso beans over medium heat until the mixture just comes to a boil, about 6 to 8 minutes. Turn off the heat, cover, and steep for 30 minutes.

Meanwhile, in a large bowl, whisk the egg yolks and sugars until light and pale. Strain the cream mixture through a fine-mesh strainer into a large bowl. Temper the eggs with the cream by slowly adding one quarter of the hot cream mixture into the yolks a little at a time until it is completely mixed. Chill the mixture until cool.

Pour the chilled custard mixture into six 6-ounce ramekins and place the ramekins in a large baking dish. Add enough hot water to the dish to reach halfway up the sides of the ramekins. Cover the dish with foil and bake on the middle rack for 20 minutes or until set. Remove the custards from the oven and let cool to room temperature (about 45 minutes). Cover and refrigerate until chilled, at least 2 hours or overnight.

Before serving, sprinkle the tops with a thin layer of brown sugar and caramelize them with a small torch or under a broiler set on high. Garnish with whipped cream and chocolate covered espresso beans.

Serves 6

BELLWETHER FARMS PEPATO

SPRING №3

REGION:	Petaluma, California
MILK:	sheep
PROCESS:	raw
PRODUCTION:	uncooked, pressed, semi-hard, natural rind
AFFINAGE:	five months
FLAVOR:	nutty, pepper, spicy
AROMA:	spicy, grassy
TEXTURE:	medium firm - firm
SIMILAR CHEESES:	Ossau-Iraty, Petit Basque
PAIRINGS:	L'Epicurien Black Cherry Confit
	Blackberry Farm Apple Butter
	McEvoy Ranch Olio Nuovo
	Apple Compote (page 315)
	Made in Napa Apricot Fig Spread
	spiced nuts, salad greens
NOTES:	Pepato has a fine balance of salt and pepper. The addition of whole black peppercorns gives the cheese an interesting texture.

Graffeo Coffee

We've been serving coffee from Graffeo, a local coffee company, in the restaurants for over ten years. Selected in a blind tasting, we were able to taste and distinguish the flavors that we love most about coffee. Rich, strong, full-flavored, and fresh were qualities that we were looking for. The fact that Graffeo's recipe for success relies on simplicity was a bonus. Graffeo has only one blend that they offer as a Dark Roast and a Light Roast (we prefer the dark). They also offer a decaffeinated Colombian Roast produced naturally. I should mention that our staff is addicted to Graffeo and they work harder than ever after an espresso or two! Graffeo is one of California's oldest family-run artisan coffee companies and was founded in San Francisco. (See Sources, page 318 for more information.)

Colby Eierman
Expert Biodynamic Farmer

It would have been a difficult road without Colby Eierman's assistance and collaboration in the beginning of **the farm project**. We have been so lucky to be able to learn and work side by side with him; he has taught John a lot about how to keep the fresh produce coming into the restaurants every day, month after month.

A Sonoma County native, Colby grew up just a few miles from the Imagery Estate Winery. He got interested in gardening in high school and graduated from the University of Oregon with a degree in landscape architecture, specifically in edible landscaping. After an apprenticeship at UC Santa Cruz to hone his horticulture skills, he started managing gardens and farming for restaurants. Colby's first job was at the famed raw food restaurant Roxanne's in Marin County, California. After Roxanne's, he grew baby lettuce for the legendary restaurant Chez Panisse and then moved to Napa to manage the gardens at Copia: The American Center for Wine, Food and the Arts. Copia had an expansive edible garden, and he was grew all of the produce for Copia's restaurant, Julia's Kitchen.

After working in Napa, Colby returned to Sonoma and went to work for Benziger Family Winery. There he focused on biodynamic and sustainability practices, both for growing produce and raising animals. While at Benziger, Colby built the garden at Imagery Estate Winery.

Around the same time, at a Fork & Shovel Meeting (a networking event for chefs and farmers), John told Colby about his new upcoming farm project and that we would need some serious assistance in understanding biodynamic, sustainable, and organic farming methods to keep the Imagery Farm certified. Simultaneously we gained permission from the Benziger Family to take on the farming responsibilities at Imagery in early March 2010. "It was spring already and they were ready to go, so I just jumped in and got their crop plan together and helped them get the garden started," says Colby.

We began **the farm project** not knowing what it would take to create a working garden that could supply all of our restaurants and catering company. There are countless details involved in planting and sustaining a garden and Colby has been our guide, teacher, and mentor. "We collaborate on the crop plan and ask questions like, 'are we growing that from seed or ordering transplants from a local nursery? Are we going to trellis the tomatoes? How are we going to manage pests?' That's what I'm focused on," says Colby. "They call me and tell me something is eating the Swiss chard. I come out and look at it and offer solutions." Colby is literally our go-to guy for everything garden-related.

His biodynamic solutions, such as spraying neem oil to prevent garden pests, have opened our eyes to organic and biodynamic farming methods.

the farm project isn't just about growing locally for us; there has to be an economic advantage to harvesting our own produce. Colby knows how to work with restaurants to plant the right crops. "When you're growing for restaurants, we start with an evaluation of what products the restaurant is using, decide what we can do well with, and then we do a financial analysis," he says. "We can't grow everything, and that's not the goal of the project." Colby first looks at what is available in the community. "If we're happy with a certain product, we're not going to make the effort to grow that. If there is a product that isn't available, we can try it out," he says.

Colby is passionate about working with restaurants because the crops can lead to culinary inspiration. While some growers gripe about a bumper crop of zucchini or tomatoes, Colby sees opportunity. "When you've got so many tomatoes you don't know what to do with them, it will open up an opportunity to use that product in a way you wouldn't necessarily have thought of," says Colby. "It's a wellspring of inspiration for the chefs, and it's exciting for them to be that close to the source." One of our goals with the garden was to reduce waste, by asking the sous chefs and other staffers to work the land and harvest crops. "They've [the staff] made the investment and know how much effort goes into growing, and hopefully that leads to less waste and the food costs can come down because everything is utilized," notes Colby.

John had some basic garden knowledge before we started but Colby has guided him through the process of a working farm. "John's a farmer now. It's cool to work with a guy like that, who is motivated to understand every part of the business he's involved with. It's inspiring for me because he is so inspired. He's a good resource on that front," says Colby. "He's the right person for the job because he's got great chefs that are at the helm that he can trust to deliver the food in the right way, so he has the ability to get out and manage **the farm project** and elevate the quality of the project."

Entrée
Chilled Asparagus Soup, Chervil Cream

Plat
Slow Cooked Rabbit & Spring Vegetables,
Creamy Polenta

Dessert
Rhubarb Tart

Fromage
Bohemian Creamery Bo Peep

Chilled Asparagus Soup, Chervil Cream

Truchard Vineyards Roussanne, Carneros, Napa Valley, California
Zaca Mesa Winery & Vineyards Roussanne, Santa Ynez Valley, California

Spring has arrived when I start seeing asparagus at the local market and on menus all over town. We don't always buy the first case available, but check the quality for the best spears; they shouldn't be too woody in flavor or texture or too soggy from excess moisture. There are so many ways to love this gorgeous vegetable, whether it's blanched and wrapped in prosciutto or just drizzled with extra-virgin olive oil. Asparagus is quite stunning in its pure shape, and it's nice to show off Nature's magic by leaving them whole.

For the soup:

2½ tablespoons unsalted butter

1 small yellow onion, chopped

3 celery stalks, chopped

1 leek, white part only, cleaned and chopped

2 shallots, chopped

4 garlic cloves, crushed

2 bunches green jumbo asparagus, peeled and cut in
   ¾-inch rounds (reserve tips for garnish)

½ cup heavy cream

Salt and white pepper to taste

For the Chervil Cream:

1 bunch chervil (reserve 12 stems for garnish and
   chop remaining leaves)

½ cup crème fraîche

1 tablespoon heavy cream

Salt and white pepper to taste

To prepare the soup:

Melt the butter in a large saucepan over medium-low heat. Add the onion, celery, leek, shallots, and garlic and sauté until the vegetables are soft, about 7 minutes. Stir the vegetables occasionally to prevent browning. Add the asparagus and stir together.

Add 1½ quarts of water and season with salt and pepper. Bring to a boil. Reduce the heat and cook until the asparagus are tender, about 5 minutes. Add the heavy cream. Remove the soup from the heat and purée the mixture with a hand immersion blender, food processor, or a blender. Strain the mixture through a fine-mesh sieve into a container over an ice bath. Adjust the seasoning if necessary.

Blanch the reserved asparagus tips for the garnish.

To prepare the Chervil Cream:

Mix the chopped chervil with the crème fraîche and the heavy cream. If it is too thick, adjust the consistency with a little more of the heavy cream or water.

To serve:

Garnish each soup with a dollop of the Chervil Cream, a few asparagus tips and a sprinkling of chervil leaves.

Serves 6 to 8

Asparagus

I know spring is here when crates of asparagus arrive at the restaurants. It truly is a spring vegetable: asparagus grows only when temperatures start to rise and the shoots will emerge when the soil reaches 50 degrees F. This long-stemmed vegetable is actually the shoot of a perennial plant that's part of the lily family. Originally a wild seacoast plant from Great Britain, it has been cultivated for more than 2,000 years. California leads the U.S. in asparagus production—the marshes along the Sacramento River are a perfect environment for growing asparagus. (Which is why we don't try growing it at the Imagery Estate farm!) It's a labor-intensive crop; workers must hand-harvest each spear and it takes at least two years for the first shoot to appear after the seeds are planted.

Asparagus comes in several colors: green, white, and purple. White asparagus is from the same plant as green asparagus but has been deprived of sunlight. White asparagus is very common in Europe and has a more delicate flavor than the green variety.

The size of asparagus varies and affects cooking time. Different sizes also work better for certain recipes—you wouldn't grill pencil-thin asparagus but it's a delicious and easy way to prepare the larger-sized spears.

Asparagus season runs from February through June. Look for bunches with tight tips. The best way to store asparagus is upright in an inch or two of water, like a bunch of flowers, in the refrigerator for up to 3 days.

To prepare fresh asparagus, simply trim the woody ends. (Some say you should take the spears individually and gently bend the tops over until they snap.) Fresh asparagus can be used in salads but cooked asparagus is extremely versatile: steamed, it makes a beautiful, healthy side dish (asparagus is rich in fiber). Or simply blanch the spears and then sauté in butter for the perfect spring accompaniment to a piece of meat or fish. It's also easy to stir-fry or grill, where it will cook in just a few minutes. We often blanch asparagus, chop it, and add it to pastas, risotto, and even frittata or egg dishes.

Slow Cooked Rabbit & Spring Vegetables, Creamy Polenta

Failla Wines Viognier, Alban Vineyard, Edna Valley, California
Quivira Vineyards and Winery Grenache, Wine Creek Ranch, Dry Creek Valley, California

Has anyone ever told you that rabbit tastes like chicken? If so, they should freshen up their taste buds. Rabbit tastes like rabbit and in our restaurants rabbit braised with fresh spring vegetables provides a hearty, earthy dish that highlights the delicate meat, the vibrant vegetables, and the rich sauce. This dish, served over polenta, would be just as delicious served with mashed potatoes or farro. You can find rabbit at specialty butcher stores and some farmers markets; you often have to order it ahead.

For the rabbit:
1 fresh whole rabbit (2½ to 3 pounds)
¼ cup blended oil
1 large carrot, chopped
2 celery ribs, chopped
1 large yellow onion, chopped
4 garlic cloves, peeled
3 Roma tomatoes, chopped
1 cup red wine
2 bay leaves
1 bunch fresh thyme
10 black peppercorns
5 cups Veal (page 313 or Chicken Stock can be
   substituted, page 313)

For the vegetables:
3 bunches baby carrots, blanched
½ cup fava beans, blanched and peeled
1 bunch scallions, blanched
2 leeks, white parts only, blanched and sliced into
   ¼-inch rounds
2 ounces pancetta, diced into ¼-inch slices and
   cooked
2 tablespoons unsalted butter
Salt and pepper to taste

For the polenta:
2 tablespoons blended oil
1 large onion, chopped
1 clove garlic, sliced
3 cups whole milk
1½ cups coarse grain polenta
6 tablespoons chopped fresh herbs, such as thyme,
   sage, and parsley

½ cup mixed fresh herbs (whole leaf), for garnish

Preheat the oven to 350°F.

To prepare the rabbit:
Break down the rabbit (or have the butcher do it for you) into front and hind legs and saddle. Reserve the trimmings and rib cage. Place the bones and trimmings on a baking pan and roast until golden brown. Set aside. Heat a heavy bottomed Dutch oven or similar ovenproof pan over medium-high heat. Season the rabbit legs and saddle generously with salt and pepper. Add the blended oil to the pan and sear the rabbit on all sides until golden brown, about 5 to 6 minutes per side. Remove the rabbit and set aside.

Keep the pot over the heat and add the carrot, celery, onion, garlic, and tomatoes. Cook until the vegetables have caramelized. Deglaze with the red wine and add the herbs, peppercorns, rabbit, roasted bones, trimmings, and stock. Bring to a simmer and then turn off the heat. Cover the pot and bake until the rabbit meat begins to pull away from bone, about 2 to 3 hours. Remove the pot from the oven and let it cool until you can remove the ingredients with your hands. Remove the saddle and legs from the pot and pull the meat from the bones. Set aside.

Strain the cooking liquid and skim any fat off the top. Transfer the liquid back to the pot and reduce by half over high heat. Set aside.

To prepare the vegetables:
In a medium sauté pan, large enough to hold all of the ingredients, combine the baby carrots, fava beans, leeks, pancetta, butter, and ¼ cup water. Cook until heated through, about 5 to 6 minutes. Add the butter and season with salt and pepper to taste.

To prepare the polenta:
Heat the blended oil in a large saucepan. Add the onions and garlic and cook until translucent, about 5 minutes. Add 2 cups water and the milk and bring to a simmer. Slowly whisk in the polenta and the fresh herbs. Bring to a boil, reduce the heat, and simmer for about 10 to 15 minutes or until the polenta is soft. Season with salt and pepper to taste.

To serve:
Add a spoonful of polenta to six bowls, top with the rabbit mixture, vegetables, and herbs and serve immediately.

Serves 6

Rabbit

Rabbit has been part of man's diet for centuries, from the Aztec to the Shoshone. It's also been part of European cooking for centuries; but Americans seem more reluctant to embrace this tender, lean meat. Compared to other meats, rabbit is lower in fat, higher in essential fatty acids, and higher in protein. (Farmed rabbits have a milder flavor than wild rabbit.) Rabbit meat remains rare (and expensive) in the U.S. because they are difficult to breed in large quantities and are susceptible to disease. Australia and New Zealand raise rabbits for meat. French farmed rabbits are consistently the best quality but a few small American producers are beginning to provide top-quality meat.

Some specialty butchers can get rabbit meat for you but check your local farmers market as well. You can find it whole or cut up in pieces. Rabbit can be braised, sautéed, roasted, grilled, or even fried. Because it's so lean rabbit can dry out quickly, which is why we prefer braising or preparing rabbit confit (see page 232 for more on confit).

Rhubarb Tart
Pineau des Charentes, France

Although rhubarb has been around for centuries, it seems to come back in fashion every few years. We make this tart when rhubarb is at its peak but we also use rhubarb in crisps, confit, chutney, and conserves. Sweet strawberries are a complementary spring flavor. Garden tip: if you're planting rhubarb in your garden keep your pets away from the plants—they can be quite poisonous.

For the crust:

2 cups all-purpose flour

1 teaspoon salt

1 teaspoon sugar

12 tablespoons (1½ sticks) unsalted
   butter, chilled, cut into ½-inch cubes

For the filling:

1½ pounds fresh rhubarb, peeled and
   diced into ½-inch pieces

1 cup firmly packed brown sugar

½ vanilla bean, sliced lengthwise

1 teaspoon lemon zest

1 large egg, for egg wash

2 tablespoons coarse sugar (see Sources,
   page 318)

To prepare the crust:

Place the flour, salt, and sugar in a food processor and pulse until the ingredients are combined. Add the butter and pulse until the mixture becomes granulated. Turn the food processor on and slowly add 2 tablespoons ice water until the dough just holds together. Add more water if needed, 1 tablespoon at a time. (The process should take less than 1 minute.)

Transfer the dough to the counter and form it into one piece. Wrap it in plastic wrap and chill in the refrigerator for at least 1 hour or overnight. Remove the dough from the refrigerator, divide it into 6 equal balls, and roll them on a lightly floured surface into 8-inch rounds. Line a baking sheet with parchment paper or a Silpat baking mat. Place the tart rounds on the baking sheet and chill for 15 minutes until firm.

To prepare the filling:

Place three quarters of the rhubarb in a non-reactive pot just large enough to hold all of the ingredients. Add the brown sugar, vanilla bean, and lemon zest. Heat on low and bring to a simmer. Continue to cook until the mixture has thickened to the consistency of thick jam. Add the remaining rhubarb and transfer the mixture to a rimmed sheet pan to cool. Remove the vanilla bean from the filling.

Preheat the oven to 375°F.

Place a large dollop of the rhubarb filling in the center of each dough round and fold up the edges, pinching the seams together. In a small bowl, whisk the egg with 3 tablespoons water. Using a pastry brush, brush the pastry edges with the egg wash and sprinkle the tarts with the coarse sugar.

Bake until the dough is golden brown, about 18 to 22 minutes. Serve the tarts warm with vanilla gelato or whipped cream.

Serves 6

BOHEMIAN CREAMERY BO PEEP

REGION:	Sebastopol, California
MILK:	organic Jersey cow and sheep
PROCESS:	pasteurized
PRODUCTION:	uncooked, unpressed, semi-soft, white mold ripened
AFFINAGE:	aged 2 months
FLAVOR:	grassy, light, mild, nutty
AROMA:	musty, ashy, melted butter
TEXTURE:	soft, semi-soft, velvety
SIMILAR CHEESES:	Tomme de Corse, Fleur de Maquis (without the herbs)
PAIRINGS:	Blis Bourbon Maple Syrup
	Inna Jam Seascape Strawberry Jam
	Fastachi Almond Butter
	Saltworks Sea Salt
NOTES:	Bo Peep was inspired by traditional Corsican basket cheese. This cheese is aged in Camembert forms.

Entrée
Carrot Soup, Fava Bean Pistou

Plat
Pacific Halibut,
Grilled Spring Vegetable Barigoule

Dessert
Strawberry Panna Cotta

Fromage
Nicasio Square

Carrot Soup, Fava Bean Pistou

Imagery Estate Winery Viognier, Sonoma County, California
Domaine François Villard, Condrieu de Poncins, Condrieu, France

Who knew that plain orange carrots would one day be outshined by their heirloom cousins? The color, texture, and flavor of heirloom carrots varies: some are quite fibrous and require longer cooking times and some change color when peeled. However, they all share the earthy, fresh flavor of carrots. Chantenay carrots would be a delight in this soup if you can find them, but any local, freshly picked carrot will be just as delicious. We pair this soup with Fava Bean Pistou, but you can get creative and garnish it with a variety of toppings: a dollop of crème fraîche with a hit of curry powder, a handful of marinated golden raisins, or a spoonful of chopped parsley.

For the soup:
2 tablespoons unsalted butter
1 small yellow onion, chopped
2 celery stalks, chopped
1 leek, white part only, cleaned and chopped
2 shallots, diced
4 garlic cloves, crushed
2 pounds carrots (about 6 carrots), chopped
Salt and white pepper to taste
½ cup heavy cream

For the pistou:
¼ cup pine nuts, toasted
1 garlic clove, peeled
2 tablespoons grated Parmesan cheese
⅓ cup extra-virgin olive oil plus additional
    for garnish
½ cup fava beans, blanched and peeled
1 tablespoon chopped fresh flat-leaf parsley
Salt and black pepper to taste

To prepare the soup:
Melt the butter in a medium-large saucepan over medium-low heat. Add the onion, celery, leek, shallots, and garlic and sauté until the vegetables are soft, about 10 minutes. Stir the vegetables occasionally to prevent browning. Add the carrots and sauté for about 3 minutes while stirring. Add 1½ quarts water and season with salt and pepper. Bring to a boil, reduce to a simmer, and cook until the carrots are just tender, about 5 minutes. Add the heavy cream. Remove the vegetables from the heat and purée immediately in a blender or a food processor. Strain through a fine-mesh sieve and season with salt and pepper to taste.

To prepare the pistou:
Place the pine nuts, garlic, and cheese in a food processor and purée while slowly adding the olive oil until just blended. Add the fava beans and parsley and purée to a creamy consistency. Add more olive oil if necessary and season to taste with salt and black pepper.

To serve:
Garnish each bowl of soup with 1 tablespoon of Fava Bean Pistou and a drizzle of extra-virgin olive oil.

Serves 6

Fava Beans

Fava beans have an unfortunate reputation as being difficult. This ancient bean, also known as the broad bean, requires removing the outer skin to reach the inner pod, which must be removed to reach the actual bean. This is what Chef John calls the "double shuck." The outer layer gets tougher as the beans get older, but one taste of the bright green bean tucked inside will convince you that it was worth it.

We love to get favas early in the season when they are smaller in size and treat them like edamame: we throw the whole pod in the pizza oven to steam, and we serve them hot with a sprinkling of salt. You can throw young beans on a barbecue at home for similar results, or you can blanch them to remove the outer skin. They are wonderful in dishes that allow their flavor to shine through, such as risotto or pasta.

We also add fava leaves on pizza and make a sublime fava leaf pesto. Here in Sonoma County, you'll see fava plants flourishing in the surrounding vineyards where they're used as a cover crop. We've got 1,000 fava plants planted at our Farm Project at Imagery and we use favas as a cover crop where the tomatoes are planted. Garden tip: the entire fava plant is edible, not just the bean, so be sure to harvest both!

Baby Carrots

Baby carrots look so delicate it almost seems like a shame to eat them, but their sweet flavor and tender bite are not to be missed— we use them in every spring dish we can think of and we grow rows of baby carrots on our farm. A baby carrot is simply an immature carrot, usually about 4 to 5 inches long. Don't confuse baby carrots with the tiny peeled orange carrots you'll find in plastic bags at the grocery store. Those are actually full-grown carrots cut into miniatures and their proper name is "baby cut carrot."

While some baby carrots were harvested early to reduce the harvest, certain types have been bred to eat as baby carrots. A common type is called Amsterdam Forcing, but one of our favorites is the Nantes variety. Originally from the Chantenay region of France, it's great fresh or for canning. It's considered the sweetest and most tender baby carrot, with red-orange flesh. Because of their delicate skin, baby carrots don't need to be peeled and their small, beautiful shape doesn't need much trimming, either.

We serve baby carrots sautéed, braised, or roasted but we also love to pickle them; they look beautiful standing upright in glass jars. They also make a wonderful visual and textural addition to a crudité platter, served with dip.

Gardener's note: Coffee grounds make a superb fertilizer for growing carrots, and radishes are good plant-buddies to carrots. Radishes planted in the same rows as carrots break the soil for delicate carrot seedlings and naturally prevent overcrowding. When the radishes are harvested before the young carrots, the carrots will grow into the space vacated by the radishes.

Pacific Halibut, Grilled Spring Vegetable Barigoule

JC Cellars Marsanne, Preston Vineyard, Dry Creek Valley, California
Sans Liege "Groundwork" Grenache Blanc, RBZ Vineyard, Templeton Gap, California

This light, flavorful dish could easily be prepared with other types of fish, so use whatever is available. Just be sure the fish is fresh; it should have no odor and shouldn't be waterlogged or falling apart. Creating a relationship with your fishmonger is the best way to find out which fish is the freshest and sustainably caught. Barigoule is the French word for a Provençal artichoke and mushroom dish but here we combine artichokes and other spring vegetables, making it more like a ragoût.

18 baby artichokes
Juice of 1 lemon
2 tablespoons olive oil
1 bunch thin asparagus
1 bunch small spring onions, cleaned
6 halibut filets (5 ounces each)
Salt and pepper to taste
½ cup extra-virgin olive oil
1 small carrot, thinly sliced
1 small onion, thinly sliced
2 garlic cloves, thinly sliced
2 sprigs fresh thyme
1 bay leaf
1 cup dry white wine
1 cup fish stock
3 tablespoons blended oil

To prepare the artichokes:

Clean the artichokes by removing the top ½-inch and the hard outer leaves. Quarter the artichokes and place them in a large bowl filled with water and the lemon juice.

To prepare the asparagus:

Preheat a grill.
Break off the bottom woody section of the asparagus. Toss the asparagus and onions in the olive oil and season with salt and pepper. Grill the asparagus and onions until well browned, about 2 to 4 minutes. Set aside.

To prepare the fish:

Preheat the oven to 425°F.
Season the halibut on both sides with salt and pepper.

Drain the artichokes. Heat a heavy bottomed saucepan over medium heat. Add 2 tablespoons of olive oil and sauté the carrots, onion, and garlic until soft, about 5 minutes. Add the artichokes, thyme, bay leaf, wine, stock, 1 cup water, and the remaining olive oil. Season, turn the heat to low, and simmer until the artichokes have cooked through, about 10 minutes.

While the vegetables are cooking, heat the blended oil in a large oven-proof sauté pan over high heat. Place the halibut in the pan and cook until well browned on one side. Turn the fish over and place the pan in the oven for 5 to 7 minutes or until the halibut is just cooked through.

Roughly chop the asparagus and spring onions and add them to the vegetable mixture (the barigoule). Cook for 2 more minutes.

To Serve:

Divide the barigoule equally among 6 bowls, top with a piece of halibut, and serve immediately.

Serves 6

Strawberry Panna Cotta

Anaba Late Harvest Viognier, Nelson Vineyards, Mendocino, California
Graham's 20 Year Tawny Port, Portugal

Even restaurant chefs can have trouble with recipes. Just a few weeks ago, we had to throw out several batches of Panna Cotta that did not make the grade. Panna Cotta isn't difficult to make but it does require proper ratios of gelatin to liquid to create the right texture. It's a creamy Italian dessert made from cream, milk, sugar, and gelatin that easily takes on other flavors. Feel free to substitute other fresh, very ripe berries for the strawberries. The riper the berries are, the less sugar you will need. We love to serve this creamy dessert with crunchy Chocolate-Dipped Hazelnut Shortbread (page 317).

For the Panna Cotta:

1½ cups ripe strawberries, cleaned
⅓ to ¾ cup sugar (amount will vary depending on ripeness of berries; use less if they are perfectly ripe and sweet)
1 teaspoon agave syrup (light corn syrup can be substituted)
Pinch of salt
2 tablespoons plus 1 teaspoon powdered gelatin
4 cups whole milk

For the coulis:

½ cup sugar
2 cups strawberries, hulled
1 teaspoon fresh lemon juice

For the topping:

8 medium strawberries, hulled
1 teaspoon pure vanilla extract

To prepare the Panna Cotta:

In a food processor, combine the strawberries with ⅓ cup sugar, agave syrup, and salt. Taste, adding more sugar or salt as needed. The mixture should be quite sweet because it will be diluted by the milk.

In a large bowl, sprinkle the gelatin over 2 cups of cold milk. Scald the remaining 2 cups of milk in a saucepan over medium heat. Whisk the hot milk into the cold milk until the gelatin has completely dissolved.

Stir in the strawberry purée. Pour the mixture into either a large 2-quart mold (a deep, mixing bowl lined with plastic wrap will do) or smaller individual molds, filling them three quarters full. Chill in the refrigerator until set, about 2 hours or overnight.

To prepare the coulis:

Bring ½ cup water and the sugar to a boil in a large saucepot and stir until dissolved. Add the strawberries and cook for 2 to 4 minutes. Purée the mixture in a food processor and add the lemon juice. Chill before serving.

To prepare the topping:

Dice the strawberries into a small dice, place them in a bowl, and mix in the vanilla.

To serve:

Unmold the Panna Cotta by placing the molds in a pan of hot water for 3 seconds and inverting them onto serving plates. Drizzle the Strawberry Coulis around the Panna Cotta and top with a spoonful of the diced strawberries. Serve the Chocolate-Dipped Hazelnut Shortbread on the side.

Serves 6

Watmaugh Strawberry Farm

We're lucky to get strawberries so early in Sonoma—while most of the country is still digging out of the snow! I drive by the Watmaugh Strawberry Farm every morning, and it's big news around town when the OPEN sign appears on the small wooden shack, a signal that the first strawberry treasures of the season are ready to be eaten.

You'll know you're in the right place when you see a line of cars (and then a line of customers) waiting patiently in line for these beautiful strawberries.

Owner Sam Saetern, originally from Laos, began farming the six-acre field in 2002, and it's a family affair. His wife, children, and relatives work together to weed, water, tend, harvest, and hand-box the many hundreds of cartons of luscious, deep red, sugar-ripe strawberries. Though they're not certified organic, Sam doesn't use any pesticides or herbicides on the fruit.

If you're in the area be sure to stop by the farm; it's on Watmaugh Road and Arnold Drive in Sonoma.

NICASIO VALLEY CHEESE COMPANY, NICASIO SQUARE

REGION:	Nicasio, California
MILK:	100 percent organic farmstead cow
PROCESS:	pasteurized
PRODUCTION:	semi-soft, washed rind
AFFINAGE:	at least 30 days
FLAVOR:	rich, salty rind
AROMA:	mushroom notes
TEXTURE:	semi-soft
SIMILAR CHEESES:	Tallegio
PAIRINGS:	the girl & the fig Raisin & Fig Mostarda Blis Bourbon Maple Syrup American Spoon Sour Cherry Preserves Loulou's Garden Quince Jelly
NOTES:	At press time, Nicasio Valley Cheese Company is the only certified organic farmstead cow's milk cheese made in California.

Farmers Markets

Before the idea of sustainable, local eating and the backyard edible garden craze took hold, most people bought their food in supermarkets. Meat, fish, produce, bread—it was all wrapped up in a plastic package. When we were young, my brothers and I never knew the source of the food; it just showed up in our refrigerator. The closest thing to a farmers market in Philadelphia at the time was Reading Terminal, an indoor market where the Amish came to sell their fresh food and food products. That must be why I'm so enamored with farmers markets; the mounds of just-picked fruits and vegetables, crates of brown and white eggs, buckets of fresh flowers, and baskets of fragrant herbs create such a sensory experience, one that's so different from pushing a cart through a grocery store.

I love that in Sonoma people can come to the town square twice a week and pick up fresh foods that are grown in our backyard. I love the face-to-face contact with farmers and the hustle and bustle of shoppers leaning in to pay the farmers and filling their baskets, carrot tops or curly kale hanging over the edges. It's an opportunity to connect with the community. It's also a chance to truly experience the word seasonal; when you have a conversation with a farmer you learn that this is the last week for strawberries or that this type of potato will be coming in a few weeks. I love roaming the stalls at the local markets at home and wherever I happen to be traveling. No matter where the market is located, it's a chance to connect with the people and see how the locals live.

I wish I had the time to go to the farmers market every week. Not only do I love the Sonoma farmers market, but the Tuesday and Saturday markets in Healdsburg are awesome as well. When I get some extra time I like to go the Thursday farmers market at the Marin Civic Center or to the Saturday morning market at the Ferry Building in San Francisco.

With so many farmers markets popping up around the country, it's hard to believe this boom arrived only in the past 15 years. As of 2010, there were more than 6,000 farmers markets in the U.S. while in 1994 there were only 1,755 markets, according to the USDA. Farmers markets were once found only in rural areas, a way for farmers to sell directly to the consumer. Now you can

hardly drive 10 miles without finding one, whether you live in a big city or small town. What was once fringe is now mainstream. That became clear when the White House converted part of the grounds to an edible garden in 2008. The European sensibility of buying produce daily at a local open market has finally caught on here in the States.

It's funny to think that what was once a simple way to buy direct has now turned into a hugely popular experience—so popular that many producers sell out early. New York City's Union Square Greenmarket is so popular that only the early risers score the free-range Knoll Krest chickens or the freshest eggs. The Marin County Farmers market is so crowded it takes time just to park and navigate the crowds jostling for the ripest peach, juiciest strawberry, or just-picked lettuce. More than 20,000 visitors crowd the Madison, Wisconsin, market every Saturday and similar crowds engulf the city streets of Santa Monica, California, for the Saturday morning market. At every market, chefs wheel hand trucks and wagons stacked with crates of produce amid shoppers buying produce for the evening meal. This experience takes us back to our roots—a basic exchange, but with so much more personality than swiping a head of lettuce through a supermarket checkout line.

Why shop at farmers markets? It keeps local farmers on their land and gives you a local taste of the region. Again, it's about community. You get to know the vendors, talk to them, and learn more about the food and your region. It's such an intimate way to buy food—to hold a bunch of carrots that were pulled from the ground the night before, or even early that morning, is simply an unparalleled experience. It's also a chance to learn—asking a farmer about an unusual ingredient or for a recipe is a great way to expand your culinary repertoire.

All you need at a farmers market are a few cloth bags, cash, and an open mind. Some vendors are certified organic and/or sustainable and some aren't; others can't afford organic certification but still don't spray their produce. Just ask. Also, some markets only allow local produce while others can bring in non local produce. Again, it's best to ask the farmer, or you can go online and do some research. A great resource for locating a market near you is Local Harvest (www.localharvest.org); they have a complete list of markets by ZIP code (as well as farms and CSAs). The U.S. Department of Agriculture also maintains a searchable list at http://apps.ams.usda.gov/FarmersMarkets/.

Entrée
Braised Baby Artichokes

Plat
Rabbit Leg Confit, Herb Spaetzle,
Star Anise Jus

Dessert
Rosemary Olive Oil Cake, Lemon Glaze

Fromage
Bleu d'Auvergne

Braised Baby Artichokes

Stella Artois or Sierra Nevada Hefeweizen beer

At ESTATE, artichoke plants line the east sidewalk, giving us a culinary landscape that we actually use in our cooking. Young, tender artichokes require less preparation, but as they grow larger a bit more trimming of the fibrous leaves is necessary. Grated baby artichokes add an element of earthy surprise to a salad, but this braised artichoke recipe is easy and adaptable and shows off their unique flavor. It also makes a wonderful side dish.

2 cups dry white wine
½ cup fresh lemon juice
½ cup extra-virgin olive oil plus 1½ tablespoons
1 sprig fresh thyme
3 sprigs fresh flat-leaf parsley
1 bay leaf
5 whole black peppercorns
2 pounds baby artichokes, cleaned and prepped
    (see **Food for Thought**)
1 lemon, cut in half

Sea salt and freshly cracked black pepper to taste
2 tablespoons chopped fresh flat-leaf parsley
2 tablespoons chopped fresh tarragon
2 tablespoons chopped chives
2 tablespoons chopped fresh chervil

In a large saucepan, combine the white wine, 2 cups water, lemon juice, 6 tablespoons extra-virgin olive oil, thyme, parsley, peppercorns, and bay leaf. Bring to a boil. Lower the heat and bring the poaching liquid to a gentle simmer. Submerge the cleaned artichokes in the liquid and cook until a knife easily pierces the stems, about 15 minutes.

Remove the pan from the heat and transfer the artichokes with their liquid into a container and let cool. Remove the artichokes from the poaching liquid and set aside. Discard the poaching liquid.

Heat 2 tablespoons olive oil in a sauté pan over medium-low heat. Gently sauté the onions, until translucent, about 7 minutes. Remove the onions to cool. Cut the chilled baby artichokes in half.

To serve:
Season the artichokes with the sea salt, black pepper, and 1 tablespoon extra-virgin olive oil. Divide among six chilled plates and garnish with the fresh herbs.

Food for Thought:
To prepare the baby artichokes, remove the tough outer leaves from the artichokes until you reach the tender light green leaves, rubbing them with the cut lemon as you go to prevent discoloration. Trim the ends and tops and remove any remaining tough or dark green leaves.

Serves 6

Artichokes

These thorny thistles are the epitome of California agriculture. Any native Californian worth his or her salt knows what to do when an artichoke is put in front of them! California is the source of nearly 100 percent of the U.S. artichoke production. (We can thank the Italian immigrants who settled in Half Moon Bay in the late 19th century and established Monterey County as the U.S. artichoke capital.)

While at least 100 varieties of artichokes exist, most of them developed in Italy, the most common variety is the Green Globe.

The Green Globe has less prickly spines than other varieties, making it easier to work with—and eat! Two other types are often available in farmers markets: the Purple of Romagna and the Imperial Star. We grow a few plants at ESTATE, but not enough to supply the restaurants.

Eating artichokes does take some practice: removing the edible flesh from the leaves (called bracts) with your teeth, avoiding the fuzzy floret (the choke), and diving into the flavorful heart. They can be eaten hot or cold but they must be cooked.

Artichokes always sell well when we put them on the menu at ESTATE. Artichokes braised in red wine or crispy-fried and served with a dipping sauce are two simple antipasti dishes. When in season, they also end up on special pizzas and in our brunch frittata.

One word of warning for wine lovers: wine does not pair well with artichokes. This is due to a unique organic acid called cynarin present in artichokes, which stimulates sweet receptors on the palate and changes the flavor of the wine—and not for the better. So enjoy your wine and artichokes—just not together.

Rabbit Leg Confit, Herb Spaetzle & Star Anise Jus

La Diligence Marsanne, Stagecoach Vineyard, Napa Valley, California
Prospect 772 Wine Company "The Brat" Grenache, Sierra Foothills, California
Skylark Wine Company Grenache, Mendocino, California

Chef Bryan at the fig café is our spaetzle expert, and he has a specific method for making it that we've included here. Spaetzle is a German dish of tiny dumplings made from flour and water, and it makes the perfect base for roasted meats. There are a few tricks to making perfect spaetzle; the first is using the proper perforated pan for pushing the dough through to the salted boiling water. The second is developing the proper amount of gluten, or elasticity, in the dough. This is determined by how long you mix the dough in the mixer. The perfect texture is when the dough easily pulls apart like taffy. Once the dough becomes too hard you will end up with inedible hard spaetzle. This recipe calls for fresh herbs, but you could easily substitute fresh spinach, watercress, or chard. Cook's note: this is a two-day recipe, so plan accordingly. The rabbit should marinate at least overnight and can go a few days longer if you prefer.

For the rabbit:

5 tablespoons Kosher salt
6 to 10 rabbit legs
½ large yellow onion, thinly sliced
2 teaspoons black peppercorns
2 sprigs fresh thyme
4 cups duck fat (see Sources, page 318)
6 to 10 slices prosciutto, sliced very thin
2 tablespoons olive oil

For the spaetzle:

3 large eggs
2 tablespoons chopped fresh flat-leaf
  parsley
1 tablespoon chopped fresh tarragon
1 tablespoon chopped fresh thyme
1 cup soda water
1 cup half and half
4 cups all-purpose flour
Salt and pepper to taste
Nutmeg to taste
3 tablespoons olive oil

For the vegetables:

1 bunch baby carrots, trimmed,
  blanched, and cut in half
1 bunch baby turnips, trimmed,
  blanched, and cut in half
1 bunch spring onions, cleaned,
  blanched, and cut into thirds
1 tablespoon unsalted butter

For the jus:

1 cup red wine
1 star anise
1 whole black peppercorn
3 sprigs fresh thyme
3 cups chicken or rabbit stock
2 tablespoons unsalted butter

To prepare the rabbit:

Sprinkle 2 tablespoons of salt on all sides of the rabbit legs. Toss the remaining salt with the onions, peppercorns, and thyme and mix with the rabbit legs. Place the rabbit in a perforated pan, cover, and place in the refrigerator overnight.

Preheat the oven to 350°F.
Remove the rabbit and wipe it clean with a damp towel. Place the rabbit in a ovenproof pot, cover it with the duck fat, and cook for 2 hours or until tender. Cool the rabbit in the fat until it comes down to room temperature, about 1 hour. Remove the rabbit and chill. Once the rabbit has chilled, wrap each leg with a slice of prosciutto. If desired, reserve the fat for another use.

To prepare the spaetzle:

Whisk the eggs by hand in a bowl. Add the herbs, soda water, and half and half. Transfer the mixture to the bowl of a stand mixer fitted with a dough hook attachment. On slow speed, slowly add the flour. Mix on medium speed for 6 to 8 minutes. The dough should be stretchy like taffy. Let the spaetzle rest for at least 2 hours while the rabbit is cooking. Bring a large pot of salted water to a boil. Place a colander over the pot and push the spaetzle dough through the colander using a spatula or a pastry scraper. Cook until the spaetzle floats to the top, about 2 to 4 minutes. Transfer the spaetzle to a water bath to chill.

To finish the dish:

Preheat the oven to 375°F.
Heat 2 tablespoons of olive oil in a large sauté pan over medium heat. Sear the rabbit on the top side and place it in the oven to warm through, about 10 to 12 minutes. Meanwhile, heat 3 tablespoons of olive oil in another large sauté pan over medium heat until slightly brown. Toss the spaetzle until lightly brown and heated all the way through, about 5 to 7 minutes.

To prepare the vegetables:

In a small pan place the carrots, turnips, onions, 2 tablespoons of water, and the butter. Season with salt and pepper to taste and heat through on medium-low heat for about 5 to 7 minutes.

To prepare the jus:

Place the red wine, star anise, pepper, and thyme in a sauce pot and reduce by half over high heat. Strain the wine to remove the herbs and spices. Return the wine to the pot, add the stock, and reduce again by a little more than half over high heat.

To serve:

Divide the spaetzle among six plates and top with equal amounts of the warmed vegetables. Place the rabbit over the top and drizzle with the jus.

Serves 6

Rosemary Olive Oil Cake, Lemon Glaze

Domaine de Durban Muscat de Beaumes de Venise, France
Bonny Doon "Vinferno", Late Harvest White Blend, California

Rosemary Olive Oil Cake has a rich, subtle flavor with a delicate texture and is very simple to make. You wouldn't think that olive oil belongs in cake or pastries—or desserts in general—but it's quite common in Europe and adds a subtle earthy, grassy element. Feel free to play around with the recipe by substituting orange or lemon zest for the rosemary, adding a honey glaze, or serving it with warm fruit such as warm marmalade or macerated strawberries.

For the cake:

2 cups sugar

4 large eggs

1 cup extra-virgin olive oil

1 cup dry white wine

2½ cups all-purpose flour

½ teaspoon salt

2¼ teaspoons baking powder

1 teaspoon pure vanilla extract

1 vanilla bean

2 tablespoons chopped fresh rosemary

For the glaze:

1 cup fresh lemon juice

1¼ cups powdered sugar, sifted

Preheat the oven to 350°F. Line the bottom of a 9-inch round cake pan with parchment paper.

To prepare the cake:

Beat the sugar and the eggs together in a mixer on medium speed for 30 seconds. Add the oil, wine, flour, salt, baking powder, vanilla, and rosemary. Continue to mix for 1 minute. Pour the batter in the baking pan.

Bake until the cake pulls away from the sides, about 30 minutes. Let the cake cool in the pan for about 5 minutes. Remove the cake from the pan and let it cool on a wire rack for 2 hours.

To prepare the glaze:

In a small saucepan, cook the lemon juice and powdered sugar over medium heat and stir until smooth. Let the mixture cool slightly and pour it over the cake.

To serve:

Slice the cake in 6 to 8 wedges. Put a slice of cake on a plate and add a dollop of crème fraîche or whipped cream.

Serves 6

BLEU D'AUVERGNE

REGION:	Auvergne, France
MILK:	cow
PROCESS:	raw and pasteurized
PRODUCTION:	uncooked, unpressed, semi-soft with veins of blue mold, natural rind
AFFINAGE:	in a humid cellar for 5 - 15 weeks
FLAVOR:	slightly salty, spicy, tart, tangy, rich
AROMA:	pungent, strong
TEXTURE:	sticky, moist, creamy, grainy
SIMILAR CHEESES:	Roquefort, Fourme D'Ambert
PAIRINGS:	Savannah Bee Orange Blossom Honey Rustic Bakery Three Seed Pan Forte Sarabeth's Kitchen Chunky Apple San Giacoma Saba Chestnut Honey Toasted Pistachios
NOTES:	Bleu D'Auvergne pairs wonderfully with Banyuls, a dessert wine from France.

Devil's Gulch Ranch
Marin County
California

My first taste of rabbit was fifteen years ago in the French town of Ampuis. It was a leisurely meal, with bottle after bottle of amazing wine and a big platter of rabbit confit wrapped in salty ham. That meal inspired me to include rabbit on our menu and while it's not the most popular dish on the menu, it's one of our staples. In Europe, rabbit is hugely popular, but Americans seem reluctant to embrace this lean, delicate meat. John likes to braise rabbit and serve it over pappardelle or cook it in a stew with loads of vegetables.

We're lucky to get rabbits from Devil's Gulch Ranch, a sustainable family farm in Marin County, just over the hill from Sonoma County. Owners Mark and Myriam Pasternak raise the rabbits (as well as pigs, lamb, and quail) without hormones or antibiotics. The Pasternaks have been raising rabbits for meat for 15 years, thanks to his wife's French family, who grew up eating rabbit. What started as a 4-H project for their children quickly developed into a rabbit business once Myriam's mother offered a French friend and chef a taste of rabbit. Orders from top California restaurants like Chez Panisse, The French Laundry, Manka's, and Spago soon followed. "I'm not sure what came first: that the restaurants didn't have rabbit on the menu so nothing was available, or there was nothing available so no one could put it on the menu," says Mark. Today Devil's Gulch is one of the largest producers of rabbits in the U.S.; they process 100 rabbits a week and are increasing to 500 rabbits this year. In contrast, the large suppliers of rabbit in Europe process 5,000 per week.

The challenge for the Pasternaks in raising rabbits is their susceptibility to predators, disease, and stress. "You can eliminate the predator issue, but you can't eliminate stress and disease," says Mark. While large rabbit producers in Europe solve these problems by creating a climate-controlled factory and dosing the water with antibiotics, the Pasternaks are vehemently opposed to anything like this. Mark says their "secret weapon" is Myriam, a rabbit expert. One of the top meat animal veterinarians in the country, Myriam is the production manager and creates an environment where the rabbits have more room and airflow to combat weather and stress, which prevents the need for antibiotics.

The rabbits are fed alfalfa meal, a few vitamins, and plenty of water. This extra effort—and a high mortality rate—is why rabbit meat tends to be pricier than chicken or pork, on par with grass-fed beef. (Cheaper frozen rabbit meat from China is available but contains antibiotics and is not as fresh.) Myriam is so dedicated to rabbit production as a farming technique that she has been working in Haiti and other undeveloped countries to demonstrate how small-scale agricultural production like raising meat rabbits can transform an economy.

The Pasternaks crossbreed three types of rabbits (California, New Zealand, and Rex), but Mark won't sell rabbit to just anyone—it has to be local. The only reason he sells to Spago in Los Angeles is that his neighbor, a lamb farmer, sends a truck down to Los Angeles every week. It's this devotion, coupled with their knowledge, that has led to this superior product, and we are so lucky to get it in the restaurants. "I encourage local participation, and you really have to twist my arm to get me to ship you rabbit," says Mark. "I really try to walk my talk as much as I can and really examine how I'm doing everything so that it's in the most environmentally sound way possible."

Devil's Gulch rabbit is only available wholesale in California and in one San Francisco grocery store, as well as at the Marin County Farmers Market on Sundays, but Mark urges you to ask your local farmer if he knows a local source for rabbit; the more local the meat, the fresher the product.

Entrée
Fried Green Tomatoes,
Tomato Corn Relish

Plat
Bay Scallops, Hazelnuts, Carrot Purée

Dessert
Chocolate Polenta Cake

Fromage
Epoisses

Fried Green Tomatoes, Tomato Corn Relish

Zaca Mesa Winery & Vineyard Roussanne, Santa Ynez Valley, California
Peay Vineyards Estate Roussanne/Marsanne, Sonoma Coast, California

One year, we prepared 2,500 fried green tomatoes for the annual Tomato Festival at Kendall-Jackson Winery in Sonoma County. The quantity seemed insane, but it was worth it every time a guest popped one in their mouth. Their happy faces said it all! Last year the weather abruptly changed, and what would have been a stellar tomato season resulted in hundreds of pounds of unripened green tomatoes. This created an opportunity to produce green tomato jam, pickled green tomatoes, and green tomato relish-which translated to hearty BLT's with green tomatoes and salumi plates with green tomato pickles. This recipe has many components, but you can make the Corn Stock and the Tomato Corn Relish a day ahead.

For the Corn Stock:
2 tablespoons unsalted
   butter
½ large white onion,
   diced
1 leek, diced
1 celery stalk, diced
1 shallot, diced
1 garlic clove, minced
1 cup dry white wine
3 ears yellow corn
   (reserve 1 cup kernels
   for velouté; set cobs
   aside)
Herb sachet (3 sprigs
   fresh thyme, 1 bay leaf,
   and 5 whole pepper-
   corns tied in cheese-
   cloth)
Pinch of saffron

For the velouté:
2 tablespoons unsalted
   butter
3 tablespoons all-purpose
   flour
Corn Stock (see above)
1 cup heavy cream
Salt and pepper to taste

For the relish:
1 pint cherry tomatoes,
   cut in half
1 cup corn kernels
   (reserved from velouté
   sauce)
1 tablespoon balsamic
   vinegar
1 garlic clove, minced
2 tablespoons chopped
   chives
1 teaspoon salt
½ teaspoon pepper
1 tablespoon olive oil

For the tomatoes:
3 to 5 large green tomatoes
½ cup buttermilk
½ cup panko
¼ cup cornmeal
¼ cup all-purpose flour
¼ cup grated Vella Dry
   Jack cheese
   (Parmesan can be
   substituted)
1 teaspoon chipotle
   powder
1½ teaspoons paprika
1 teaspoon salt plus more
   to taste
1 teaspoon pepper plus
   more to taste

To prepare the corn stock:
In a medium saucepan, heat the butter over medium heat and sauté the onion, leek, celery, shallot, and garlic. Season lightly and cook until translucent. Deglaze with the wine and reduce until almost dry. Add the reserved corn cobs, and the herb sachet and just cover with water (about 2½ cups). Bring the mixture to a boil, reduce to a simmer, add the saffron, and cook for 25 minutes. Remove the cobs and sachet. Add 1 cup corn kernels and purée the mixture. Strain and keep warm.

To prepare the velouté:
Melt the butter in a saucepan over low heat. Add the flour all at once and cook, stirring constantly, until the flour and butter have created a smooth roux. Do not brown. Slowly add in the corn stock, stirring constantly. Bring to a low simmer and slowly add the cream, stirring constantly. Reduce the sauce to the desired consistency and season with salt and pepper to taste.

To prepare the relish:
In a separate bowl, mix the cherry tomatoes, corn, vinegar, garlic, chives, salt, pepper, and olive oil together.

To prepare the tomatoes:
Remove the ends of the tomatoes and slice the tomatoes into ½-inch slices. Place the buttermilk in a shallow bowl. In another bowl combine the panko, cornmeal, flour, cheese, chipotle powder, paprika, 1 teaspoon salt, and 1 teaspoon pepper.

In a heavy bottom skillet, heat the oil to 350°F degrees. Place the tomatoes in the buttermilk, allowing the excess buttermilk to fall free, and toss them in the flour mixture. Place the tomatoes in the oil over high heat and cook for 1 minute on each side. Remove the tomatoes and season them lightly with salt and pepper to taste.

To serve:
After frying all the tomatoes, spoon the sauce on the plate and place two slices of tomato in the middle of the sauce. Garnish with the Tomato Corn Relish and serve immediately.

Serves 6

EPOISSES

REGION:	Burgundy, France
MILK:	cow
PROCESS:	raw and pasteurized
PRODUCTION:	uncooked, unpressed, soft, washed rind
AFFINAGE:	minimum 5 weeks in a cool, dark cellar
FLAVOR:	intense, fruity, milky, rustic, grassy
AROMA:	pungent, unctuous, aroma is stronger than the flavor
TEXTURE:	gooey, smooth, melts in your mouth
SIMILAR CHEESES:	Livarot, Munster
PAIRINGS:	Harvest Song Fresh Walnut Preserves Blue Chair Fruit Co Apricot - Plum Jam Loulou's Garden Pickled Cherries Candied Pecans (page 315) Poached Prunes
NOTES:	During affinage the cheese is washed with water flavored with Marc de Bourgogne. Epoisses dates back to the 16th century when the monks made it.

Alex Benward during the 2010 Olive Harvest

Beltane Ranch
Glen Ellen, California

Driving down Highway 12 you might notice a yellow ranch house set back from the road along the Mayacamas, surrounded by towering oak trees, rows of vineyards, and lush gardens, with a stone wall that runs along the vineyard. It looks like a snapshot of Sonoma from 100 years ago, and it actually is a piece of local history; once a territory of the Wappo Indians, and later a part of Rancho Los Guilicos, it has been known as Beltane Ranch since the main house was built in 1892.

I've known the current owners, Rosemary Wood and her daughter, Alexa, for years through local community and hospitality events, and more recently we've catered dozens of weddings held at the ranch. They're also loyal customers at all three restaurants. (Rosemary's grandchildren, Lauren and Alex Benward, still live on the property and help run the ranch and the winemaking program.) Rosemary Wood's aunt and uncle bought the ranch in 1936, and Rosemary began renovations and opened it up to guests in 1970. Rosemary has been devoted to the ranch from the beginning. In 1974 she rebuilt the stone wall—by hand!—that runs along the vineyard. She remains an active, vibrant part of the ranch. "She certainly keeps us all on our toes!" says Lauren.

Rosemary Wood in one of the property's Olive Groves

Longtime Beltane Ranch Gardener, Victor Torres

In the 1980s, the family planted 32 new acres of vineyards and an additional 4 acres of olive trees. (Their estate Sauvignon Blanc is delicious and really shows off the terroir.) The 105-acre Beltane Ranch is one of the top bed-and-breakfasts in the state, mentioned in every travel magazine and newspaper you can imagine. It's a magical place, with six cozy guest rooms and sensational breakfasts that utilize produce and eggs from the ranch. They grow their own vegetables and fruit, including heirloom orchards and their famous raspberries that were first planted by Lauren's great-great-aunt in the 1930s. The gardens are glorious, with a mix of herbs and flowers that bloom year-round. Each year they press seven types of olives for their estate olive oil, which has a beautiful buttery, grassy flavor. Most recently, they started raising their own cattle and they sell the grass-fed beef to local customers.

I love that the ranch is a family-run operation that is run in tune with the seasons. It truly exemplifies the region. (In 2004, the Sonoma County Agricultural Preservation & Open Space District purchased 1,300 acres of the ranch, which protects it from development in perpetuity.) For an only-in-Sonoma experience, plan a stay at Beltane Ranch to experience the ranch for yourself and get a little glimpse of Sonoma life!

104

summer

There are so many things to love about summer. I adore the bright, cooling flavors of the summer bounty and the long, cool evenings. Those are the things to remember when the temperature reaches the 90s and traffic crawls along the town square. The golden-brown hills have given up hope of rain until autumn and the horses and cattle lounge under the shade of the oak trees while munching on fields of yellow grass. Green and purple lavender bushes flourish in the summer heat, perfuming the air with their scent. Summer is our busiest season, when the restaurants fill up with visitors and the patios overflow with alfresco diners sipping chilled white wine or rosé. Wine festivals bring the wine lovers who drive from vineyard to vineyard.

The farm seems to explode in the summer months, it takes all hands on deck to keep up with the abundance. John likes to get to the farm extra early on those summer mornings to check the crops; if you don't pick by 8 a.m., everything seems to wilt in the midday heat. The Tuesday night farmers market is in full swing, with locals lingering on the square in the evenings with baskets of fresh produce and a bottle of wine. The kids are out of school, riding their bikes in the neighborhood and playing baseball in the local parks until the last bits of sunlight remain.

On the menu, tomatoes are the stars of summer. We wait patiently for them, hoping the morning fog will lift long enough to ripen the San Marzanos, Juliets, and Green Zebras that grow in neat rows on the farm. Two varieties of cucumbers fill the picking bins and the bright earthy scent of basil remains on any hand that touches the emerald-green leaves. Lemon verbena is another summer herb; the delicate hint of lemon is a perfect flavor for cocktails and custards. Baskets of bright green string beans ("haricots verts" in French) arrive from the farm, ready for a quick blanch or sauté to accent their earthy essence, and who can forget green zucchini and yellow squash, which seem to envelop the garden? We quickly transform them into bowls of ratatouille or roast them whole, and we save the blossoms for stuffing and frying, a truly seasonal dish. I'm partial to fresh corn—those sweet kernels just scream summer to me. Peaches, plums, blackberries, and watermelons are the quintessential summer fruit in Sonoma, and they get transformed into crisps, pies, and refreshing summer salads.

With the busy Sonoma square and the frenzy of the summer rush, time flies by so quickly that we often forget to enjoy a lazy summer day. It's hard to imagine that our busy season will continue right through the fall.

summer cheese

Summer cheeses bring an entirely new dimension of flavor. The rich grass of spring is gone, often replaced by more feed and hay. The animals have shed much of their hair and/or wool to keep cool, and they graze under shady trees to escape the midday heat. I love watching the sheep ramble through the paddocks and pastures as I drive home on a summer afternoon.

In regions where the weather provides summer grass for the animals to graze on, the milk has more acidity and is higher in fat than spring milk. This produces a more robust cheese. As summer ends and the weather cools, the animals' grazing habits become more selective and the milk is more concentrated in flavor.

Milk production for cows, sheep, and goats drops dramatically in the summer months, which is why summer is not the cheesemakers favorite season, especially those in hot climates. However, in some regions summer is a wonderful time for milk. For traditional European mountain cheeses, the cows graze on flowers, herbs, and grasses and produce a rich milk. The cheese is more yellow in color and has more flavor than cheese made from winter milk.

(Clockwise from top left; Pont l'Eveque, Crescenza, Humboldt Fog, Rogue River Blue, Pondhopper, Red Hawk).

WATERMELON MOJITO

MAKES 2 COCKTAILS

16 TO 20 FRESH MINT LEAVES
1 CUP CUBED WATERMELON, SEEDED AND SKINNED
JUICE OF 2 LIMES
4 OUNCES LIGHT RUM
2 OUNCES SIMPLE SYRUP (PAGE 36)
CLUB SODA

DIVIDE THE MINT LEAVES BETWEEN TWO PINT GLASSES.
MUDDLE THE MINT AND ADD THE WATERMELON.
CONTINUE TO MUDDLE UNTIL THE WATERMELON IS
COMPLETELY BROKEN UP. FILL THE GLASSES WITH ICE
AND ADD THE LIME JUICE, RUM, AND SIMPLE SYRUP.
SHAKE WELL WITH A COCKTAIL SHAKER AND TOP
EACH DRINK WITH A SPLASH OF CLUB SODA.

FIG KISS
MAKES 2 COCKTAILS

3 OUNCES ST-GERMAIN LIQUEUR
1 OUNCE FIGCELLO DI SONOMA
2 OUNCES CRANBERRY JUICE
FRESH MINT OR LEMON TWISTS, FOR GARNISH

COMBINE THE ST-GERMAIN, FIGCELLO, AND CRANBERRY JUICE
IN A COCKTAIL SHAKER. TOP WITH ICE. SHAKE VIGOROUSLY TO
INCORPORATE AND STRAIN INTO CHILLED MARTINI GLASSES.
GARNISH WITH MINT OR LEMON TWISTS.

Elderberry/Elderflower

While the creamy white-colored flower and the black-purple fruit of the elder tree are quite common in Europe, they're less familiar to Americans. The floral essence is what makes the flowers so popular, and it's made into tea, syrup, and a liqueur. (A popular elderflower liqueur is St-Germain, made from elderflowers harvested in the Alps.) The small, sour elderberry has been used as a medicinal herb for centuries because it is rich in antioxidants; it's difficult to find fresh in the States.

We use elderflower syrup in our non-alcoholic cocktails instead of vanilla (vanilla contains alcohol), which adds a floral flavor. We rely on elderflower liqueur for many of our cocktails; it adds a subtle floral note without overpowering the drink.

CUCUMBER COSMOPOLITAN
MAKES 2 COCKTAILS

½ MEDIUM CUCUMBER (½ CUP), PEELED, SEEDED, AND CUBED
2 OUNCES CHARBAY BLOOD ORANGE VODKA
1 OUNCE COINTREAU
JUICE OF 1 LIME
1 OUNCE SIMPLE SYRUP (PAGE 36)
2 OUNCES CRANBERRY JUICE
ENGLISH CUCUMBER SLICES, FOR GARNISH

IN A COCKTAIL GLASS MUDDLE THE CUCUMBER WITH THE
VODKA. ADD THE ICE, LIME JUICE, SIMPLE SYRUP, AND
CRANBERRY JUICE. TOP WITH ICE. SHAKE VIGOROUSLY TO
INCORPORATE AND STRAIN INTO CHILLED MARTINI GLASSES.
GARNISH WITH THE ENGLISH CUCUMBER SLICES.

summer

"GIN"–GER BASILTINI

MAKES 2 COCKTAILS

12 BASIL LEAVES (RESERVE 2 LEAVES FOR GARNISH)
JUICE OF 2 LIMES
4 OUNCES HENDRICK'S GIN
1 OUNCE GINGER SIMPLE SYRUP (SEE BELOW)

MUDDLE 10 BASIL LEAVES WITH THE LIME JUICE
IN THE BOTTOM OF A COCKTAIL SHAKER. FILL
WITH ICE. ADD THE GIN AND THE GINGER SIMPLE
SYRUP. SHAKE VIGOROUSLY TO INCORPORATE AND
STRAIN INTO CHILLED MARTINI GLASSES. GARNISH
WITH THE REMAINING BASIL LEAVES AND SERVE.

GINGER SIMPLE SYRUP

1 CUP SUGAR
NUGGET OF GINGER, PEELED AND SLICED
    (ABOUT THE SIZE OF YOUR THUMB)

COMBINE 1 CUP WATER AND THE SUGAR IN A
MEDIUM SIZE SAUCEPAN. BOIL FOR 10 MINUTES,
STIRRING OCCASIONALLY UNTIL THE SUGAR IS
COMPLETELY DISSOLVED. REMOVE THE MIXTURE
FROM THE STOVE AND ADD THE GINGER. LET THE
GINGER STEEP UNTIL THE LIQUID IS COOL. STRAIN
THROUGH CHEESECLOTH OR A FINE–MESH STRAINER
INTO A CLEAN GLASS JAR. REFRIGERATE AND USE
WITHIN 2 WEEKS.

Infusions

An infusion is used with herbs or plants
that dissolve readily in liquid to release
their active ingredients. (Tea is the most
common infusion.) An infusion is a way to
release the flavor for use in a dessert or a
cocktail; certain herbs can only be used if
they are first infused, such as lavender and
hibiscus flowers. Infusions can be made with
ingredients such as chilies, garlic, and lemon.
Infused oils and vinegars are a delicious way
to add flavor without overpowering the main
ingredient. (For more on herb oils, see page
114.)

The amount of steeping time depends on what
you're making; usually 15 to 30 minutes does
the trick. The herb is then strained, and you're
left with a flavorful liquid. You can make an
infusion with almost any liquid: water, milk
or cream, and oil are the most common. The
ratio of herb to liquid is generally one-to-one,
but it varies depending on the herb.

SUMMER NIBBLES
CORN CAKES, HEIRLOOM TOMATO JAM
MOZZARELLA, TOMATOES, OREGANO ON CROSTINI

CAPRESE PANZANELLA
"BLT" GOUGÈRES

CORN CAKES, HEIRLOOM TOMATO JAM

These are a perfect summer bite that will please both tomato and corn lovers. If you have a jar of pepper jelly sitting in your pantry, substitute that for the Heirloom Tomato Jam.

3 cups corn kernels (from about 6 medium ears)
2 tablespoons diced red onion
1 tablespoon chopped flat-leaf parsley
4 tablespoons crème fraîche
2 large eggs, lightly beaten
2 teaspoons baking powder
¼ cup firmly packed brown sugar
1 teaspoon smoked paprika
½ cup cornmeal
1 tablespoon fresh lime juice
2½ cups panko, for breading
1 cup Heirloom Tomato Jam (page 315)

In a food processor, purée 2 cups of corn. In a large bowl combine the corn purée, the remaining corn kernels, onion, parsley, crème fraîche, eggs, baking powder, brown sugar, smoked paprika, cornmeal, and lime juice. Mix well. Add 1 cup of panko and mix until the mixture is moist but not sticky, add more panko if needed. Form the mixture into 36 miniature cakes and turn each cake in the panko to coat the outside.

Place a large sauté pan over medium heat, fill it with ¼-inch of canola oil, and heat the oil to 375°F. Pan fry the corn cakes until golden brown, flip them over, and cook, about 1 to 3 minutes per side.

To serve:
Place the corn cakes on a large platter, add a dollop of the Heirloom Tomato Jam on each one, and serve. These can be served warm or at room temperature.

Makes 36 nibbles

CAPRESE PANZANELLA

When summer hits, the first ingredient I think of is the tomato. That is why you will see tomatoes in every form at the restaurants. This small bite is a riff off panzanella, the traditional Italian tomato and bread salad. Be sure to use your favorite olive oil, a smidgen of salt, and, of course, the ripest tomatoes.

½ cup balsamic vinegar
Two ½-inch slices sourdough bread
¼ cup plus 2 tablespoons extra-virgin olive oil
Salt and pepper to taste

One 8-ounce ball fresh mozzarella, cut in small dice
30 cherry tomatoes, cut in half
¼ cup micro basil or regular basil, cut in chiffonade
1 tablespoon Maldon Sea Salt (see Sources, page 318)

Place the vinegar in a saucepan over high heat and reduce by half. Cool and set aside. Remove the crust from the bread, dice the bread in small cubes, and set aside.

Heat 2 tablespoons of the olive oil in a sauté pan and cook the bread until golden brown. Season with salt and pepper and set aside.

In a bowl, combine the bread, mozzarella, cherry tomatoes, and the remaining olive oil. Place the mixture in a small spoon and garnish with the basil, a few pinches of sea salt, and a drizzle of the reduced balsamic vinegar.

Makes 30 nibbles

MOZZARELLA, TOMATOES, OREGANO ON CROSTINI

What a crowd pleaser! You can't go wrong with these flavorful bites. Play around with the type of cherry tomatoes—add whatever herbs you have in your kitchen garden, or simply sprinkle the crostini with Lavender Sea Salt. You can also prepare this bite without the bread by serving the mozzarella and tomatoes on a spoon or a skewer.

For the tomatoes:
54 cherry tomatoes, about 1 to 2 pints depending on size
3 cups olive oil
2 sprigs fresh thyme
2 garlic cloves, sliced
½ tablespoon salt
1 teaspoon pepper

For the crostini:
Eighteen ½-inch slices ciabatta bread
¼ cup extra-virgin olive oil

To finish:
8 ounces fresh mozzarella cheese, torn into 18 pieces
2 tablespoons fresh oregano leaves
½ tablespoon Maldon Sea Salt (see Sources, page 318)

To prepare the crostini:
Preheat the oven to 425°F. Using a pastry brush, brush the oil evenly on both sides of the bread and season with salt and pepper to taste. Place the bread on a baking sheet and bake until the edges begin to color, about 10 to 14 minutes. Set aside.

To prepare the tomatoes:
Place the tomatoes, olive oil, thyme, garlic, salt, and pepper in a medium saucepan and heat to a simmer. Remove from the heat and let the tomatoes cool to room temperature. Remove the tomatoes from the oil using a slotted spoon and set aside. (The oil can be used again to cook more batches of tomatoes but must be refrigerated after use.)

To finish:
Place the crostini on a platter, cover with the mozzarella, and then place 3 tomatoes on top of each crostini. Sprinkle the tops with the oregano and salt.

Makes 18 nibbles

Mozzarella

I've yet to meet anyone who doesn't love soft, creamy mozzarella cheese. This fresh cheese is made by dipping the curd into hot whey and then stretching and kneading the curd to the desired consistency. Originally, mozzarella was made only from water buffalo milk but cow's milk is now the norm. There are two forms: fresh and regular. Fresh mozzarella is made from whole milk and has a softer texture and delicate flavor; it's usually packed in whey or water. Regular mozzarella is available in low-fat and nonfat varieties and has a semisoft, elastic texture. It's drier than fresh mozzarella.

Buffalo mozzarella (labeled Mozzarella di Bufala) is the most prized of the fresh mozzarellas and is made from milk from the domesticated water buffalo; it's rich in fat and has a silky, soft texture and buttery flavor. It literally melts in your mouth.

When preparing our small bites and some salads, we use little bocconcini balls that are usually made with a blend of buffalo and cow's milk. At ESTATE, we prefer large spoonfuls of fresh mozzarella to top our Margherita pizzas.

Herb Oils

We use vibrant, herbaceous, spicy oils to add a hit of flavor to salads, pastas, pizzas, and most fish and meat dishes. They are so simple to make at home and they are also wonderful hostess or holiday gifts.

There are just a few things to remember to make a great herb oil:

- Use a high-quality olive oil.
- Use organic herbs and flavorings (if not organic than make sure they are pesticide-free).
- Sterilize jars and bottles.
- Use the herb oils within four to six months after bottling.
- If you see any bubbles forming in the oil, discard it right away. Bubbles could indicate contamination.
- Store herb oils in a cool, dark place.
- Fresh herbs should be slightly wilted to minimize moisture content. Any excess moisture can cause mold in the oil.

Rosemary Oil
2 sprigs fresh rosemary
1 pint extra-virgin olive oil

Wash the rosemary and dry thoroughly. (It must be completely dry to prevent mold from growing.) Put the rosemary and the olive oil in a bottle and leave for 2 to 3 months in a dark, cool place.

Mint Oil
¼ cup fresh mint
1 pint canola oil

Wash and dry the mint and put it in a blender. Add the oil to the blender and blend until the blender cup feels warm, about 3 minutes. Strain the liquid through a fine-mesh sieve and place it in an ice bath until chilled, about 10 minutes. Mint Oil must be refrigerated and will keep for 2 to 3 weeks.

Lemon Oil
2 lemons (preferably organic)
1 pint extra-virgin olive oil

Zest the lemons carefully, making sure not to get any of the white pith. Lightly crush the zest to release some of the natural oils. (You can use a mortar and pestle or the side of a knife.) Transfer the lemon zest to a large bowl with a tight-fitting lid. Pour the oil over the lemon zest and preserve for at least 3 weeks in a cool, dark place. Then strain the contents and transfer to a bottle. Lemon Oil will keep for 2 to 3 weeks in a dark, cool place.

"BLT" GOUGÈRES

This is a tongue-in-cheek version of a BLT sandwich. Gougére, the classic French cheese puff, can be made ahead and frozen for an impromptu gathering, but mini-brioche toasts can also be substituted.

2 tablespoons unsalted butter
1 teaspoon salt
1 cup all-purpose flour
3 to 4 large eggs plus 1 egg yolk
¼ cup grated cheese (Parmigiano-Reggiano and Gruyère work well)
¼ cup Tarragon Aioli (page 314)
25 cherry tomatoes, cut in half
12 slices bacon, cooked crispy and cut into quarters
½ cup baby arugula

Place 1 cup of water in a medium saucepan, add the butter and salt, and bring to a simmer. Remove the pan from the heat and add the flour all at once. Stir with a wooden spoon until a smooth dough forms.

Place the saucepan back on the stove over low heat and keep working the dough lightly until it is soft but not sticky, about 2 minutes. Transfer the dough to a mixer and let it cool for a few minutes. Turn the mixer on low and add one egg at time, waiting until the egg is fully incorporated before adding the next. (The fourth egg might not be needed depending on the consistency of the dough, which should be firm and smooth.) Add the cheese and mix to incorporate.

Preheat the oven to 350°F.
Mix the egg yolk with a few tablespoons of water.

Using a pastry bag with a wide plain tip or a cut Ziploc bag, pipe the dough into 1-inch balls onto a sheet pan. Brush the gougères with the egg wash and bake for 15 to 20 minutes or until just brown on top.

Cut each gougère three quarters of the way through to create a open mouth (as John would say, "like a Pacman.") Stuff each one with a tiny spoonful of aioli, 1 cherry tomato half, 1 piece of bacon, and 1 piece of arugula.

These are best eaten the day they are baked. You can pipe out the gougères on parchment paper, carefully roll them, and freeze them for at least 2 months until you are ready to bake them.

To serve:
Place the gougères on a large serving platter.

Makes 50 (1-inch) nibbles

summer

summer menus

Entrée
Cornmeal-Dusted Tiny Fish, Salsa Roja

Plat
*Roasted Chicken, Roasted Peppers,
Olive and Thyme Sauce*

Dessert
Apricot & Blackberry Cobbler

Fromage
Bellwether Farms Crescenza

Cornmeal-Dusted Tiny Fish, Salsa Roja

Très Bonnes Années "the girl & the fig" Blanc, Russian River Valley, California
Peter Mathis Wine Grenache, Sonoma Valley, California

When I think about crunchy little fish, I am transported to a small café in the south of France. I was determined to recreate this memory for our guests. Flour, panko, or cereal would all work just fine as a coating, but I love the texture of the cornmeal and the additional heartiness it provides with that first bite.

For the salsa:

1 tablespoon blended oil
½ medium onion, roughly chopped
1 tablespoon chopped garlic
8 ounce-can stewed tomatoes
1 ancho chili, toasted, seeded, and chopped
2 New Mexico dried chiles, chopped and seeded
¼ teaspoon cumin seeds, toasted and ground
½ teaspoon coriander seeds, toasted and ground

For the fish:

½ cup Wondra flour (see Sources, page 319)
½ cup cornmeal
½ cup semolina
1 tablespoon smoked paprika
1 tablespoon garlic powder
½ tablespoon salt
½ tablespoon pepper
1 bunch fresh basil, leaves picked
1 cup buttermilk
1 lemon, thinly sliced
2 pounds smelt

To prepare the salsa:

Place a small saucepan over medium heat, heat the oil, and sauté the onions and garlic until they become translucent, about 3 minutes. Add the tomatoes, chiles, cumin, and coriander and bring to a boil. Reduce to a simmer and let cook for 30 to 40 minutes. Remove from the heat and transfer the mixture to a blender or food processor. Purée the mixture and season with lime juice, salt, and pepper to taste. (Depending on how much sauce you like, you may have extra salsa left over. Use the remaining sauce for another dish or snack.)

To prepare the fish:

In a medium bowl combine the flour, cornmeal, semolina, paprika, garlic powder, salt, and pepper.

Set a deep fryer to 375°F (a deep saucepan filled with canola oil will work as well as a deep fryer) and fry the basil leaves until crispy, about 1 minute. Transfer the bail leaves to a paper towel to drain the excess oil and season with salt. Set aside.

Place the buttermilk in a bowl. Dip the lemon slices into the buttermilk, dredge them in the flour mixture, and fry until golden brown and crispy. Transfer the lemons to paper towels to drain the excess oil. Repeat the dredging and frying process with the smelt.

To serve:

Spread some of the salsa on each of the 6 plates, arrange the smelt on top, and garnish with the fried basil and lemon slices.

Serves 6

Roasted Chicken, Roasted Peppers, Olive and Thyme Sauce

Maison Bouachon "La Rouviere," Tavel, France
Elyse Winery "Les Corbeau" Grenache, Hudson Vineyard, Carneros, California

Roasted chicken is the ultimate comfort food. It reminds me of family dinners growing up, sitting around the table and talking about our day at school. Sonoma County has long been known for having some of the oldest chicken and duck farms in the region, so we're lucky to have access to amazing chickens from local farmers.

3 chickens (2½ pounds each, have your butcher debone and cut in half)
Salt and pepper
3 tablespoons olive oil
½ cup red wine
1½ cups Chicken Stock (page 313)
2 Roasted Red Peppers, peeled and seeded (page 311)
1 cup Castelvetrano olives, pitted (see Sources, page 320)
5 tablespoons capers, drained
3 tablespoons chopped fresh thyme
2 tablespoons unsalted butter

To prepare the chicken:
Preheat the oven to 475°F.

Season the chicken liberally on both sides with salt and pepper. Place a large ovenproof roasting pan over two burners on high heat and add the olive oil. Add the chicken one piece at a time, skin side down, to the HOT pan. Baste the flesh side with a bit of the hot liquid from the pan and cook until the skin begins to brown, about 8 to 12 minutes.

Transfer the pan to the oven for about 12 to 15 minutes or until the temperature by the thigh reaches 155°F on a meat thermometer. Remove the chicken from the pan and set aside.

To prepare the sauce:
With the pan back on the heat, add the red wine, chicken stock, peppers, olives, capers, and thyme. Reduce the liquid by half. Add the butter, and season with salt and pepper to taste.

To serve:
Place each chicken, flesh side down, on a plate and top with the sauce.

Serves 6

Deboning Chicken

Place the whole chicken, breast side up, on a clean cutting surface. Stretch out each wing flat against the board by pulling the tip.

With a boning knife, cut off the wing tip and the joint next to it. Leave the largest wing bone still attached.

Position the chicken so the back is facing up and the drumsticks are pointing towards you.

Using a pair of kitchen shears, cut all the way down one side of the backbone. The cut should be made through the small rib bones, not through the center of the backbone itself. Cut close to the backbone so you don't lose too much meat.

Cut all the way down the other side of the backbone and remove it completely. Position the chicken so the drumsticks are pointing away from you.

Use a paring knife to make a small cut in the white cartilage that conceals the top of the breastbone and bend both halves of the carcass backward at the cut to expose the breastbone. It should pop right up through the cut. Using your knife, separate it from the meat and then pull the bone out.

The chicken should lay flat at this point. Cut down the center between the breasts to break in half.

Turn one side of the chicken over with the thigh closest to you. Using a boning knife, cut on top of the thigh bone to the leg joint. Make a couple of passes to free the bone from the flesh. Place your blade underneath the bone and follow to the leg joint and cut through to release bone. Repeat on other half.

Apricot & Blackberry Cobbler
Paul Jaboulet Muscat, Beaumes de Venise, France

I tend to take liberties when naming our dishes, and cobblers, pie, crisps, and tarts certainly qualify. We get creative because restaurant menus need to sound interesting and must change from time to time—today's Apricot & Blackberry Cobbler could be tomorrow's Blackberry & Apricot Crisp! Cobbler or crisp, this is the quintessential summer dessert. The best, ripest fruit doesn't need much help as the sun has already done its job. A squirt of lemon and a nice crispy crust is sufficient.

For the dough:
1 cup all-purpose flour
¾ cup sugar
1 teaspoon ground cinnamon
1 teaspoon baking powder
1 teaspoon ground allspice
1 teaspoon salt
1 large egg
5 tablespoons unsalted butter, melted

For the filling:
12 fresh apricots
2 tablespoons fresh lemon juice
2 tablespoons cornstarch
4 pints blackberries
¼ cup lightly packed brown sugar
3 tablespoons unsalted butter, cut
    into pieces

To prepare the dough:
In a mixer on slow speed, combine the flour, sugar, cinnamon, baking powder, allspice, and salt. Add the egg to the dry ingredients. Add the melted butter and mix. Form the dough into a ball, wrap it in plastic and chill the dough for at least 2 hours and up to overnight.

Divide the chilled dough into 6 portions. Roll out the dough between pieces of wax paper so the dough is at least ½-inch larger than the size of the ramekin on all sides if making individual cobblers.
Preheat the oven to 375°F.

To prepare the filling:
Quarter the apricots and coat them with lemon juice. In a separate bowl, dissolve the cornstarch in 2 tablespoons water. Add the blackberries, apricots, and brown sugar to the bowl with the apricots and mix gently. Place an equal amount of the filling into each baking dish. Add ½ tablespoon of butter over each portion. Cover with a layer of solid dough or create a lattice topping by trimming the dough into 14 to 16 ½-inch strips using a knife or a pizza wheel. Weave the dough strips over the filling by going over and under to create a lattice. Let the strips come a bit over the edge of the baking dish as the dough will slightly shrink as it bakes. Bake the cobbler for 40 to 50 minutes until the crust is golden brown. Let cool.

To serve:
Serve each portion with a scoop of ice cream or gelato.

Makes 6 to 8 individual cobblers or 1 large 8x8-inch cobbler

BELLWETHER FARMS CRESCENZA   SUMMER №1

REGION:	Petaluma, California
MILK:	Jersey cow
PROCESS:	pasteurized
PRODUCTION:	uncooked, unpressed, soft rising
AFFINAGE:	two weeks, ages quickly
FLAVOR:	soft, sweet, tangy, rich, milky, buttery
AROMA:	very mild, yeasty
TEXTURE:	creamy, gooey, thick, luscious
SIMILAR CHEESES:	Teleme
PAIRINGS:	ellelle Central Coast Raspberry Jam
	Frog Hollow Farm Asian Pear Chutney
	Pasolivo Extra-Virgin Olive Oil
	fresh herbs, salad greens
NOTES:	Crescenza is a rindless cheese that is cut into large curds. This cheese is great to cook with and works well with pastas, risotto, and pizza.

the girl & the fishmonger

Over the past few years, our meat and poultry orders have gone down and our fish orders have increased significantly. As with most food trends, there is usually a high and a low before things balance out again. To many folks, fish means a healthy, fresh, and light meal, and from those three words we concentrate primarily on "fresh." Our fishmongers know that we will never accept fish unless it is perfectly fresh, has a taut texture, and is free of unpleasant aromas. A bond of trust is made with our fishmongers because they realize how important food safety is. Our chefs need to order accurate amounts daily, practically using a crystal ball to decide how much fish our guests will order the next day. Ordering too much means the fish goes to waste and drives the cost up. The same is true for properly cooking fish. Most fish are extremely delicate and simply must not be overcooked. If that point is reached, there is nothing to do except cook another piece, resulting in more waste. As a result, subsequently, we're extremely careful, selecting the freshest fish possible and cooking it properly.

Fish: Farmed versus Wild

In the past ten years, a debate has developed over wild versus farmed fish. Aquaculture, as fish farming is properly known, has environmental and nutritional consequences that need to be considered. We've included some basic facts here to help you make a more informed decision. At the restaurants, we are committed to serving only fish that is sustainable and caught in an environmentally friendly manner, whether it is farmed or wild.

Aquaculture developed as the world's wild fish supply diminished. Today, more than 70 percent of the world's fisheries are exploited or depleted, according to the nonprofit trade association Seafood Choices Alliance, and half the seafood consumed in the U.S. is farmed, according to the Monterey Bay Aquarium's Seafood Watch program.

There are several types of fish farming methods, and some are better than others. Open net pens and cages, ponds, and raceways are used according to the types of fish being bred, but fish farms have an environmental impact that can't be ignored: the high concentration of fish leads to disease and antibiotic use. This affects the entire species when the farmed fish escape and breed with their wild counterparts, permanently changing the gene pool. Pollution is the second issue, with antibiotics, fish waste, and other pollutants released into the water. There can be—and are—viable aquaculture facilities, particularly for shellfish. These "smart" farms are able to limit pollution, limit or reduce the amount of fishmeal fed to the fish, and limit the number of farmed fish that escape.

The other problem with farmed fish is what they eat. Both artificial and natural additives are given to the fish to improve the color and texture, and polychlorinated biphenyls (PCBs) have been found in farmed fish samples. PCBs are toxic industrial compounds that have been found to cause cancer in lab rats. They were banned by the U.S. in 1976 but still exist in the sediment of some rivers, and then are absorbed by the fish. In addition, wild fish are used as feed for farmed fish. It takes three pounds of wild fish to raise one pound of farmed salmon, according to Seafood Watch. This affects the wild fish population, which is already decreasing at a rapid rate.

Nutritional differences in wild and farmed fish also exist. Some studies have shown that farmed salmon has lower levels of omega-3s than wild salmon, and a higher fat content.

There is a plethora of information available to help you make a decision about what kind of fish to buy. Two trusted sources are Seafood Choices Alliance (www.seafoodchoices.org), an international nonprofit trade association that looks at ocean-friendly seafood, and the Monterey Bay Aquarium's Seafood Watch program (www.montereybayaquarium.org).

Fish at the fig

Local wild salmon: Local wild salmon is troll-caught using barbless hooks, a sustainable method of harvest.

Other Pacific wild salmon: If you must have salmon and can't find anything local, Pacific Northwestern or Alaskan wild are the best choices. (There are many reliable online sources for Alaskan wild salmon.)

Sand dabs: This San Francisco favorite is harvested two ways: by hook and line or trawling. Ask your fishmonger which method was used.

Sardines: Sardines are harvested locally in California, but they are generally a good, sustainable seafood choice no matter where you live.

Sole: The method of catch for these ground fish is sometimes disruptive to sea floor ecosystems, but the fishery is generally healthy, and they are listed as a good alternative by the Seafood Watch. Ask for locally caught fish when possible, although Dover sole, caught in the Atlantic and Mediterranean, is the most common.

Pacific halibut: Harvested in Alaska and Canada, and also known as Alaskan halibut, it's a sustainable option; no fish farms exist for halibut. The largest flatfish in the ocean, Pacific halibut season runs from March through October 1st for recreational fishermen, although commercial fishing season varies.

Pacific cod: Harvested in Alaska and Canada, it's an ecologically sound option.

Dungeness crab: This brown-gray crab is found only in the Pacific Ocean and is a sustainable choice. It turns bright red when cooked and has a wonderful, sweet meat. Dungeness crab season runs from November through May or June, but 80 percent of the Northern California catch is brought in by late December.

California Salmon

The most shocking change we've seen in our food at the restaurants is the decline of local salmon. We used to rely on a local supply of Chinook and Coho salmon, but starting in 2005 the commercial salmon season in California virtually came to a standstill. The Pacific Fishery Management Council, a federal agency that regulates all fisheries off the coasts of Oregon, Washington, and California, works with states to determine the viability of the salmon population. They base their determination on the number of fish that return to their natural spawning ground, and then decide whether or not to open up the fishing grounds to commercial fishermen. The commercial season was closed in 2005, 2007, 2008, and 2009, but opened with a sigh of relief in 2011.

The salmon population is affected by disease and by the increase in water temperatures, which is determined by water flow (set by the Federal Bureau of Reclamation). Most of the salmon caught in the waters off the coast of California come from two major river basins, the Klamath and the Sacramento. The salmon hatch in the rivers, swim to the ocean to mature, and then return to the rivers to spawn and then die. The Chinook salmon's life cycle is three to four years, meaning that water decisions made three years prior will affect the current salmon population. As of 2006, the current Klamath salmon population is estimated to be only about 10 percent of historic levels. The issue is water, something that is always a controversial topic in California, and one that looks like it will continue for some time.

When it happens, wild salmon season runs from May through July. If you can find local wild salmon, be sure it's line-caught salmon from small-scale fishermen. The decline of salmon fishing affects not only our plates, but the livelihood of thousands of fishermen. According to the California Department of Fish and Game, the 2008 salmon season closure resulted in a loss of $255 million and 2,263 jobs. Until California salmon fishing recovers, wild salmon from Alaska and Washington State are good alternatives.

In the first book, we introduced you to Ray, the fisherman who brought us fresh salmon during the salmon season. Although still an avid fisherman, he has had to shift to local halibut as salmon fishing is not always reliable and has became more restricted in the past few years. It is stories like these that really raise our awareness about our food sources and our responsibility to be advocates of environmental and sustainable methods.

Scallops

This sweet, delicate shellfish is such an extraordinary ingredient when cooked properly. Fresh scallops are so versatile—raw, broiled, sautéed, or gratinéed, we serve them every few months in the restaurants.

There are two types of scallops available in the market: bay (½ to 1 inch in size) and sea (1½ to 2 inches). Day-boat scallops, which can be either bay or sea, are caught on a boat that has returned to shore within 24 hours and are not treated with any preservatives or additives. Occasionally, you'll see diver scallops in a seafood store or restaurant menu; these are harvested in the ocean by hand and are the most expensive type of scallop. The season for diver scallops from the Atlantic Ocean is November through April, but frozen scallops are available year-round. While Europeans enjoy the beautiful coral-colored shell that covers a scallop, in the U.S. they are sold shucked. The ivory-colored "meat" of a scallop is actually the animal's adductor muscle.

Because scallops are so perishable, they are often treated with preservatives to extend their shelf life, and sometimes whiteners are used to enhance their color. These scallops are labeled "treated," so check the package or ask your fishmonger if you want to avoid these preservatives. The Northeastern U.S., Canada, Japan, and China are the main sources of scallops.

When buying fresh scallops, look for those with a pinkish-ivory color; they should also be practically odorless. (Sometimes sea scallops have a muscle on the side that should be removed before cooking.) Cooking scallops is simple but be careful not to overcook them—overcooked scallops become unbearably tough and dry. Allow about 2 minutes per side in a skillet, or 5 minutes in a very hot oven. Grilling them for a minute or two on each side is another tasty way to prepare them, and butter is always a perfect complementary flavor to this delicate seafood.

Entrée
House Cured Sardines,
Meyer Lemon Vinaigrette

Plat
Grilled Lamb Loin, Summer Beans,
Sun-Dried Tomato Vinaigrette

Dessert
Pistachio & Cherry "Mille Feuille"

Fromage
Rogue River Blue

House-Cured Sardines, Meyer Lemon Vinaigrette

Copain Wine Cellars Roussanne, James Berry Vineyard, Paso Robles, California
Domaine Pierre Gaillard Saint-Joseph Blanc, Saint-Joseph, France

Sardines always remind me of the South of France; not the word as much as the image of small silvery fish glistening on a plate. Other than the annoying bones, sardines are a pleasure to eat. The fish is tender and the flavor is full and hearty and perks up nicely with the Meyer Lemon Vinaigrette. These sardines are a delicious, simple starter, but would also make a nice dinner on their own with a crusty baguette and a glass of chilled white wine. This recipe is not difficult but it does require marinating the sardines overnight.

For the sardines:

15 sardines

1¼ cups apple cider vinegar

1 cup verjus (see Sources, page 318)

½ cup sugar

½ cup salt

3 tablespoons pickling spice

3 tablespoons Meyer lemon zest, for garnish

3 tablespoons Pickled Shallots, for garnish, (page 313)

1 tablespoon chopped chives, for garnish

1 tablespoon extra-virgin olive oil, for garnish

To prepare the sardines:

Remove the head of each sardine and cut it lengthwise down the belly. Open up the body and flush out the insides, rinse, and pat dry. Place the sardines on a flat surface and using a sharp knife remove the top filet starting at the top. Next, pull the bones out with your fingers.

Place the sardines, flesh side down, in a large, shallow baking dish. Place the vinegar, 2½ cups water, verjus, sugar, salt, and pickling spice in a saucepan and heat to 150°F using a candy thermometer. Remove from the heat, and cool the mixture to 130°F, and pour it over the sardines. Refrigerate the fish overnight.

To serve:

Remove the sardines from the liquid. Place 5 sardine halves on each plate and garnish with the lemon zest, shallots, chives, and olive oil.

Serves 6

Meyer Lemons

Meyer lemons are a true California winter treat. They bloom and fruit all winter long in our mild climate so we're able to take advantage of their slightly sweeter, less acidic flavor. Their deep yellow color reminds me of an egg yolk and brightens up any kitchen. They have an herbal, almost floral aroma that perfumes the air. Thought to be cross between a lemon and a mandarin orange, the Meyer lemon originated in China and was brought to America by a USDA employee named Mr. Meyer in 1908.

They tend to be rounder with a thinner, more fragrant skin than regular lemons so we use Meyers in our vinaigrettes, fish sauces and sorbets. But Meyers are so versatile; from wonderful lemon desserts to delicious cocktails, you just can't resist their sweet flavor.

Their thin skin means they don't transport well, so Meyers are found primarily in California, although a few specialty produce companies offer them by mail. Look for Meyers that have an even-colored yellow skin and no blemishes and that feel heavy for their size. They'll last in the refrigerator for up to two weeks.

Grilled Lamb Loin, Summer Beans, Sun-Dried Tomato Vinaigrette

Audelssa "Maelstrom" Syrah, Sonoma Valley, California
Two Hands Wine "Angels Share" Shiraz, McLaren Vale, Australia
Paul Lato Wines "Il Padrino" Syrah, Bien Nacido, California

In the first week in March, dozens of baby lambs graze at the Benziger Winery. Inevitably, these lambs end up on our menus through the next few months. We are conscious of using the whole animal in our cooking, so we get creative and combine the different cuts of lamb with various cooking methods. Summer means grilling; the meat's flavor is in its prime and the grill provides just the right amount of heat without melding the flavors.

For the lamb:

3 pounds lamb loin
1 bunch fresh rosemary, chopped
2 garlic cloves, crushed
1 cup extra-virgin olive oil
Salt and pepper to taste

For the beans:

1 pound haricots verts, blanched
1 pound yellow wax beans, blanched
2 pounds fresh Shelling Beans, cooked (page 313)
1 tablespoon blended oil

For the vinaigrette:

1 cup sun-dried tomatoes, julienned
½ cup extra-virgin olive oil
Salt and pepper to taste
2 tablespoons sherry vinegar

¼ cup fresh flat-leaf parsley leaves, for garnish
2 tablespoons fresh oregano leaves, for garnish
2 tablespoons chives, cut into 1-inch pieces, for garnish
¼ cup oil-cured olives, such as Nyons, pitted and cut in half, for garnish

To prepare the marinade:

In a large pan place the lamb loin, rosemary, garlic, and olive oil. Cover and marinate overnight in the refrigerator.

To prepare the vinaigrette:

In a small bowl rehydrate the sun-dried tomatoes in warm water for 15 minutes. Drain the tomatoes, place them in a food processor, and purée with the olive oil and vinegar. Season with salt and pepper to taste.

To prepare the lamb:

Preheat a grill to high. Remove the lamb loin from the marinade, removing any excess oil and the garlic. Season the lamb with salt and pepper. Cook the lamb on a hot grill for 2 to 3 minutes per side.

To prepare the beans:

While the lamb is cooking, place a large sauté pan over medium heat. Heat the blended oil and add the beans. Season with salt and pepper to taste and heat through, about 5 to 6 minutes. Remove from the heat and toss the beans with half of the vinaigrette.

To serve:

Slice the lamb into 12 portions. Place two pieces of lamb on each plate and distribute the beans evenly over the top. Garnish with the herbs and olives and drizzle the remaining vinaigrette around each plate.

Serves 6

Pistachio & Cherry "Mille Feuille," Lemon Verbena Custard

Yalumba Antique Tawny Port, Australia
Cave de Rasteau Vin Doux Naturel, Rasteau, France

This is a visually stunning dessert that is also fun to prepare. Light and delicate, it tastes even better when the cherries are ripened to perfection. The Lemon Verbena Custard adds a slightly tart, herbal flavor and contrasts nicely with the dark fruit.

For the phyllo sheets:

4 sheets phyllo dough, thawed according to
    package directions (see Note)

3 tablespoons unsalted butter, melted

4 teaspoons sugar

For the custard:

2 cups whole milk

6 large egg yolks

½ cup superfine sugar

1 teaspoon pure vanilla extract

4 tablespoons cornstarch

Pinch of salt

6 large fresh lemon verbena leaves (see
    Sources, page 320)

36 ripe cherries, pitted and halved (about ½
    pound)

¾ cup shelled pistachios, toasted and finely
    chopped

Stone Fruit

Stone fruit appears on our menus whenever possible —apricots, peaches, cherries, and plums are used liberally by our chefs through the spring and summer months. We make an endless array of desserts but also incorporate stone fruit into savory dishes, as an accompaniment to meat dishes or transform it into chutney. We also use a variety of stone fruit to make jams, marmalades, and preserves for brunch dishes and cheese plates.

Spring is a temperamental time for stone fruit growers in California because the weather is completely unpredictable. Every year we cross our fingers that the crop will be good and provide us with a reliable source of fruit from our local growers.

Preheat the oven to 350°F.

To prepare the phyllo:

Butter a large baking sheet and set 1 phyllo sheet on top. (Cover the remaining phyllo with a damp cloth while you are working.) Lightly brush the phyllo sheets with butter and sprinkle with 1 teaspoon sugar. Layer another phyllo sheet on top and press down. Repeat layering until you use all of the sheets, ending with 1 teaspoon sugar on top. Cut the phyllo stack into 18 equal triangles. Bake until the phyllo triangles are golden brown and crisp, about 10 minutes.

To prepare the custard:

Whisk ¼ cup milk, the egg yolks, sugar, and vanilla together. Add the cornstarch and salt and set aside. Bring the remaining milk and lemon verbena to a boil in a saucepan. Remove from the heat, cover, and steep for 10 minutes. Taste the milk to check the strength of the lemon verbena flavor. Continue to steep if needed. If the flavor is assertive enough to your taste, pour the hot milk in a small stream into the egg mixture, whisking constantly as you pour. Once incorporated, pour the mixture back into the saucepan.

Whisk the mixture over medium heat until it thickens and firms up. Remove from the heat. Pour the hot custard into a bowl and place the bottom of the bowl into a larger bowl of ice water to cool, giving it a whisk occasionally. Once it reaches room temperature, cover the surface of the cream with plastic wrap to prevent a skin from forming. Refrigerate for 30 minutes or until chilled. Put the chilled pastry cream into a pastry bag fitted with a star or round tip and twist the open end to seal. Keep in the refrigerator until ready to use. The pastry cream can be made 1 day ahead.

To assemble:

Pipe a small dot of pastry cream onto the center of each chilled plate. Arrange a rectangle of phyllo on the pastry cream at the center of the plate. Pipe the pastry cream down the length of the rectangle and sprinkle with 1 teaspoon of pistachio nuts. Arrange 6 cherry halves on top of the pastry cream the length of the rectangle and top with a new phyllo sheet, pressing gently to set. Repeat this process and top with the third and final phyllo sheet. Garnish with more pistachios and repeat with the remaining plates.

Note: Standard phyllo sheets come 40 (9x4-inch) sheets per box. For this recipe you will need 4 full sheets. Our recommendation is the following: Cut each sheet 3 across and 3 down, providing 9 squares. Cut each square on the diagonal to get 18 triangles.

Serves 6

summer

ROGUE CREAMERY ROGUE RIVER BLUE

REGION:	Central Point, Oregon
MILK:	cow
PROCESS:	raw
PRODUCTION:	uncooked, unpressed, soft, with veins of blue mold
AFFINAGE:	8 months - 1 year
FLAVOR:	vigorous, complex, balanced, butterscotch, caramel, hints of brandy
AROMA:	tart, fruity, earthy, sherry
TEXTURE:	creamy, buttery, moist
SIMILAR CHEESES:	Fourme d'Ambert
PAIRINGS:	Hector's Honeycomb
	L'Epicurien Quince Paste
	Panevino No 6 Grissini
	Matiz Fig & Walnut Cake
NOTES:	Rogue River Blue is only made with autumn milk. At about four months, the wheels are wrapped in Syrah grape leaves that have been steeped in Clear Creek Pear Brandy and matured for another four months.

Entrée
Heirloom Tomato & Watermelon Salad

Plat
*Panko-Crusted Soft Shell Crabs,
Warm Bacon Vinaigrette*

Dessert
*Grilled Peaches,
Pistachio Crème Anglaise*

Fromage
Cypress Grove Humboldt Fog

Heirloom Tomato & Watermelon Salad

Kunde Family Estate Viognier, Sonoma Valley, California
Quenard Chignin "Les Terrasses" Roussanne/Bergeron, Savoie, France

This is one of the most popular menu items at the girl & the fig. You don't normally think of pairing tomatoes with watermelon, but peak tomato season is usually the same for watermelon. The two fruits are somewhat similar in texture and color, as well. The watermelon's sugar content, though higher than a tomato's, ties the two fruits together. The addition of the salty sheep's milk feta and a sprinkling of sea salt create a nice contrast to the sweetness of the salad. We use fresh oregano as the main herbal flavor, but it would be just as good with fresh basil or thyme.

For the vinaigrette:
1 medium yellow tomato, blanched, peeled and seeded
1 tablespoon Dijon mustard
1 tablespoon champagne vinegar
½ cup extra-virgin olive oil
Salt and white pepper to taste

For the salad:
½ cup feta cheese
3 tablespoons extra-virgin olive oil

1 pound seedless watermelon, rind removed, sliced into ½ x 2-inch
   rounds
2 pounds assorted heirloom tomatoes, sliced into ½-inch pieces
2 tablespoons fresh oregano leaves, for garnish
Sea salt, for garnish

To prepare the vinaigrette:
Place the yellow tomato in a blender. On medium speed add the mustard and then the vinegar. Slowly add ½ cup of olive oil. Taste and season with salt and white pepper as needed and set aside.

In a separate bowl, crumble the feta and mix it with 3 tablespoons olive oil.

To serve:
Divide the heirloom tomato slices and the watermelon slices equally among 6 plates. When plating, alternate the slices and garnish with a bit of feta. Drizzle the vinaigrette over each portion and garnish with the oregano leaves. Add a touch of sea salt to the salad if desired.

Serves 6

Panko-Crusted Soft Shell Crabs, Warm Bacon Vinaigrette

Qupé Winery Roussanne, Bien Nacido Estate, Santa Maria Valley, California
Cave Yves Cuilleron "Les Challets," Condrieu, France

My first soft shell crab was love at first sight. Though I like my soft shells quickly sautéed to maximize the lingering salt water flavor, I also like them with a rich, textural coating from panko. Panko has a larger flake than typical bread crumbs and attaches easily to the crab. Sautéing them in a hot pan ensures a crispy texture as they cook. For this version of soft shells we chose a warm, slightly salty bacon vinaigrette that will be absorbed by the coating.

For the vinaigrette:

2 tablespoons extra-virgin olive oil
3 strips thick-sliced bacon, cut into ¼-inch strips
2 tablespoons minced shallots
½ cup champagne vinegar
1 tablespoon whole-grain mustard
1 tablespoon chopped fresh tarragon
Salt and pepper to taste

For the tomatoes:

2 pints cherry tomatoes
2 cups extra-virgin olive oil
3 sprigs fresh thyme
2 garlic cloves

For the crabs:

3 cups panko
1 tablespoon smoked paprika
½ tablespoon salt
½ teaspoon white pepper
1 cup all-purpose flour
3 large eggs, lightly beaten
6 medium soft shell crabs, cleaned
Salt and pepper to taste

2 heads frisée, trimmed, for serving
1 bunch chives, cut into 1-inch pieces, for serving

To prepare the vinaigrette:

Heat the olive oil in a medium sauté pan and cook the bacon over medium heat, tossing occasionally until browned, about 6 to 8 minutes. With tongs or a slotted spoon, transfer the bacon to a paper towel-lined plate to drain. Set aside.

Pour off all but 2 tablespoons of the bacon fat from the sauté pan and return the pan to the heat. Add the shallots, vinegar, and mustard to the pan. Stir, scraping up any browned bits, until the dressing is combined. Add the tarragon and season to taste.

To prepare the tomatoes:

Place a small saucepan over low heat and add the tomatoes, olive oil, thyme, and garlic. Bring to a simmer, remove from the heat, and let the tomatoes cool to room temperature. Remove the tomatoes from the oil using a slotted spoon and set aside. (The oil can be used again to cook more batches of tomatoes, but must be refrigerated after use.)

To prepare the crabs:

In a medium bowl, mix the panko, paprika, salt, and white pepper together. Place the flour and the eggs in two separate bowls. Arrange the bowls in the following order: flour, egg, and panko.

Place a large sauté pan over medium heat, fill it with ¾-inch of canola oil, and heat the oil to 375°F. Dip the crab in the flour, then the egg, and then the panko mixture. Add the crab to the pan and fry until golden brown. Turn over and repeat, about 2 minutes per side. Place the crabs on paper towels to drain and season lightly with salt and pepper to taste.

To serve:

Toss the frisée and the chives with the bacon, tomatoes, and 6 tablespoons of the vinaigrette. Divide the mixture equally among the 6 plates, top with the crabs, and drizzle a little vinaigrette around the edge of each plate.

Serves 6

Grilled Peaches, Pistachio Crème Anglaise

McCrea Cellars Late Harvest Roussanne, Yakima Valley, Washington

Peaches right off the tree and on to the grill—you couldn't dream up a simpler or more delicious dessert to celebrate summer! This recipe is best when using very ripe peaches. Underripe peaches will take longer to cook and will not have the luscious flavor.

For the crème anglaise:

3 large egg yolks

¼ cup sugar

½ cup whole milk

½ cup heavy cream

1½ tablespoons pistachio nut paste
   (see Sources, page 318)

For the peaches:

1 tablespoon brandy

1 tablespoon pure vanilla extract

1 teaspoon salt

1 tablespoon sugar

¼ teaspoon ground cinnamon

9 ripe peaches, cut in half, pits
   removed

½ cup shelled pistachios, toasted
   and seasoned with salt, for garnish

To prepare the crème anglaise:

In a medium bowl, whisk the egg yolks and the sugar until pale and thick. Set aside. Place the milk and cream in a medium saucepan and heat to just below a simmer. Temper the eggs by whisking half of the milk mixture into the egg mixture. Pour the mixture back into the saucepan and whisk in the pistachio paste. Place the mixture over medium heat and cook, stirring often, until the mixture is thick enough to coat the back of a spoon, about 5 to 7 minutes. Strain the mixture into a bowl set over an ice water bath to chill. Set aside. Preheat a grill to medium heat.

To prepare the peaches:

In a stainless-steel or glass bowl, combine the brandy, vanilla, salt, sugar, and cinnamon. Add the peaches and toss to coat. Set aside at room temperature for about 15 minutes to let the peaches soak up the liquid.

Place the peaches face down on the hot grill for about 3 minutes. Turn the peaches over and spoon some of the liquid from the marinating bowl into the cavity. Close the grill lid or cover the peaches with foil and cook for an additional 3 to 5 minutes or until the peaches have warmed through.

To Serve:

Pour a small pool of the crème anglaise on each plate and cover with a peach half, cut side up. Drizzle a little more of the crème anglaise in the pit cavity. Repeat so that each plate has 3 peach halves. Distribute the remaining crème anglaise among the plates and garnish with the pistachios.

Serves 6

CYPRESS GROVE HUMBOLDT FOG

SUMMER Nº3

REGION:	Arcata, California
MILK:	goat
PROCESS:	pasteurized
PRODUCTION:	lactic acid set curd, uncooked, unpressed, bloomy rind
AFFINAGE:	at least three weeks
FLAVOR:	elegant, subtle tang, bright, lemony, hints of flowers and herbs,
AROMA:	fresh, buttermilk, floral
TEXTURE:	creamy, soft, elegant, chalky
SIMILAR CHEESES:	Sainte Maure, Valençay
PAIRINGS:	the girl & the fig Black Mission Fig Jam INNA jam nova Raspberry Jam Calivirgin Bountiful Basil Olive Oil persimmons, dates
NOTES:	Each handcrafted wheel has a decorative layer of edible ash in the center and a coating under its exterior.

Chris Benziger
Glen Ellen, California

The Benzigers have been growing grapes in Sonoma County for more than 30 years, and few families are as devoted to biodynamic farming as they are. They own and farm two properties in Glen Ellen: Benziger Family Winery and the Imagery Estate Winery property. Chris Benziger, the youngest of seven siblings, is responsible for the Imagery property, where we started **the farm project**. We've known Chris for years, from the day we opened the girl & the fig in Glen Ellen, just a few blocks from the Benziger Winery. The Benziger story is a lesson in learning from the land and paying attention to what nature is telling you, something that we try to do in the kitchen with **the farm project**.

What we love most about the Benzigers is how deep their commitment is to the land. They haven't jumped on the "green" bandwagon; rather, they live it every day. When they started growing grapes in 1980 at their main property in Glen Ellen, they were conventional farmers, using chemical pesticides and fertilizers, but they realized these sprays had a direct impact on the fruit and the land. "We thought the chemicals were diminishing the quality of our fruit and our land and we decided to go biodynamic and organic," says Chris. So during the 1980s and 1990s they transitioned their land from conventional to organic and biodynamic. "The principle is biodiversity. You can't have one crop. Think of an old European estate; they have woodlands, orchards, vineyards. It's a mosaic of farming. They didn't just plant corn," he says. The Benzigers tore out vineyards and replaced them with olive and fig trees, built insectaries (intense gardens for animals such as insects and hummingbirds who then eat the "bad bugs" in the vineyards); and used compost instead of chemical fertilizers. These are principles that they later adopted at the Imagery Estate Winery property. The process took

about three years, but the family saw the health of the property slowly come back. "You end up increasing the biological capital of your property," notes Chris. In 2000, Benziger Family Winery was the first winery in Napa and Sonoma to become certified biodynamic.

In the late 1990s the Benzigers bought a 20-acre parcel of land on Highway 12 in Glen Ellen and decided to start a brewery. They ripped out the Merlot grapes (a move that made the front page of the *New York Times!*), planted hops, and tapped an aquifer that ran below the property as a water source, but the beer market went downhill and the family realized they had the perfect site for another winery. "We had Imagery as a second label [of Benziger Family Winery] for years, so we decided to give it a home," recalls Chris. They replanted the vineyards with varietals such as Sangiovese, Barbera, Viognier, and Grenache, what Chris calls the "esoteric grapes." Imagery Estate Winery now produces 10,000 cases a year under Joe Benziger, Chris' brother and head winemaker.

After the vineyards, winery, and production facilities were established, acres of land remained. Chris decided to plant orchards and vegetables, hiring Colby Eierman to establish the garden. In keeping with the organic and biodynamic principles, Chris also introduced livestock to the property. He keeps a flock of about 100 Dorper sheep which roam the hills year-round, their white woolly coats visible through the trees. "The sheep do wonderful things," says Chris. "They eat the grass in the vineyards and fertilize as they go and push over-wintering leaves to prevent mildew on the grape leaves." Chris harvests about 30 males each year, selling the meat to local restaurants. (We've been lucky enough to get the lamb every spring and it is simply delicious. Because the sheep graze on fresh clover and other wild greens, the meat has a wonderful, distinctive flavor.) Besides lamb, Chris raises cows (for their manure) and chickens (for their eggs).

Chris realized he needed a partner in the venture. "I needed a good active partner, because farming is a full-contact sport," says Chris. "I needed someone who wasn't afraid to get their hands dirty, and I needed someone who had the passion to do it right." John had been talking about expanding our farming efforts, and it seemed like a natural fit. We've had a wonderful symbiotic relationship ever since, establishing the Sharecropper program and working together to maximize the harvest while respecting the land. "The relationship with the girl & the fig brings it back to what it's all about it: a farm growing veggies for the restaurant right there," says Chris. "John and Sondra are such great stewards of what Sonoma has to offer. It's great to partner with them. You don't want to truck in your food from Chile when you've got food that is seasonal from right down the road. This is food that is grown with respect to the land; it's got authenticity and it's got a ZIP code."

Chris is also a foodie, which makes it even more fun to work with him. Last summer, he fell in love with the heirloom varieties of potatoes we planted. "I was always a tomato guy, and always thought potatoes were just a common vegetable," Chris confesses, but he was quickly persuaded by the German Creamers and the Russian Blues. "I got into making French fries. I bought a deep-fryer and made garden-fresh French fries." When he's not busy making heavenly French fries, Chris is working to create even more environmentally friendly projects on the farm. He helped create a cutting-edge water recycling system at the estate that saves a tremendous amount of water. The system essentially works like a wetlands, and the waste water is recycled back into the land, saving 2 million gallons of water each year. In 2010, the Benzigers won a Growing Green Award from the Resource Defense Council for their water conservation efforts. "Water is the biggest resource in California, and we have to be conscious about it," says Chris.

The next steps for the Imagery Estate Farm include plans for a greenhouse, where Chris will nurture seed starts and cuttings. "I want to keep the relationship going and perfect what we have going on right now," he says. "I'd like to have full seasonality in our growing and perfect the winter harvest. Growing in winter is tough because there isn't a lot of sunlight and there are big frosts, but there are a lot of root vegetables you can grow. You just have to be creative."

We're lucky to have such a great working relationship with the Benzigers, and we look forward to seeing what the years ahead will bring. The amazing wine and food that flourish on their land is possible because of their farming techniques and dedication, a type of farming that thinks about the bigger picture.

Entrée
Sweet Corn Cakes

Plat
Pan-Seared Trout,
Lemon Butter Sauce, Haricots Verts

Dessert
Lavender Crème Brûlée

Fromage
Tumalo Farms Classico Reserve

Sweet Corn Cakes

Fess Parker Winery Viognier, Santa Barbara, California
Sebastiani Vineyards & Winery Roussanne, Carneros, California

Corn is one of my top five favorite summer ingredients. This dish can be served as a starter, a small bite, or as a side to an entrée. These corn cakes have a great flavor with a crisp exterior and are even tastier with marinated cherry tomatoes. The abundance of summer vegetables allows for a variety of sauces and dips that will enhance the corn cakes all summer long. Try them with Salsa Roja (page 118) or Tomato Corn Relish (page 94).

For the tomatoes:
1 pint cherry tomatoes, cut in half
1 tablespoon chopped chives
2 tablespoons extra-virgin olive oil
1 tablespoon balsamic vinegar
Salt and pepper to taste

For the corn cakes:
3 cups corn kernels (from 6 medium ears)
2 tablespoons diced red onion
1 tablespoon chopped fresh flat-leaf parsley
4 tablespoons crème fraîche
2 large eggs, lightly beaten
2 teaspoons baking powder
¼ cup firmly packed brown sugar
1 teaspoon smoked paprika
½ cup cornmeal
1 tablespoon fresh lime juice
2½ cups panko

To prepare the tomatoes:
In a bowl mix the tomatoes, chives, olive oil, and vinegar together. Season with salt and pepper to taste and set aside. (The tomatoes can be made 1 day ahead.)

To prepare the corn cakes:
In a food processor, purée 2 cups of corn. In a large bowl, combine the corn purée, the remaining corn kernels, onion, parsley, crème fraîche, eggs, baking powder, brown sugar, smoked paprika, cornmeal, and lime juice. Mix well. Add enough panko until the mixture is moist but not sticky. Form the mixture into 12 cakes and coat the outside of each cake with panko.

Place a large sauté pan over medium heat and fill it with ¼-inch of canola oil. Heat the oil until bubbly (about 375°F). Pan-fry the corn cakes in batches until golden brown, about 2 to 3 minutes per side. Flip the cakes over and repeat. (Be careful when frying the cakes; the corn kernels may pop when heated.)

To serve:
Place the corn cakes on a large platter and spread a spoonful of the tomatoes over the top of each cake.

Serves 6

Corn

Corn is part of every American's history lesson, Native Americans taught pilgrims how to grow corn, and corn sat on the first Thanksgiving table next to the turkey. When the early European settlers arrived corn was a well-established crop throughout South, Central, and North America and each area had its own indigenous varieties. (The sweet corn that Americans eat by the ton was discovered along the Susquehanna River in central New York.)

We love corn in the summer. Sweet and crunchy, we make corn relish, corn cakes, and corn fritters and we add the sweet kernels to soups and sauces. Bacon and corn is a match made in culinary heaven; the salty, fatty bacon plays off the sweet corn flavor beautifully. Boiled, grilled, or creamed, it's a true taste of summer.

We don't grow corn because we don't have room in the garden. Growing corn is a heroic effort—each plant produces only two cobs. This is why genetically modified (GMO) corn came to be—they got the plant to set more corn, and increased the per acre ratio. The result is more corn, but also the need for more commercial fertilizer. The bottom line is that GMO corn has a significant environmental impact, so it's better to look for local organic corn in season.

When buying fresh corn, look for ears with evenly spaced, tight rows, and slightly plump kernels. Ignore any with shriveled or enlarged kernels. The corn silk should be dry but not brittle and the stems should be light green rather than yellow. Corn should be consumed very soon after harvesting, preferably the same day, though you can store unhusked ears of corn in a plastic bag in the refrigerator for up to two days.

Pan-Seared Trout, Lemon Butter Sauce, Haricots Verts

Atmosphere "Dos Burros" Marsanne/Roussanne, La Prenda Vineyard, Sonoma Valley, California
Starlite Vineyards Viognier, Sonoma County, California

Trout is a simple fish to prepare and works nicely with a wide variety of flavors. I like the clean, fresh taste and the texture of trout. The dish is very similar to the traditional "Trout Meunière." Meunière sauce is a variation on brown butter sauce with the addition of parsley and lemon. Our guests are delighted whenever we feature a fish with this sauce. It definitely means we need to order more fish for the following day. We have a few guests that come a few times a week just to have it!

½ pound haricots verts, stemmed and blanched

For the trout:
½ cup all-purpose flour
Salt and freshly ground white pepper to taste
6 trout (10 ounces each), bone out, cleaned
   (heads left on or off)
⅓ cup blended oil
8 tablespoons (1 stick) unsalted butter, diced
¼ cup fresh lemon juice
6 tablespoons lemon segments, (from about 4
   lemons)
3 tablespoons capers, drained
4 tablespoons finely chopped fresh flat-leaf parsley
¼ cup Meyer Lemon Vinaigrette (page 312)
2 heads frisée, washed and green leaves removed
1 cup fresh picked fines herbs (such as tarragon,
   parsley, chives, and chervil)
Salt and white pepper to taste

To prepare the trout:
Season the flour well with salt and pepper and spread it over a flat dish. Place the trout in the flour and coat thoroughly. Remove the trout from the flour and shake off any excess.

Heat the oil in a large frying pan over medium-high heat and add the trout one or two at a time. Cook until golden brown, about 3 minutes on each side, basting with oil to keep the trout moist. Remove the trout to a platter and place it in a warm oven (200°F) until all of the trout are sautéed.

To prepare the salad:
Heat the vinaigrette and haricots verts in a medium sauté pan over medium-low heat until warm. Remove from the heat, toss with the frisée and herbs, and season with salt and pepper to taste. Keep warm.

To finish:
Pour off the fat from the trout pan and return the pan to the heat. Melt the butter and cook until it turns hazelnut brown in color without burning. Add the lemon juice and season lightly with salt. Add the lemon segments, capers, and parsley to the pan.

To serve:
Place one trout on each plate and pour the lemon butter over the fish. Divide the salad among the plates and serve.

Serves 6

summer

Lavender Crème Brûlée

Bonny Doon Vineyards Muscat Vin de Glaciere, Central Coast, California

The lavender used in this recipe is the key to success. Make sure to use culinary lavender and try to get a sense of the intensity. The stronger the scent, the shorter the steep time should be. There is a very delicate line between making a blissful Lavender Crème Brûlée and what tastes like a decadent bath lotion.

2¼ cups heavy cream

¾ cup whole milk

3 to 4 sprigs fresh lavender or 1½ tablespoons dried
   culinary lavender, plus additional for garnish

8 large egg yolks

½ cup sugar plus about 4 tablespoons sugar

2 tablespoons wildflower honey

Preheat the oven to 350°F.

Place the cream and milk in a saucepan and add the lavender. Bring to a boil and turn off the heat. Let the lavender steep for about 15 minutes or until the milk has a lavender flavor. (For a stronger flavor, allow the lavender to steep longer.) Meanwhile, beat the egg yolks, ½ cup sugar, and honey until smooth. Whisk it into the lavender-cream mixture. Strain though a fine-mesh sieve and skim off any foam. Refrigerate for at least 4 hours or overnight.

Pour the mixture into 6 ramekins or brûlée dishes. Set the ramekins in a baking pan and add enough hot water to reach halfway up the sides of the ramekins. Cover the baking pan with foil and bake for 40 minutes or until set. (The custards are done when they stop jiggling.) Remove the baking pan from the oven and allow the ramekins to cool in the water bath for 5 minutes. Refrigerate, covered, for at least three hours or overnight.

Before serving, sprinkle the tops of the ramekins with a few teaspoons of sugar and caramelize with a small torch or under a broiler set on high. Garnish each crème brûlée with a lavender blossom.

Serves 6

TUMALO FARMS CLASSICO RESERVE

REGION:	Bend, Oregon
MILK:	farmstead goat
PROCESS:	pasteurized
PRODUCTION:	semi-hard, cooked, pressed
AFFINAGE:	cave aged for at least 12 months
FLAVOR:	slightly sweet brown butter, nutty, honeysuckle
AROMA:	butter, hazelnuts
TEXTURE:	firm, smooth
SIMILAR CHEESES:	Pleasant Ridge Reserve
	Vermont Shepherd (sheep's milk)
PAIRINGS:	the girl & the fig Apple-Fig Mostarda
	Loulou's Garden Pickled Cherries
	Sonoma Syrup Co Hazelnut Syrup
	Grilled Figs
	fresh fruit, medjool dates
NOTES:	During affinage this 20 pound wheel of cheese is turned and wiped daily.

Entrée
Padrón Peppers

Plat
Grilled Flat Iron Steak, Eggplant Purée,
Anchovy Butter

Dessert
Decadent Chocolate Brownies

Fromage
Pont-l'Evêque

Padrón Peppers

Treana Winery White Rhône Blend, Mer Soleil Vineyard, Central Coast, California
Kunde Family Estate Viognier, Sonoma Valley, California

Padrón peppers are a wonderful treat. They are simple, quick to cook, and make a surprising addition to most summer meals. However, not all Padróns are the same; some are delicate and mild in flavor and others surprise you with a spicy bite. There is no way of knowing how spicy they are just by looking at them; you just have to go for it. Other than washing the peppers, there is no preparation before cooking them and you can eat them right up to the stem, making Padróns the ultimate finger food.

1 pound Padrón peppers

3 tablespoons olive oil

½ tablespoon Maldon Sea Salt

2 tablespoons Herbed Bread Crumbs (page 311)

2 tablespoons balsamic vinegar (condimento or saba can be substituted)

Heat a heavy-bottomed skillet over high heat until almost smoking.

In a small bowl combine the peppers and oil and add them to the skillet. Sear the peppers on all sides until browned, about 4 to 6 minutes. Remove from the heat.

To serve:
Place the peppers on a serving dish and sprinkle them with the salt and bread crumbs. Add a drizzle of the balsamic vinegar over the top.

Serves 6

Grilled Flat Iron Steak, Eggplant Purée, Anchovy Butter

Preston of Dry Creek Carignane, Dry Creek Valley, California
Villa Creek "Damas Noir" Mourvèdre, Paso Robles, California
Beckman Vineyards Grenache, Purisma Mountain, Santa Ynez Valley, California

We have many options available when selecting cuts of meat from our meat purveyors, but we keep coming back to the Flat Iron steak. The Flat Iron comes from the shoulder and has a good amount of marbling, which gives it a great flavor. Not only is the price right, it's also a great tasting piece of beef. If you plan on cooking this piece of meat any further than medium, you may want to switch to a Ribeye.

For the steaks:
2 shallots, sliced
3 tablespoons extra-virgin olive oil
1 tablespoon chopped fresh thyme
1 tablespoon chopped fresh rosemary
1 tablespoon chopped fresh flat-leaf parsley
6 Flat Iron steaks (6 ounces each and 1-inch thick)

For the anchovy butter:
8 tablespoons (1 stick) unsalted butter, at room
   temperature
4 anchovy filets
1 tablespoon diced shallots

For the eggplant:
2 large eggplants, halved lengthwise
½ cup extra-virgin olive oil
Salt and pepper to taste

To finish:
1 tablespoon unsalted butter
1 cup cress (water, pepper or ancho, or a mixture)
1 tablespoon extra-virgin olive oil

To prepare the steaks:
In a large baking dish combine the shallots, olive oil, thyme, rosemary, and parsley. Add the steaks, cover, and refrigerate for 4 hours or up to overnight.

To prepare the anchovy butter:
In a food processor, purée the butter with the anchovy and shallots. Place the butter in a small dish and refrigerate. (The anchovy butter can be made up to 1 week ahead.)

To prepare the eggplant:
Preheat the oven to 400°F.
Using a knife, slice ½-inch deep crosses into the flesh side of the eggplant. Drizzle ¼ cup of the olive oil over them and season generously with salt and pepper. Place the eggplant flesh side down on a baking sheet and bake until the flesh has fully cooked, about 35 to 45 minutes.

When the eggplant is cool, scoop out the flesh into the bowl of a food processor and discard the skin. Purée the eggplant with the remaining ¼ cup olive oil and add water to thin the consistency to a thick purée. Season with salt and pepper to taste and set aside.

To finish:
Preheat the grill to high.
Remove the steaks from the marinade and scrap off any excess. Season the steaks with salt and pepper and grill them to the desired temperature (for rare, about 5 to 7 minutes; for medium rare, about 7 to 10 minutes).

In a saucepan heat the eggplant purée with 1 tablespoon of butter over medium heat until the butter is incorporated and the purée is hot. Spoon a large spoonful of the purée on each of six plates and spread it with a spoon. Place one steak over the eggplant purée and crumble the anchovy butter over each steak. Toss the cress with the olive oil, season with salt and pepper to taste, and divide it among the steaks.

Serves 6

Decadent Chocolate Brownies

Broc Cellars Grenache, Dry Stack Vineyard, Sonoma Valley, California
Domaine Madeloc Pierre Gaillard Banyuls, France

Over the years, I've over-indulged on one or more of our products. Some years I say, "That is the year that I gained twenty pounds on cheese," while other years I say, "That was the year I gained ten (maybe more) pounds on our chocolate brownies!" Our brownies are so good they should be illegal. Rich and chocolatey, they work great as a mini-bite on a dessert buffet or as a base for a decadent ice cream sundae. Grab your favorite vanilla ice cream for this recipe.

For the chocolate sauce:

6 ounces bittersweet chocolate (we use 60%)

½ cup plus 2 tablespoons heavy cream

2 tablespoons corn syrup

1 teaspoon pure vanilla extract

For the brownies:

9 ounces bittersweet chocolate (we use 60%)

24 tablespoons (3 sticks) unsalted butter

3 cups sugar

6 large eggs

1 teaspoon pure vanilla extract

½ teaspoon salt

¼ cup unsweetened Dutch-processed cocoa powder

1½ cups all-purpose flour

Vanilla ice cream, for serving

½ cup Candied Pecans (page 315), for garnish

To prepare the chocolate sauce:

Chop the chocolate into small pieces, place them in a small stainless-steel bowl, and set aside. In a saucepan over medium heat bring the cream, corn syrup, and vanilla to a simmer. Pour the cream over the chopped chocolate, cover for 5 minutes or until the chocolate has melted, and then stir until completely smooth. Set the bowl in a warm place until needed or cover and refrigerate and melt it at a later time. (The chocolate sauce can be made ahead and refrigerated for at least 1 week.)

To prepare the brownie:

Preheat the oven to 350°F. Grease a 9 x 12-inch baking pan and line it with parchment paper. Melt the chocolate and butter together in a double boiler over medium heat. In a separate bowl, whisk the sugar and eggs until light and pale. Remove the chocolate mixture from the heat and slowly fold the egg mixture into the chocolate mixture. In a separate bowl, sift the salt, flour, and cocoa powder together and fold the mixture into the chocolate mixture. Pour the batter into the baking pan and bake for about 40 to 45 minutes or until a toothpick inserted into the middle comes out clean. Let the brownies cool before cutting.

To serve:

Cut the brownies into the desired size. Reheat them in a 350°F oven until warmed through, about 8 minutes. Place each brownie on a plate and top with one scoop of vanilla ice cream. Drizzle chocolate syrup over the top and garnish each brownie with the pecans.

Serves 6 to 12

PONT-L'EVEQUE

REGION:	Basse-Normandy, France
MILK:	cow
PROCESS:	raw and pasteurized
PRODUCTION:	uncooked, unpressed, soft, washed rind, sometimes a natural mold
AFFINAGE:	can not be sold before 20 days, optimum flavors between 28 to 45 days
FLAVOR:	trace of sweetness, mild and grassy, fruity
AROMA:	pungent, aromatic
TEXTURE:	soft, supple
SIMILAR CHEESES:	Munster
PAIRINGS:	the girl & the fig Dried Fig Compote June Taylor Peach & Fennel Conserves American Spoon Bartlett Pear Preserves
NOTES:	Pont-L'Evêque is considered one of the top ten most pungent cheeses. Currently only six dairies provide milk for this cheese.

Entrée
Burrata, Heirloom Tomatoes & Basil

Plat
Provençal Petrale Sole

Dessert
Black Mission Fig Clafouti

Fromage
Tumalo Farms Pondhopper

Burrata, Heirloom Tomatoes & Basil

Guigal Saint-Joseph Blanc, Saint-Joseph, France

Until we opened ESTATE, burrata was not on our radar, but soon after we saw burrata on menus everywhere. Now we know why. The California burrata we serve is truly luscious, (but of course so is Italian burrata). Enriched with cream, this velvety cheese is the perfect pairing with the ripest tomatoes and artisan sea salt. Grab a crusty loaf, a handful of fresh basil leaves, and some aged balsamic vinegar and you are all set.

8 medium assorted heirloom tomatoes, cored and sliced into
   1-inch wedges
12 fresh basil leaves, torn into 1-inch pieces
¾ pound burrata cheese, pulled into ½-inch chunks
¾ cup high-quality extra-virgin olive oil
1 tablespoon Maldon Sea Salt

Place an assortment of the heirloom tomato wedges on a serving platter. Loosely cover the tomatoes with the burrata and the basil. Drizzle with olive oil and sprinkle with salt right before serving.

Serves 6

Basil

I can't imagine a culinary life without basil. We use the green Sweet variety in so many ways: to make basil oil, for pesto, as a garnish, in cocktails—basically whenever we can! It's integral to Italian dishes as well as French food, and it's one herb that is strong enough to stand up to the robust flavor of garlic.

Thai basil is another variety that has become more common, a beautiful blend of green leaves, pinkish-purplish flowers, and red-purple stems. Popular in many Asian dishes, it has a distinctive minty aniseed flavor. Opal basil is another variety you'll find and it's hard to miss: the deep purple leaves are captivating and the mild flavor is deeply satisfying.

We have rows of Sweet, Thai, and Opal basil plants at our farm, and they love the spring and summer sun. Picking fresh basil is hardly a chore—your hands smell wonderful for hours afterward!

Look for fresh bunches of basil with brightly colored leaves—there should be no brown leaves. Refrigeration causes brown spots on the basil leaves so the best way to store a bunch is upright in a jar of water on your countertop; it should last two to three days. Ideally, eat your basil the day you buy (or pick) it!

Provençal Petrale Sole

Beckman Vineyards Grenache Blanc, Purisma Mountain Vineyard, Santa Ynez Valley, California
Domaine Ott Côtes de Provence Rosé, Provence, France

What makes this dish so delicious is the vinaigrette. The combination of olives, capers, tomatoes, fennel, and fresh herbs makes a refreshing sauce for this delicate fish. Castelvetrano olives have been in the spotlight for past few years. They are harvested early, and because of that these olives are bright green in color and have a very wonderful fresh flavor similar to Olio Nuovo (fresh olive oil). If you are unable to find these olives, another fresh green olive can be substituted.

½ fennel bulb, shaved thinly
1 tablespoon fresh lemon juice
2 tablespoons lemon zest
1 orange, segmented
10 Castelvetrano olives, pitted and halved (see Sources, page 320)
10 oil-cured black olives, pitted and halved
1 red pepper, roasted, peeled, and diced
2 tablespoons fresh thyme leaves
¼ cup extra-virgin olive oil
Salt and pepper to taste
½ cup all-purpose flour
blended oil, for cooking
6 pieces Petrale sole (5 ounces each)

In a bowl toss the fennel, lemon juice, zest, orange segments, olives, red pepper, thyme, and olive oil together. Season to taste and set aside. Let the mixture sit at room temperature for 1 hour to let the flavors meld.

Season the flour well with salt and pepper and spread it over a flat dish. Lightly dust the sole with the flour. Place a large sauté pan over high heat. In several batches, heat the blended oil in a sauté pan and sear the sole until brown, about 2 minutes per side. Turn the fish over and repeat.

To Serve:
Place one piece of sole in the center of each plate and top with a few tablespoons of the vinaigrette.

Serves 6

Fennel

Fennel comes to the restaurant in many forms: fresh, seed, and pollen. The stalk and root are the vegetable, and the stems and leaves are all edible. Known as finocchio in Italy, it's also called common fennel, sweet fennel, wild fennel, and sweet cumin.

Fresh fennel is my favorite substitute for celery when making mirepoix. Anytime I want to add a nuance of flavor and a celery-like crunch, I grab a fennel bulb. You have to have a taste for licorice to love fennel, though. (My love for pastis and absinthe developed from my licorice adoration, but that's another story.) Stuff the leaves into oily fish such as mackerel and sprinkle finely chopped stems and leaves on salads.

Cooked fennel mellows the anise flavor and it's easy to sauté or braise. Fresh fennel is also a natural addition to soups and stuffings and is in season in spring, summer, and autumn, depending on the region. Fennel bulbs will keep in the refrigerator for two to three days.

Fennel seed is similar to anise seed but sweeter and milder. It's a natural pairing with pork and fish but Italians also like to add it to sauces, meats, and sausages. John adds fennel seed to a few of our salumi products, as well.

One of my favorite forms of fennel is fennel pollen. It's not only the strongest form of fennel but also the most expensive—it's actually the pollen from fennel flowers and must be harvested by hand. Luckily a little goes a long way. We like to use fennel pollen on everything from fish to pork, drink rims, and whenever we want a touch of Provence. You'll find it in specialty grocery and spice stores.

summer

Black Mission Fig Clafouti

JC Cellars Late Harvest Marsanne, Ripken Vineyards, Lodi, California
M. Chapoutier Rasteau, Côtes du Rhônes, France

A clafouti is a traditional French dessert that can be prepared with a wide variety of fruit and makes a lot of sense for our seasonal menu. It won't surprise you to learn that a clafouti with Black Mission figs is my favorite. When fresh figs are available, we use them in our clafouti but off-season we use dried Black Mission figs from our friends at Valley Fig Growers in California. We purchase the finest quality organic figs that have been tree-ripened and harvested at their peak of flavor. These are also the figs that we use in our FIGfood product line.

For the clafouti:

1⅓ cups all-purpose flour

1⅓ cups sugar

Pinch of salt

2½ cups whole milk

½ cup plus 1 tablespoon unsalted butter, melted

6 tablespoons Armagnac or brandy

8 large eggs

12 fresh figs, halved (1 cup rehydrated dried figs, quartered, can be substituted)

For the caramel sauce:

1 cup sugar

6 tablespoons unsalted butter

½ cup heavy cream

Powdered sugar, for garnish

To prepare the clafouti:

Preheat the oven to 350°F. Butter a 9-inch cake pan and set aside.
Sift together the flour, sugar, and salt in a large bowl. Form a well and using a fork, mix in the milk, melted butter, Armagnac, and eggs. Beat until smooth and strain through a fine-mesh sieve.

Place the figs face down in the cake pan and cover with the clafouti mixture. Bake for 45 minutes or until a toothpick inserted into the middle of the clafouti comes out clean.

To prepare the sauce:

Heat the sugar in a stainless-steel pan over medium-high heat and stir occasionally until the sugar turns brown, about 5 to 7 minutes. Remove the pan from the heat, add the butter, and whisk until the butter has melted. Add the cream and continue to stir constantly until the cream is completely incorporated. (Makes about 1 cup)

To serve:

Slice the clafouti into 6 slices and transfer each slice to a plate. Drizzle each slice with the caramel sauce and dust with powdered sugar. You can also warm the clafouti in a low oven before serving.

Serves 6 to 8

TUMALO FARMS PONDHOPPER

SUMMER № 6

REGION:	Bend, Oregon
MILK:	farmstead goats
PROCESS:	pasteurized grade A farmstead milk
PRODUCTION:	washed, cooked, pressed, semi-soft
AFFINAGE:	2 to 3 months
FLAVOR:	hops, toffee, caramel, tangy, mild, sharp
AROMA:	lemony, citrus
TEXTURE:	semi-firm, dense paste
PAIRINGS:	fresh fruit
	Matiz Apricot & Almond Cake
	B & R Farms Blenheim Sun-Dried Apricots
	Harvest Song Fresh Walnut Preserves
NOTES:	Local microbrew hops are added to the milk during the cheesemaking process. Pondhopper makes a flavorful Macaroni and Cheese.

summer

Mary Matos

Joe Matos Cheese Factory
Santa Rosa, California

There is one cheese I simply cannot imagine doing without, a cheese that is essential to our grilled cheese sandwich and the Croque Monsieur: Joe Matos's St. George. It's a semi-soft, pale-yellow cow's milk cheese reminiscent of Havarti but with more bite to it. I like eating it out of hand or in a sandwich; it melts nicely but still retains its flavor. We've had Joe's cheese on our menu since 1997, and it was one of the first California cheeses I tasted when I moved here. It's another ingredient that is quintessential Sonoma County—the product of two people, a herd of cows, and a lot of hard work.

Driving down the rutted dirt road to the Matos farm in Santa Rosa doesn't give you a clue about the intensely flavored cheese that sits in the aging room. Past the wooden fences, acres of grass, a friendly dog, and a large brown barn lies a plain white door. This is where the magic happens. Joe and Mary Matos have been making this particular cheese for five generations, and "it's the only type of cheese made where I come from," says Mary. The family is from the town of St. George in the Azores, an island in Portugal, but the

Matos settled in Petaluma, California, in 1965. Joe taught Mary how to make the cheese, and Mary made it in her home kitchen for family and friends until they moved to Santa Rosa in 1980 and built the cheesemaking facility. Joe is a compact man in a baseball hat who moves efficiently around the farm and refers affectionately to "the boss," his silver-haired, tough-talking wife, Mary.

The Matos family uses the milk from their 37 Jersey and Holstein cows—"I don't want anyone else's milk," says Mary. Joe takes care of the cows and milks them while Mary and her two assistants ("the ladies," as they're called) make the cheese six days a week. They make 10 to 13 wheels each day, "depending on how much milk we have," says Mary.

The cheesemaking room is quite small, with a large stainless-steel vat dominating the tiny white room. The milk is heat treated and then poured into the vat. When we first started serving the cheese in the restaurant, it was a raw milk product. However, the county caught up with them and, they've been heat-treating the milk since 2000.

The curds and whey are separated in the vats, and then the cheese is transferred to presses in a small cement-floored room. Joe made the presses himself from cement and metal weights; the cheese is entirely handmade except for the heat-treating machine. (When Mary first started making cheese she used a coffee can with holes punched in it and a wooden press to shape it.)

After the cheese is shaped and pressed it's transferred to the aging room, a narrow room filled with brown wooden shelves that reach ten feet high. The wooden shelves allow the cheese to breathe and age evenly. Mary checks the cheese every day, and it's turned over once a day and rubbed with a dry rag. "It gets tangier the longer it ages," says Mary. "It has to be aged properly." The cheese ages for two to eight months and is then cleaned and scraped and ready for customers—chefs, wholesalers, and locals—to pick up. The cheese is shipped around the country, as well.

It was lovely watching Mary's eyes light up when we visited the farm. She proudly told us the story about how a few years ago she shipped a wheel of her cheese to the priest in her hometown in Sao Jorge. He claimed it to be finer than the original versions sold on the islands. I am not surprised—a combination of an age-old tradition, Sonoma County's terroir, and good animal breeding would do it! That sense of pride keeps the quality high in the production of a family cheese.

Don't expect to find St. George in your local grocery store. "We keep making it a little bit at a time," says Mary. "That's how I was raised." You might find it in local cheese shops in Sonoma County and some specialty stores and you can always find it on our menu. (See Sources, page 318, for more information.)

"The Ladies"

Grilled Cheese Sandwich with St. George Cheese & Tomato Confit

Entrée
Parsnip & Cipollini Soup

Plat
Fig & Verjus Braised Pork Shoulder

Dessert
Apple-Fig Sorbet

Fromage
Cowgirl Creamery Red Hawk

Parsnip & Cipollini Soup

Anaba Wines Viognier, Landa Vineyard, Sonoma Valley, California
Sebastiani Vineyards & Winery Roussanne, Carneros California

This is a transitional soup, one that teases you with hearty fall flavors on the verge of abundance but still retains some of the bright flavors of summer. The Chive Oil is a flavor element that adds a color contrast and complements the sautéed cipollini garnish perfectly. This is a hearty soup that will fill you up.

For the Chive Oil:
1 bunch chives
½ cup extra-virgin olive oil

For the soup:
¼ cup olive oil
12 cipollini onions, peeled
2 tablespoons unsalted butter
1 small yellow onion, chopped
2 celery stalks, chopped
1 leek, white part only, chopped
2 shallots, diced
4 garlic cloves, crushed
2 pounds parsnips, chopped (about 6)
Salt and white pepper to taste
½ cup heavy cream

Cipollini Onions

These small, flat onions are known for their delicate flavor—and, amazingly, they are actually the bulb of a hyacinth plant. (The name means "little onion" in Italian.) Cipollinis have a higher sugar content than most onions and a flavor that's a cross between a red onion and a shallot. They have a thin yellow-gold exterior with white flesh. Unlike most onions they don't fall apart when you slice them and you can serve them raw or cooked. We love to roast or stew them with meat as they add such a wonderful sweet contrast to the meat. Cipollinis roasted with balsamic vinegar is a traditional—and tasty—way to serve them.

Cipollinis are available year-round and will keep in a dry, cool place for up to one month.

To prepare the Chive Oil:
Bring a small saucepan of water to a boil. Add the chives and blanch them for 10 seconds. Drain the water and transfer the chives to an ice bath. Remove them and pat dry on paper towels, squeezing to remove as much of the excess water as possible. Roughly chop the chives and place them in a blender. Slowly add the olive oil while the blender is on low and process until smooth.

Transfer the Chive Oil to a bowl and refrigerate overnight. Strain the oil through a fine mesh sieve, pressing against the solids with the back of a spoon to extract as much oil as possible. Transfer the oil to a squeeze bottle and refrigerate until needed, up to 2 weeks. (Bring it to room temperature before using.)

To prepare the soup:
Preheat the oven to 350°F.
In a medium ovenproof sauté pan, add the olive oil and cipollini onions and cook them over medium-high heat until browned on all sides, about 8 minutes. Place the pan in the oven and bake for an additional 10 minutes or until the onions are caramelized and cooked through. Remove the onions from the pan, chop them, and keep warm.

Melt the butter in a large saucepan. Sauté the onion, celery, leek, shallots, and garlic until the vegetables are soft, about 12 to 15 minutes. Stir the vegetables occasionally to prevent browning. Add the parsnips to the vegetables and sauté for about 3 minutes while stirring. Add 1½ quarts of water and season with salt and pepper to taste. Bring the soup to a boil. Lower the heat and simmer until the parsnips are just tender, about 10 minutes. Add the heavy cream. Remove the vegetables from the heat and immediately purée the soup in a blender or food processor. Strain the soup through a fine-mesh sieve and season with salt and pepper to taste. Reheat the soup before serving.

To serve:
Ladle the soup in 6 bowls. Add a heaping spoonful of the onions in the center and drizzle the Chive Oil on top.

Serves 6

Figs

To me, biting into a luscious, fresh fig is one of the great joys in life. (Why else would I name our flagship restaurant after this seductive fruit?) What a shame that most people know figs only from Fig Newtons, because the fruit is simply spectacular. Figs thrive in California and are a common backyard tree and a familiar sight at farmers markets.

The Black Mission fig is one of the most common, and it gets it name from fig history; the sweet fruits were brought to California in 1759 by Franciscan monks from Mission San Diego. (Today, California is the only state with a significant commercial fig production.) Four varieties of fresh figs dominate the markets with colors ranging from light purple to pale yellow, and each has a distinctive personality. The dark purple to black-colored Black Mission is one of the most recognized, with its pink flesh and earthy flavor. Brown Turkeys are in fact light purple in color, with pink flesh and a robust flavor. The amber-colored Kadota has a delicate flavor, while the Calimyrna is a large, yellow variety with a sweet, nutty flavor.

Black Missions, Brown Turkeys, Kadotas, and Calimyrnas make up the majority of California's fig crop although a few small farmers grow the Adriatic variety. The Adriatic has the highest sugar content and is most often used in bars and spreads.

Many fig varieties have two harvests. The first happens in June and is called the breba crop, which produces more acidic, less sweet fruit. The second, and main, fig crop come after and brings more flavorful fruit.

We work with thousands of figs each year, both fresh and dried. Luckily, the fig is such a versatile ingredient. As a fig-centric restaurant, it would be boring if we only served figs one way. However, figs show up in many of our dishes: in season, our signature Fig & Arugula Salad (page 196) is adorned with freshly grilled figs drizzled with bacon drippings. We also use dried figs in our luscious housemade Fig & Port Ice Cream, make a Fig & Thyme Crisp, and we add dried figs to our Braised Short Ribs for another layer of flavor. Our Fig Kisses, whole dried figs dipped in bittersweet chocolate, make a perfect finishing touch to any meal!

Because we're so devoted to figs we've developed a long-standing relationship with the Valley Fig Growers in Fresno, California. They act as a cooperative of more than 30 grower members that represent 40 percent of the California fig industry. The figs that are brought in from the growers are sorted by quality and dried before being sold around the world. Both the processing plant in Fresno and the figs themselves are certified organic under the Blue Ribbon Orchard Choice label. This has always been an important aspect to us, because the figs are the star ingredient in each of our FIGfood products. The Valley Fig Growers also offer figs in other unusual forms, such as fig paste, fig nuggets, fig concentrate, and fig powder.

Because fresh figs are so delicate and make transport difficult, the bulk of California figs are sold dried. Generally, fresh figs are at their peak in August and September but some figs may be available as late as November; it depends on the variety. Look for unbruised fruit and plan to eat the figs within a few days. Then simply use your imagination; figs are particularly tasty with anything salty. Wrap a fig slice in prosciutto for a salty-sweet bite, or drizzle a platter of fresh figs with balsamic vinegar and shaved Parmigiano-Reggiano cheese — simply divine.

California Fresh Fig Season, by variety:
Black Mission: May through November
Brown Turkey: May through December
Kadota: June through October
Calimyrna: July through September

Source: California Fig Advisory Board

summer

autumn

One word defines autumn in wine country: harvest! While autumn is often a slower time in some regions, we're still enjoying 90-plus degree days. Folks from all over the world arrive in droves to tour the region, our guests are still dining on the patio, and the grape harvest is in full swing. For us, autumn is more like summer; some years it's almost as if we have six seasons rather than four.

Throughout the valley, there are signs of autumn everywhere: traffic slows for tractors and trucks packed with grape picking bins and for the yellow school busses picking up and dropping off the kids. It's serious work time now, with workers lined up in the vineyards to pick the grapes and the wineries operating at full capacity, usually right through the night. When you drive through Sonoma Valley, the smell of fermenting grapes fills the air.

Tomatoes and corn are summer ingredients for most people but depending on the weather we'll have tomatoes through October. This is also my favorite time for figs. In the midst of the second crop, the figs have been kissed by the sun and are ripening magnificently on the trees. Calls from friends and neighbors offering us their crop adds to the fig fest.

We slowly adjust the menu to incorporate the autumn bounty. Soft-skin squashes like zucchini are replaced with the hard-skin winter squashes such as Acorn, Delicata, and Butternut. What would autumn be without pumpkin? We celebrate the festive orange squash in soups, stews, and in cheesecake! Heirloom apples arrive, and we waste no time adding them to salads, tarts, and crisps. Baskets of earthy mushrooms such as porcini and chanterelles are highlighted in soups and alongside the braised meat dishes that we start serving in late autumn.

The autumn pace is a constant, steady stream of guests, harvest festivals, and weddings. We keep our heads down and work and enjoy the warm days and the crisp air, knowing they will soon be replaced by the chill of winter.

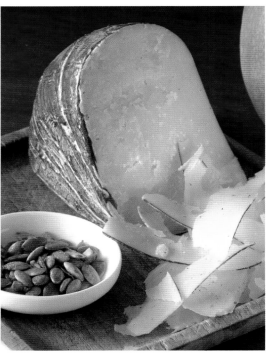

autumn cheese

Most cheeses are aged in autumn rather than produced during this season. (In some regions the milk supply dries up by October.) The cheeses are developing their flavor during the autumn months, with new molds growing as the weather changes. Some cheeses are considered at their peak in autumn, including Parmigiano-Reggiano from Italy, with its full, rich flavor.

The animals that are grazing during this time are usually munching on slow-growing grass, which has a different flavor from the fresh grass of spring.

(Clockwise from top left; Morbier, Cabecou, Carmody, Fleur du Maquis, Vella Dry Jack, Blue d'Auvergne).

APERITINI
MAKES 2 COCKTAILS

3 OUNCES HENDRICK'S GIN
1 OUNCE ST-GERMAIN LIQUEUR
½ OUNCE LILLET BLANC
JUICE OF 1 LEMON
ENGLISH CUCUMBER SLICES, FOR GARNISH

COMBINE THE GIN, ST-GERMAIN, LILLET, AND LEMON JUICE IN A COCKTAIL SHAKER. TOP WITH ICE. SHAKE VIGOROUSLY TO INCORPORATE AND STRAIN INTO 2 CHILLED MARTINI GLASSES. GARNISH WITH THE CUCUMBER SLICES.

Mixing It Up

Mixology has not only become a hot topic in the hospitality industry, but mixologists are becoming the new celebrity chefs. The creative process for making cocktails is sometimes more fun than creating new food items, but tends to be much more dangerous, especially in the morning. We have found that the hardest part of creating a new cocktail is naming it.

As more artisanal liquors are popping up, it has been truly fun trying them out and supporting our local friends with their new elixirs. We are lucky to have HelloCello, Firelit, Hangar One, Junipero Gin, Charbay, Skyy and more right in our backyard or should I say our Back Bar!

Our philosophy for our cocktail menu follows the path of the restaurant: we aim for seasonality, freshness, innovation, and a hint of France. We always want to offer our guests new and unique flavors that they may not have tried before. We've certainly achieved that with our house cocktails, including our Lavender Mojito (page 37) and "Gin"-ger Basiltini (page 111).

SAZERAC
MAKES 2 COCKTAILS

PERNOD (OR ABSINTHE)
3 OUNCES MITCHER'S RYE
6 DASHES PEYCHAUD'S BITTERS
1 OUNCE SIMPLE SYRUP (PAGE 36)
LEMON PEEL

CHILL 2 ROCKS GLASSES. POUR A DASH OF
PERNOD INTO EACH GLASS AND TWIRL TO COAT
THE INSIDE OF THE GLASSES. COMBINE THE RYE,
BITTERS, AND SIMPLE SYRUP IN A COCKTAIL
SHAKER. TOP WITH ICE AND STIR GENTLY. STRAIN
INTO THE CHILLED GLASSES. TWIST A PIECE OF
LEMON PEEL OVER EACH GLASS TO RELEASE THE
FRAGRANT OILS INTO THE GLASS. DISCARD THE
TWIST AND SERVE.

APPLE HOT TODDY
MAKES 2 COCKTAILS

2 CINNAMON STICKS
1 TEASPOON WHOLE CLOVES
1 STAR ANISE
3 CUPS NANA MAE'S APPLE JUICE
2 TABLESPOONS CARAMEL
3 OUNCES CAPTAIN MORGAN'S SPICED RUM

PLACE THE CINNAMON STICKS, CLOVES,
AND STAR ANISE IN A SQUARE OF
CHEESECLOTH AND MAKE A SACHET.

POUR 3 CUPS OF APPLE JUICE INTO A
MEDIUM POT OVER MEDIUM HEAT. ADD
THE SPICE SACHET AND THE CARAMEL.
HEAT THE MIXTURE TO A BOIL, STIRRING
REGULARLY. ONCE THE MIXTURE REACHES
A BOIL, LOWER THE HEAT AND LET IT
SIMMER FOR 5 MINUTES. REMOVE THE
SACHET AND POUR THE LIQUID INTO 2
COFFEE MUGS, ADD 1½ OUNCES OF RUM
IN EACH MUG AND SERVE.

autumn

SPARKLING
FRENCH PEAR
MAKES 2 COCKTAILS

3 OUNCES GREY GOOSE POIRE
1 OUNCE PINEAU DES CHARENTES
1 OUNCE SIMPLE SYRUP (PAGE 36)
SPARKLING WINE

ADD THE GREY GOOSE POIRE,
PINEAU DES CHARENTES, AND
THE SIMPLE SYRUP IN 2 ROCKS
GLASSES FILLED WITH ICE. TOP
WITH SPARKLING WINE AND
SERVE.

Apple Cider

Living in apple country, we love apple cider! We use it both in cooking and as a cocktail ingredient (and serve it straight). It's typically made from blends of several different apples to give it a balanced flavor and the best apple cider is made from blends of heritage, or heirloom, apple varieties such as Gravenstein, Gala, Freedom, and Snowapple.

Though pasteurized apple cider is now the norm, unpasteurized cider was once the standard. Today, you can usually find unpasteurized apple cider only at orchards and farms. Without pasteurization, the naturally occurring yeasts in the cider are not killed, and they cause fermentation with time. Some bacteria can grow in unpasteurized cider, including E. coli, which is why most states mandate a warning label on unpasteurized beverages. The fermentation process turns sugar into alcohol, which some producers use to produce hard cider.

Aperitifs

We love introducing the French tradition of the aperitif—a before-dinner drink—to our guests. We truly believe it stimulates the appetite! There are several classic liqueurs that are served as aperitifs and we've included two here to inspire you.

Pastis is a famous French licorice-flavored liqueur that is popular in the south of France. (In the 1930s, the French city of Marseilles was wild about anise-flavored liqueurs.) It's strong (90 proof) and is usually mixed with water; interestingly, it's related to absinthe. The unique flavor comes from a combination of licorice and the seeds of star anise, and the remaining ingredients can include black and white peppercorns, cardamom, sage, nutmeg, cloves, cinnamon, and sugar. The exact recipe varies according to the brand. One of the most familiar brands is Ricard, a bright yellow pastis created by Paul Ricard in 1932.

We serve several different brands of pastis at the girl & the fig, including Pernod, Herbsaint, Ricard, and a local version from Charbay. People generally have a preference when drinking pastis; I prefer to have a nice pour over ice with a side of cold water that I can add to achieve the perfect balance.

Pineau des Charentes is a grape-based liqueur that was made by happy accident. The story goes that a winegrower in the 16th century accidentally poured grape must into a barrel that contained Cognac eau de vie and a few years later when he opened the barrel, he was pleasantly surprised at the results. Pineau des Charentes was born.

Pineau des Charentes continues to be a tradition in France, and today there are two types of Pineau des Charentes produced: white and rosé. There are strict methods that control the production of Pineau des Charentes. To be labeled Pineau des Charentes, the Cognac eau de vie and grape juice must come from the same property and be aged in oak casks for a minimum of 18 months.

Pineau des Charentes is consumed as an aperitif or made into a cocktail, such as Pineau and tonic water. It's also used in sauces and often served with the cheese or dessert course. At the restaurants, we serve it over ice with an orange slice, straight up and chilled, or in a cocktail.

AUTUMN NIBBLES

MANCHEGO SCONES WITH PROSCIUTTO
CORNBREAD, CHORIZO, PEPERONATA

CHICKEN BOUDIN, PEAR MOSTARDA, SABA
POLENTA, BRAISED LAMB, GREMOLATA

MANCHEGO SCONES WITH PROSCIUTTO

To spice up your cocktail party, we've included this scone recipe that features sharp Manchego cheese and crispy prosciutto. These bite-size scones can take on any flavors you like so feel free to experiment. Add a bit of fig jam or a dollop of red onion confit for a truly delectable bite.

2 cups all-purpose flour

1½ teaspoons baking powder

Pinch of salt

⅔ cup grated Manchego cheese

4 tablespoons (½ stick) very cold unsalted butter, cubed

¾ cup buttermilk

2 large egg whites plus 1 egg yolk

¼ cup crème fraîche

2 ounces prosciutto, thinly sliced, fried and broken into 40 pieces, for garnish

Makes 40 (1½-inch) nibbles

Preheat the oven to 350°F.

Set aside 2 tablespoons of the cheese.

Place the flour, baking powder, salt, and the remaining cheese in a food processor and process to combine. Add the butter and pulse until the dough takes on a crumbly texture.

In a separate bowl whisk the egg whites until light but peaked. Add the buttermilk to the flour mixture and fold in the egg whites. In a small bowl mix the egg yolk with a few tablespoons of water and set aside.

Knead the dough lightly on a floured surface until the dough is not sticky. Roll the dough out to ½-inch thickness. Cut out the dough with a 1½-inch ring mold and place the circles on a baking sheet. Brush the circles with the egg wash and sprinkle with the remaining 2 tablespoons of cheese.

Bake the scones for 12 to 15 minutes until browned.

Note: Let the scones cool before adding a dollop of crème fraîche. Top with the crispy prosciutto pieces.

CORNBREAD, CHORIZO, PEPERONATA

This little bite highlights the peppers of late summer. Sun-kissed and sweet, peppers have a luscious flavor that will soak into the cornbread and complement the spicy chorizo. When selecting chorizo at the store, ask to taste it prior to purchasing if possible. Select your favorite as the flavors can vary greatly.

1 cup all-purpose flour
1 cup cornmeal
⅓ cup sugar
⅓ cup firmly packed brown sugar
1 teaspoon Kosher salt
1 tablespoon baking powder
1 large egg
½ cup crème fraîche plus additional for garnish
½ cup whole milk
⅓ cup blended oil
¼ pound chorizo link, cut in julienne
1 cup Peperonata (page 311)

Preheat the oven to 350°F. Grease a large shallow baking sheet. Place the flour, cornmeal, sugar, brown sugar, salt, and baking powder in a large bowl. In a separate bowl, combine the egg, ½ cup of crème fraîche, milk, and blended oil until well incorporated. Make a well in the dry ingredients and add the liquid ingredients to the center, using a fork to stir them together. Pour the batter in the greased baking sheet and bake until a fork comes out clean about 15 to 20 minutes. Let cool. Cut out desired shapes, (squares, triangles or circles) using a ring mold.

To serve:

Top with a dollop of crème fraîche, a spoonful of peperonata, and a few pieces of chorizo.

Makes 70 (1-inch) nibbles

CHICKEN BOUDIN, PEAR MOSTARDA, SABA

Sausages are always popular as small bites at a cocktail party. When sliced, they are perfect little rounds for holding other flavors. If you don't have the time to make your own Chicken Boudin or Pear Mostarda from scratch, you can find variations in any specialty gourmet market. We've recently created two versions of mostarda that are included in our FIGfood line, one with apples, figs, and raisins and another with raisins and figs. We use both of these mostardas in menu items like this one to add an intensive dash of flavor that will spice up chicken or pork.

For the mostarda:
1 firm D'Anjou pear, ¼-inch dice (Bosc can be substituted)
⅓ cup sugar
1 tablespoon yellow mustard seeds, toasted
1 lemon, juice and zest
Pinch of ground ginger
Pinch of salt

2 chicken boudin (6 ounces each) cooked, chilled and sliced into ¼-inch pieces, (another type of sausage can be substituted)
30 crostini
2 tablespoons saba (see Sources, page 318)

To prepare the mostarda:

Combine the diced pear, sugar, ½ cup of water, mustard seeds, lemon juice and zest, ginger, and salt in a small saucepan over low heat. Bring to a simmer and cook until the pear has softened and the liquid has thickened to a thick syrup about 15 to 20 minutes. Chill overnight.

To serve:

Place a boudin slice on top of each crostini. Top with a spoonful of mostarda, a tiny drizzle of saba and serve.

Makes 30 nibbles

POLENTA, BRAISED LAMB, GREMOLATA

I recommend making this appetizer a night or two after you've served braised lamb for dinner; otherwise, it will be a lot of work just for a nibble unless you are preparing it for a large cocktail party. Having a base for small bites is the first step to success, and the options are endless and interchangeable. Consider polenta cakes, chickpea fries, toast, cornbread, baguette slices, endive, cucumber slices, risotto cakes, potato chips…they would all make a wonderful base for the lamb.

For the polenta:
1 teaspoon salt
1 tablespoon unsalted butter
1 cup polenta
½ cup pecorino cheese, grated
¼ cup blended oil

For the lamb:
10 ounces braised lamb (page 278)
1 cup lamb stock (beef broth can be substituted)

For the gremolata:
Zest of 1 lemon
¼ cup Herbed Bread Crumbs (page 311)
1 tablespoon extra-virgin olive oil
3 tablespoons fresh flat-leaf parsley leaves

To prepare the polenta:
Bring 1 quart of water, salt, and butter to a boil in a medium saucepot. Whisk in the polenta and cook over low heat for 5 minutes or until the polenta comes together. Spread the polenta evenly onto a greased 8x8-inch baking pan and chill until the polenta sets.

Using a 1-inch ring mold or cookie cutter, cut the polenta into coin shapes and set aside.

Heat a small amount of blended oil (enough to cover the bottom of the pan) in a sauté pan over medium heat. Add the polenta coins (working in batches to fit the pan) and brown them on both sides, about 1 to 2 minutes per side. Repeat this process until all of the polenta coins have been cooked. Season them lightly with salt and set aside in a warm place.

To prepare the lamb:
Place the braised lamb in a small saucepan and add the lamb stock. Cook over medium heat until the lamb's texture becomes "wet and shredded," about 7 to 8 minutes. Season to taste and set aside.

To prepare the gremolata:
Combine the lemon zest, bread crumbs, olive oil, and parsley in a small bowl.

To assemble:
Top each polenta coin with a small teaspoon of the lamb and garnish with a spoonful of gremolata.

Makes 40 nibbles

Saba

Considered the first balsamic vinegar, saba dates back to the Egyptian period. Originally, Lambrusco and Trebbiano grapes were used and cooked until the liquid thickened to a "must." It was used as a sweetener in drinks, served as a digestif, and as an accompaniment with meat and grains. Saba eventually lost its popularity and was overtaken by balsamic vinegar, but many chefs today like to work with saba (we use it at ESTATE), and you can still source excellent versions made by the same producers that produce quality balsamic vinegar. When a recipe calls for saba and it's unavailable, we substitute a tiny drizzle of reduced aged maple syrup or balsamic vinegar reduction.

autumn menus

Entrée
Steamed Mussels,
Chorizo & Roasted Pepper Broth

Plat
Café Pot Roast,
Mashed Potatoes, Wilted Greens

Dessert
Chocolate Caramel Tart,
Brown Butter Gelato

Fromage
Fleur du Maquis

Steamed Mussels, Chorizo & Roasted Pepper Broth

Domaine Tempier Rosé, Bandol, France
Cline Cellars Viognier, Sonoma Coast, California

For those of you who love our Pernod steamed mussels, here is a new version for your repertoire. This version is more Basque-like in style than our original dish, with the addition of a little spicy chorizo, diced peppers and onions, and fresh tomatoes. Don't forget a crusty baguette on the side to soak up all the juices.

¼ cup extra-virgin olive oil
1 medium carrot, shredded, liquid reserved
1 small onion, shredded, liquid reserved
2 celery stalks shredded, liquid reserved
1 medium red pepper, shredded, liquid reserved
Salt and pepper to taste
3 garlic cloves, thinly sliced
1 tablespoon smoked paprika

2 tablespoons blended oil
6 ounces chorizo, sliced into ¼-inch half-moons
3 pounds mussels, cleaned and de-bearded
2 cups dry white wine
3 tablespoons unsalted butter
1 tablespoon chopped fresh flat-leaf parsley,
    for garnish
12 large pieces toasted bread, for serving

Heat the olive oil in a medium sauté pan over low heat and add the carrots, onion, celery, and red pepper along with the vegetable liquid from shredding. Season with salt and pepper to taste and simmer for 10 minutes. Add the garlic and paprika and cook until the liquid begins to evaporate and the mixture starts to darken into one dark orange color, about 12 to 15 minutes. Remove the pan from the heat and set aside.

Place a large, heavy-bottomed pot over high heat. Add the blended oil and sear the chorizo until browned on all sides. Add the vegetable mixture and the mussels and stir well to incorporate. Add the white wine and season with salt and pepper. Cover the pot and cook until the mussels have just begun to open, about 5 to 6 minutes. Add the butter and cook until all the mussels have opened, about 2 to 4 additional minutes. Mussels need to be watched; they must open or they should not be eaten. Don't overcook them because they won't taste very good.

Distribute the mussels evenly among 6 large bowls. Sprinkle each serving with the parsley and serve with the toasted bread for dunking.

Serves 6

Mussels

As much as we try to source our food as locally as possible, there are a few items that we are unable to find close to home. One of our favorites and most popular are mussels. Though mussels can be found all over the world, some of the most common are the blue-black mussels from the North Atlantic and more specifically, Prince Edward Island (PEI), a province in the Canadian Maritimes. We source our mussels from PEI, where they are abundant and consistently delicious. Even though we realize that they travel across the country, we are relieved to know that they are farmed in clear clean water by the rope-grown method. Farming mussels on suspended ropes is known to be the most environmentally gentle form of aquaculture.

Café Pot Roast, Mashed Potatoes, Wilted Greens

Margerum Wine Country "M5" Red Rhône Blend, Santa Barbara County California
Cline Cellars "Ancient Vines" Mourvèdre, Contra Costa, California
Bonny Doon "Le Cigare Volant" Red Rhône Blend, Central Coast, California

Pot roast and mashed potatoes is the perfect comfort dish. It is also one that pairs well with so many of the "Rhône-Alone" wines on our wine list. Like the other braised meats in our book, the trick is to buy the meat from a reputable butcher, use great ingredients in the marinade and braising liquid, and don't be cheap with the wine; the wine reduction will only be as good as the wine you start with. Pot roast is a dish that builds excitement as the aromas fill your kitchen. It tastes even better on day two (if you have leftovers)!

For the pot roast:

4 pounds beef roast, butcher-tied,
   (see Note)
2 tablespoons blended oil
3 large onions, quartered
3 large carrots, cut into medium dice
3 celery stalks, cut into medium dice
1 head fennel, diced
1 whole head garlic, top half cut off
2 tablespoons all-purpose flour
½ bunch fresh thyme
1 sprig fresh rosemary
2 bay leaves
5 whole black peppercorns
1 star anise
2 whole cloves
1 (750mL) bottle red wine (preferably a
   full-bodied Syrah)
1 tablespoon Worcestershire sauce
1 quart Veal Stock (page 313, beef broth
   can be substituted)

For the potatoes:

4 russet potatoes, peeled and cubed
⅔ cup heavy cream
4 tablespoons unsalted butter, at room
   temperature
1 tablespoon salt
¼ teaspoon white pepper

For the greens:

2 pounds greens, such as chard or kale,
   stemmed
2 tablespoons olive oil
1 tablespoon minced garlic
2 tablespoons minced shallots
¼ cup dry white wine
1 tablespoon unsalted butter
Salt and pepper to taste

To prepare the pot roast:

Preheat the oven to 325°F.

Season the meat liberally with salt. Heat the oil in a large roasting pan on high heat and sear the meat on all sides, getting good color on the meat, about 4 to 6 minutes per side. Remove the meat from the pan and set aside.

In the same pot, add the onion, carrot, and celery and sauté until the vegetables are golden brown. Add the garlic, flour, thyme, rosemary, bay leaves, peppercorns, star anise, and cloves, stirring well to remove any browned bits from the bottom of the pan. Add the red wine and Worcestershire sauce. At a medium simmer reduce the liquid by half, about 10 minutes, and continue stirring to ensure that all of the ingredients are incorporated. Add the Veal Stock and bring to a simmer. Return the meat to the pan and cover the pan loosely.

Roast for 2½ hours or until a knife inserted into the meat pulls out without resistance. Let the meat rest for 10 to 15 minutes and strain the sauce onto the pot roast, discarding the vegetables.

To prepare the potatoes:

Place the potatoes in a pot, cover them with cold water, and cook until soft, about 15 to 20 minutes. Drain the potatoes and run them through a food mill or potato ricer. Place the cream and butter in a saucepan and heat until the butter has melted completely. Season with salt and pepper to taste. Place the potatoes in a large bowl and, using a whisk, slowly work in the cream mixture. Once all of the liquid has been added, whisk the potatoes until they have a light and fluffy texture. (Be careful not to overwhip or the potatoes will have a glue-like texture.) Season with salt and pepper to taste.

To prepare the greens:

Tear the greens into large pieces. Heat the oil in a large pan and sauté the garlic and shallots until translucent, about 2 to 4 minutes. Add the greens and cook until they begin to wilt, about 1 to 2 minutes. Add the white wine, stir, and cook until most of the liquid has evaporated. Add the butter and season with salt and pepper to taste.

To Serve:

In each medium bowl, place the greens and the potatoes side by side. Add a few slices of pot roast on top of the potatoes and drizzle the sauce on top.

Cook's Tip:

The pot roast will cook more evenly if it is contained in a uniform shape. We suggest butcher-tying the meat to accomplish this. Whether you are stuffing a piece of meat or just holding its shape, tie the meat with twine almost like you are tying a roll of paper towels or a newspaper. This will help to hold in the juices and will be easier to slice.

Serves 6

Chocolate Caramel Tart, Brown Butter Gelato

Beckman Vineyards Late Harvest Grenache, Santa Ynez Valley, California
Buena Vista Winery Syrah Port, Ramal Vineyards, Carneros, California

Can you say DIVINE? This is my new go-to dessert when I need something sweet and yummy. This dessert is relatively new to our dessert repertoire, and it's definitely a winner. What makes this tart sing is the way the Maldon Sea Salt contrasts with the caramel and the chocolate. This is not a quick recipe to make and does require cooling time between steps but you can make the caramel, the ganache, and the gelato a few days prior to save time. Once you make this for your friends they will be asking you to make it again and again!

For the crust
¾ cup all-purpose flour
⅛ cup Dutch-processed cocoa powder
Pinch of salt
5 tablespoons unsalted butter, cubed and
    softened
¼ cup powdered sugar
1 large egg yolk
¼ teaspoon pure vanilla extract
¼ teaspoon heavy cream

For the caramel:
1½ cups sugar
3 tablespoons light corn syrup
¼ teaspoon salt
6 tablespoons unsalted butter
6 tablespoons heavy cream
1 tablespoon crème fraîche

For the ganache:
¾ cup heavy cream
4 ounces bittersweet chocolate

For the gelato:
1½ cups whole milk
1½ cups heavy cream
½ cup sugar
6 large egg yolks
1 cup Brown Butter (page 314)
1 teaspoon salt

1½ teaspoons Maldon Sea Salt, for garnish;
    (see Sources, page 320)

To prepare the crust:
Preheat the oven to 350°F. Combine the flour, cocoa powder, and salt in a medium bowl and set aside. Using a mixer fitted with a whisk, cream the butter and sugar until the mixture is pale and fluffy. Add the egg yolks, cream, and vanilla and mix well. Add the flour mixture and mix until just combined.

Roll the dough into a ball and chill for at least 20 minutes. Using a very small amount of flour roll out the dough to ⅛-inch thickness. Cut out 6 pieces of dough using a 4-inch ring mold. Place each disk in a 3½-inch ring mold and place them on a parchment-lined sheet pan. Prick the tart shells all over with a fork and bake until cooked through, about 20 minutes. Transfer the shells to a cooling rack and let them cool.

To prepare the caramel:
In a small saucepan, whisk the sugar, corn syrup, salt, and 6 tablespoons of water together and bring to a boil over high heat. Cook without stirring until the syrup reaches 340°F on a candy thermometer. Remove the pan from the heat and whisk in the butter, cream, and crème fraîche until smooth. Pour 3 to 4 tablespoons of the caramel into each cooled tart shell and let cool slightly; refrigerate until firm, about 4 to 5 hours.

To prepare the ganache:
Bring the cream to a boil in a small saucepan over medium heat.
Place the chocolate in a small bowl and pour the hot cream over the chocolate. Let sit for 1 minute and then stir the mixture slowly until smooth. Pour the ganache evenly over each tart and refrigerate until set, about 4 to 5 hours.

To prepare the gelato:
In a small saucepan, heat the cream and milk over medium-high heat until simmering. In a medium bowl, whisk the sugar and the egg yolks until light and pale. Whisk the egg yolk mixture into the cream and heat the mixture until it reads 160°F on a candy thermometer. Add the Brown Butter and stir until well incorporated. Chill the mixture, transfer it to an ice cream maker, and follow the manufacturer's directions.

To Serve:
Place one tart on each plate, top with a scoop of gelato, and sprinkle with the Maldon Sea Salt.

Note:
The picture to the right shows this dish with a garnish of Hazelnut Praline (page 317) and a drizzle of Mint Oil (page 114).

Serves 6

FLEUR DU MAQUIS

REGION:	Corsica, France
MILK:	sheep or goat or both
PROCESS:	pasteurized or raw
PRODUCTION:	uncooked, unpressed, soft, natural mold, sometimes ash
AFFINAGE:	12 months
FLAVOR:	lemony, slightly sour, savory, herbal
AROMA:	aromatic, dried herbs
TEXTURE:	semi-firm when young, softer as it ages
SIMILAR CHEESES:	Brin d'Amour
PAIRINGS:	Robert Lambert Orange Marmalade the girl & the fig Red Onion Confit Blue Chair Fruit Co. Early Girl Tomato Jam Made in Napa Fig & Roasted Shallot Tapenade
NOTES:	Fleur du Maquis, coated with juniper berries, red peppercorns, and dried thyme should be one of the last cheeses served on a cheese plate. This cheese is relatively a newcomer, it was created in the 1950's.

"The Farmer's Wife"

Nana Mae's Organics
Sebastopol, California

Eating locally can seem like a lot of talk, but when you live and work in a place like Sonoma County it's easier than you think. We're particularly fortunate to have an apple tradition in the county, home to the celebrated Gravenstein apple. When I met Kendra Kolling at a luncheon in Napa and tasted her Gravenstein apple juice, I knew I wanted to know this person, support her family's business, and introduce our guests to their product. Paul and Kendra Kolling own Nana Mae's Organics, an organic apple company that cultivates more than 300 acres of organic apples, pears, berries, plums, and quince in Sonoma County and produces a wide array of certified organic products: apple juice, Bartlett pear juice, applesauce, apple cider vinegar, and honey. The company is named after Paul's grandmother, a native of Northern California. The product labels feature a wonderful black-and-white photo of her from 1910.

The Kollings farm Gravenstein and other heirloom apples, as well as Bartlett pear trees in their orchards, which are located throughout Sonoma County. Paul has farmed the land for more than 30 years and every year he and Kendra plant new apple varieties, waiting six years for the trees to bear fruit. They use an heirloom blend of apples in their applesauce, apple cider vinegar, and apple juice and the blends "change year to year according to Paul's palate and Mother Nature," says Kendra. What doesn't change is where the fruit comes from. Unlike other mass-produced brands and private label apple juice and applesauce, 100 percent of the fruit in their products is grown in Sonoma.

Every year, the Kollings anticipate (and hope for) good, if not great, conditions for the critical blossom and fruit set on the fruit trees as well as for the ripening and maturity of their award-winning fruit. "Mother Nature always ends up having the final say," Kendra says, laughing, "but in the end it's the nutritious food my family eats and the thank-yous from satisfied foodies and those concerned for the state of Sonoma County's historic orchards that keep us going!"

There is a finite amount of fruit the Kollings grow and a finite amount of product they make each year. Their fresh fruit and products are sold at local farmers markets, San Francisco Bay Area markets, and directly to consumers through their website. Distribution is limited primarily to the West Coast, with two purveyors bringing their products east of the Rockies.

Both Paul and Kendra have been working for years

with the Slow Food Organization to increase awareness of Sonoma County's endangered Gravenstein apple in order to help prevent the apple, the orchards, and the industry from becoming a thing of the past. Apple production in Sonoma County is now only a tiny fraction of its historic high levels and continues to diminish as small farmers struggle to market their heirloom fruit. Often the cost of picking the fruit is just too high to justify, and farmers leave the fruit to rot in the orchards, notes Kendra. Many farmers are hanging up their picking bags and selling off their tractors and their land to developers and/or grape growers.

Among the many reasons that Nana Mae's is no ordinary apple juice is that the Kolling family are stewards of the land and an actual family behind the brand. Paul's keen sense and palate tell him when to pick and when not to pick, resulting in perfectly nuanced flavors and sublime texture. The juice is delicious—it actually tastes like apples! For us to have access to a local product that also tastes superior was our good fortune and made it an easy decision to carry their juice.

Besides serving it straight, we've incorporated Nana Mae's Apple Juice into seasonal cocktails, mostly in fall and winter. One of the more creative cocktails was the Candied Ginger Apple, which combined ginger-infused vodka, Nana Mae's Organic Apple Juice, and sparkling wine served over ice. A well-loved cocktail from the past few winters has been our Apple Hot Toddy (page 178), a blend of Captain Morgan's spiced rum, Nana Mae's Organic Apple Juice, spices and a spoonful of caramel, served warm.

Beyond carrying their apple juice in our restaurants, over the years Kendra and I established a friendship and talked about collaborating on a food project. We share our apple recipes with the couple and Kendra talks to John about recipe ideas, and finally in 2010 we created a mostarda (an Italian condiment similar to jam; for more on that see page 21): Gravenstein Apple, Raisin & Fig Mostarda. "I recognized that in order to take my brand to the next level and have any chance of sending my kids to college I would need to draw on my chef friends for new and delicious ways to showcase my family's fruit," says Kendra.

When Kendra came to me, she was looking for a way to create a local apple condiment that would work in the specialty cheese case in grocery stores. Starting with a unique apple jelly or apple lavender compote, John and I started brainstorming about potential new creations. We knew for us to create a new product that would complement our FIGfood lineup, it would need to incorporate figs. After a few months of experimenting and tasting, we created a few condiments that morphed into mostardas. Again, we took liberties with what a true mostarda is, but the bottom line is that it is truly delicious.

"It's been a great product," says Kendra. "Sondra gifted us an opportunity and the recipe. She's kind and generous, and we are forever grateful for her efforts in saving Sonoma County's apple orchards through our collaboration. The mostarda has received rave reviews and sales have greatly helped our bottom line, no doubt about it." The mostarda may be amazing but the real success of the project is due to Kendra being out there every day, selling it, and getting folks to taste it.

We strongly believe that the connection between a farmer and a local restaurant is crucial to keep both businesses thriving. "We're an important part of the Sonoma County foodshed and local Bay Area food economy and are supported by chefs, markets, and families that buy our products," says Kendra. "There's an honest-to-goodness hard-working family behind Nana Mae's, keeping hundreds of Sonoma County acres in organic agriculture. Sondra, as both a businesswoman and foodie, understands the importance of supporting the local farmer, our foodshed, and sustaining a healthy food economy. Together we are a living model of the Slow Food Movement, building community and creating culture with our food."

Paul and Kendra are committed to passing both the importance of farming and the love of wholesome food along to their three children, who grew up picking apples and following Paul around the orchards. Their lives are in tune with the seasons and the local bounty, a lifestyle that we talk about and try to convey through our menus. We hope there will always be Gravensteins—and Nana Mae's Apple Juice—in the county!

Kendra's Pantry

Entrée	**Dessert**
Grilled Fig & Arugula Salad	*Lemon Verbena Pots du Crème*
Plat	**Fromage**
Pork Shoulder Roulade,	*Laura Chenel Cabecou*
Chanterelle Mushrooms	

Grilled Fig & Arugula Salad

Qupé Winery Marsanne, Santa Ynez Valley, California
Peay Vineyards Estate Roussanne/Marsanne, Sonoma Coast, California

What can I say about our famous fig and arugula salad? We get rave reviews from our guests all year long about this salad. This salad truly represents what I love most about food: the way different ingredients can come together and create a whole new taste, and the notion that a forkful of arugula, goat cheese, crispy pancetta, and toasted pecans can give you the most perfect bite of food. This salad has been on the menu since the day we opened, and the only thing that has changed in fifteen years is the pancetta, only because we now make our own. Our Fig and Port Vinaigrette is now available in hundreds of stores throughout the country and through our website, so it's easy to recreate this delectable salad at home.

For the vinaigrette:

3 dried Black Mission figs
1 cup ruby port
¼ cup red wine vinegar
½ tablespoon minced shallots
¼ cup blended oil
Salt and pepper to taste

For the salad:

½ cup pancetta, diced
12 fresh figs, halved (see Food for Thought)
6 bunches baby arugula
1 cup pecans, toasted
1 cup goat cheese, crumbled (preferably
   Laura Chenel Chévre)
Freshly ground black pepper to taste

To prepare the vinaigrette:

Pour the port in a bowl, add the figs, and rehydrate until soft. Transfer the port and figs to a saucepan. Reduce the port over medium heat to ½ cup, about 5 to 7 minutes. Transfer the port mixture to a food processor and add the vinegar. Purée until smooth. Add the shallots and slowly whisk in the oil. Season to taste with salt and pepper to taste.

To prepare the salad:

Sauté the pancetta in a small sauté pan over medium heat until the pancetta is crisp. Set the pancetta aside, reserving the "oil." Brush the figs with the pancetta "oil." Grill the figs for 45 seconds on each side. In a stainless-steel bowl, toss the arugula, pecans, pancetta, and goat cheese with the vinaigrette.

To serve:

Divide the salad among 6 chilled plates and surround it with the grilled figs. Grind the pepper over each salad.

Food for Thought:

If fresh figs are not in season, substitute good-quality, moist dried figs (Orchard's Choice figs from the Valley Fig Growers are my favorite). I do not recommend grilling dried figs; just cut them into small pieces and toss with the other salad ingredients.

Serves 6

Pork Shoulder Roulade, Chanterelle Mushrooms

Alban Vineyards Grenache, Edna Valley, California
Très Bonnes Années "the girl & the fig" Syrah, Sonoma County, California

This roulade technique takes a bit more time but will be well worth it! Make sure that you tie the pork nice and tight. It's also very important to get a good sear on the outside of the roulade before putting it in the oven; this will help retain the juices and keep the pork moist. Chanterelles are my favorite mushrooms—they have a nice earthy flavor but are much more delicate than you would think—but you could certainly substitute your favorite variety. Slowly cooking the chanterelles releases their flavorful juices and adds a distinctive mushroom element to the pork jus.

For the pork:

3 pounds pork shoulder, deboned (ask your butcher
    to do this for you)
Salt and pepper to taste
1 pound chanterelle mushrooms
4 tablespoons (½ stick) unsalted butter
3 garlic cloves, minced
1 bunch fresh flat-leaf parsley, chopped
1 head fennel, thinly sliced

For the sauce:

1 cup Madeira
2 teaspoons fresh thyme leaves
3 tablespoons unsalted butter

2 cups Chiogga beets, roasted and peeled (1 pound)
2 bunches baby carrots, blanched
1 bunch chives, cut into 1-inch pieces, for garnish

To prepare the pork:

Flatten the shoulder piece out into a 5 x 9-inch rectangle. Place the pork fat side down on a cutting board and season with salt and pepper. Set aside.

Preheat the oven to 325°F.

Chop half of the chanterelles. In a large sauté pan, melt 2 tablespoons of butter over medium heat and sauté the garlic, fennel, parsley, and the chopped chanterelles for 5 to 7 minutes or until soft. Set aside and let cool to room temperature.

Spread the mushroom mixture evenly over the pork. Roll the pork to enclose the stuffing and tie it with kitchen twine.

Heat 2 tablespoons of butter in a large sauté pan and sear the pork evenly on all sides. Remove the pork from the pan and place it in a medium roasting pan fitted with a roasting rack. Roast for about 2 hours or until the internal temperature reaches 165°F.

Remove the roast from the pan, place it on cutting board, and cover it with foil.

To prepare the sauce:

Remove the roasting rack from the pan and place the pan on high heat. Sauté the remaining chanterelles for 1 minute and add the Madeira and thyme. Scrape any brown bits from the pan. Remove the pan from the heat and whisk in 2 tablespoons of butter.

Place a small saucepan over medium heat and add the remaining tablespoon of butter, ¼ cup water, beets, and carrots and heat until the water has evaporated and the vegetables have warmed through, about 5 to 7 minutes.

To serve:

Slice the pork into 12 to 14 quarter-inch slices and divide them among 6 plates. Ladle the mushrooms on top, equally distribute the vegetables, and garnish with the chives.

Serves 6

autumn

Lemon Verbena Pots du Crème

Germain-Robin Viognier Grappa, California

Lemon verbena just recently came into my life. When we opened ESTATE restaurant, we discovered three huge lemon verbena plants in the front herb box. At first, I thought they were weeds and wanted to replace them, but after tasting a few recipes with lemon verbena I was convinced. When John experimented with our standard Pots du Crème recipe by steeping the lemon verbena in the milk, it gave the custard an altogether different and beautifully aromatic flavor. Lemon Verbena plants are relatively easy to grow. If you don't want to start with seed, you can purchase transplants (see Sources, page 318).

1¼ cups heavy cream

1 cup half-and-half

Pinch of salt

½ cup fresh lemon verbena leaves, loosely packed

Zest of 1 lemon

5 large egg yolks

4 tablespoons sugar

Preheat the oven to 350°F.

In a medium saucepan, heat the cream and half-and-half with the salt, lemon verbena, and lemon zest over medium heat until the mixture just comes to a boil, about 6 to 8 minutes.

Meanwhile, in a large bowl, whisk the egg yolks and sugar until light and pale. Temper the eggs with the cream by slowly adding one quarter of the hot cream mixture into the yolks a little at a time until the eggs are completely incorporated. Strain the mixture through a fine-mesh sieve into a large bowl and chill for about 20 minutes.

Pour the chilled custard mixture into six 4-ounce ramekins and place the ramekins inside a large baking dish. Add enough hot water to the dish to reach halfway up the sides of the ramekins. Cover the dish with foil and bake for 20 minutes or until set.

Remove the custards from the oven, transfer them to a cooling rack, and let them cool to room temperature, about 45 minutes. Cover and refrigerate until chilled, for at least 2 hours or overnight.

Serves 6

LAURA CHENEL'S CHEVRE CABECOU

AUTUMN №2

REGION:	Carneros, California
MILK:	goat
PROCESS:	pasteurized
PRODUCTION:	uncooked, unpressed, soft
AFFINAGE:	fresh, 15 to 17 days for the herbs to infuse
FLAVOR:	bright, citrus, clean, nutty
AROMA:	herbal, fresh cream, citrus
TEXTURE:	dense
SIMILAR CHEESES:	Haystack Mountain "Chevre en Marinade"
PAIRINGS:	Jimtown Store Fig & Olive Relish Orchard Choice Dried Figs Heirloom Tomato Jam (page 315) sunflower honey, ripe tomatoes
NOTES:	Goat milk is collected from producers seven days a week to make the cheeses at Laura Chenel's Chevre. The Cabecou is presented in a jar marinating in olive oil, bay leaf, thyme, rosemary, savory, and black peppercorns.

Polenta

You may wonder why our Plats du Jour menus include different versions of polenta. Though it may have originated in Italy, polenta is a staple in many different regions of France. One popular version is a fried porridge cake made from corn. Though not as popular in France as it is in Italy, we have found ways to incorporate Italian-style polenta into some of our French dishes.

Polenta is essentially a mush made from cornmeal that is a staple dish in Northern Italy. Each region in Italy has adopted its own style of serving polenta; it's served firm in the provinces of Veneto and Friuli and creamy in Abruzzi. We serve it as a base for many of our braised items and meat dishes. The nutty flavor is so versatile and works with a variety of flavors, from herbs and sauces to cheeses. Traditionally cooked in a copper pot and served soft, we like to cook it, shape it, and then grill or sauté the pieces. Sometimes when I've missed breakfast and lunch, I can generally talk the chefs into making me a bowl of creamy polenta topped with something simple like roasted mushrooms. This is a comfort dish—and filling, too!

My favorite type of polenta is the more rustic version, like the integrale polenta. We're able to get this from our Italian importer but there are some good versions from some of the older American grain companies like Anson Mills and Bob's Red Mill. The integrale grain has a thicker texture, which makes a nice base for sauces to cling to.

Polenta is not just for side dishes or breakfast. The use of this grain in our Chocolate Polenta Cake turns this dessert into a WOW. Aside from the chocolate, the polenta gives the cake an added texture and keeps the cake moist.

Types of artisanal polenta:

Rustic coarse polenta integrale— Milled from an Italian heirloom Red Trentino Flint that was, until recently, nearly extinct.

White polenta—This is the most common form, found in the regions of Trieste and Montfalcone in Italy. It's served as a side dish with seafood.

Red polenta—Originally from the Carnia Mountains in Friuli, it is stronger in flavor and is usually served with game meat.

Bramata—A delicious coarse-grained yellow polenta. It has a lovely delicate taste and is incredibly versatile. You can enjoy it simply with butter and soft cheese or as an accompaniment to virtually any meat dish.

Taragna—Polenta Taragna is traditionally from Valtellina in the Lombardy region of Northern Italy. It has been stone milled and mixed with buckwheat for a richer, rougher texture and a slightly nutty, bitter flavor.

Pignoletto Rosso—This is a top-quality polenta, made from the ancient Pignoletto Rosso variety of maize grown in Piedmont, Italy. It has protected "IGP" status, indicating that it's made from authentic ground organic Piedmont maize.

Winter Squash

As the days grow shorter and the temperatures dip, it's time to bring home winter squash. Even though they're harvested in the fall they're called winter squash because their hard, thick skins protect them during the winter storage, which was crucial in the days before refrigeration. Their large size and sometimes odd-looking exterior seem to intimidate some cooks but they are actually very easy to work with. Once you remove the tough outer skin or cut one in half and roast it with the skin on, you've got a very nutritious and adaptable ingredient. A sharp knife and a good recipe are really all you need.

Even though chefs long for the summer ingredients that inspire their summer recipes, the moment they feel winter coming on they start to plan the menus with winter squash in mind. Generally, they start with a light filling for ravioli or tortellini, which gradually becomes part of a squash or root vegetable ragoût. The chefs eventually create thick, rich soups that highlight the squash's flavor. Oak Hill Farm always has such a nice variety of squash in the fall—they look festive, and it's difficult to walk away without buying a few different varieties. One of my favorite ways to cook squash is to simply slice them in half, drizzle some olive oil over them, season with salt and pepper to taste, and roast them in the oven. I scoop out the roasted flesh with a spoon.

Lemon Verbena

This is an incredibly fragrant herb that few people know about. We grow many lemon verbena plants in our gardens, using it in cocktails, desserts, and in iced tea from summer through autumn. Our chefs love it because the lemon flavor holds up during cooking and lacks any bitterness. Originally from South and Central America, it was brought to Europe by Spanish explorers.

It's available dried and fresh, but use it judiciously; the lemon flavor can easily overwhelm a dish, (see Sources, page 320).

Gardener's Tip: This is a great herb for growing in window boxes. It does well indoors when placed in a sunny window.

Here are the most common varieties of squash you'll see:

Acorn squash is deep-green in color with deep ridges and orange flesh. Pick the ones with very dark green skin, almost bronze.

Buttercup is a variety of turban squash, with a light blue turban and a dark green shell. The sweet flesh is dark orange, almost red in color.

Butternut is the most common variety; it has a peachy-colored skin and bright orange flesh. Sizes range from 8 to 12 inches long and around 2 pounds in weight. Choose the darkest; it will be riper, drier, and sweeter.

Delicata squash is most recognizable by the lengthwise stripes of green down a yellowish base and grows quite easily and in large quantity. (Last fall we harvested about 300 pounds of Delicata squash!) Unlike many squash, the skin of the Delicata is completely edible.

Hubbard is a very large variety with a warty exterior; the colors range from green to orange. Hubbards are available from September to March. The flesh has a grainy texture so it's usually puréed or mashed and mixed with spices or seasonings.

Spaghetti squash is named for its fibrous creamy yellow-gold flesh that resembles spaghetti when cooked. The strands are often served like pasta, with sauce and cheese. The exterior is yellow and it looks almost like a watermelon, weighing between 4 and 8 pounds. Available year-round, this variety is at its peak from early fall through winter. Select those with a yellow exterior (any green indicates an immature squash) and avoid any with bruised spots. Store Spaghetti squash at room temperature for up to 3 weeks.

Turban ranges in size from 2 to 15 inches and has a bumpy exterior. They have colorful skins in shades of green, yellow, or orange. The flesh is not as sweet as some of the other varieties.

Entrée *Butternut Squash Soup,* *Balsamic Reduction, Fried Sage*	**Dessert** *Syrah Poached Pears*
Plat *Garlic Sausage, Puy Lentils,* *Savoy Cabbage, Walnut-Cider Vinaigrette*	**Fromage** *Roquefort*

Butternut Squash Soup, Balsamic Reduction, Fried Sage

Black Sheep Winery Cinsault, Dusty Lane Vineyard, California
Bonny Doon Vineyard DEWN Cinsault, California

When summer squash transitions to winter squash, soup always comes to mind. Butternut squash is a wonderful, hard-skin variety that when cooked just right will utterly delight you. At this time of year, you'll find several squash varieties at the market, so give the others a try in this recipe. There are a handful of options to garnish this soup. Fried sage has a nice earthy flavor and will be a wonderful flavor contrast to the creamy soup. Another option is Candied Pumpkin Seeds (page 315). They will definitely add a textural surprise!

8 tablespoons (1 stick) unsalted butter
1 small yellow onion, chopped
3 celery stalks, chopped
1 medium carrot, chopped
1 large leek, white part only, cleaned and chopped
2 shallots, chopped
4 garlic cloves, crushed
2½ pounds Butternut squash, peeled, seeded, chopped
Salt and white pepper to taste
½ cup heavy cream

1 bunch fresh sage leaves, picked, for garnish
Balsamic Reduction (page 311), for garnish

Melt 4 tablespoons of the butter in a medium saucepan over medium-low heat. Add the onion, celery, carrot, leek, shallots, and garlic and sauté until the vegetables are soft, about 7 minutes. Stir the vegetables occasionally to prevent browning. Add the squash to the vegetables and stir. Add 2 quarts of water and season with salt and pepper. Bring to a boil, reduce to a simmer, and cook until the squash is just tender, 15 to 20 minutes.

Add the heavy cream and the remaining 4 tablespoons of butter. Remove the vegetables from the heat and purée immediately in a blender or food processor. Strain through a fine-mesh sieve and adjust seasoning if necessary.

Heat a small amount of blended oil to 300°F and fry the sage leaves until crispy. Transfer the sage leaves to paper towels to drain and cool.

Ladle the soup into 6 bowls and garnish each with a drizzle of the balsamic vinegar reduction and a few fried sage leaves.

Serves 6

Garlic Sausage, Puy Lentils, Savoy Cabbage, Walnut-Cider Vinaigrette

Unti Vineyards Grenache, Dry Creek Valley, California
Leojami Wines Grenache, Pierce Ranch Vineyard, Monterey County, California
Dane Cellars Syrah, Justi Creek Vineyard, Sonoma Valley, California

One of my all-time favorite meals in France was at a friend's winery where we were served a variety—literally all shapes and sizes—of sausages. It was hard to know exactly what was in each of them, and had I not been indulging in the white Rhône wines of the evening I may have refused a few! Memorable meals are not always just about the food, but more often about the friends and family that you share them with. This garlic sausage dish is a tad more refined than the one I remember, but the focus remains on the complementary flavors of sausage, apples, cabbage, and mustard.

For the lentils:

1 cup Puy lentils
1 large carrot, diced
1 small head Savoy cabbage, halved, cored and
    cut into thin strips

For the vinaigrette:

1 celery stalk, diced
1 shallot, diced
10 chives, chopped
1 bunch fresh flat-leaf parsley, chopped
½ tablespoon apple cider vinegar
½ tablespoon whole-grain mustard
¼ cup walnut oil
Salt and freshly ground black pepper to taste
6 garlic sausages (6 ounces each)
2 tablespoons blended oil
2 tablespoons diced cooked pancetta (about 2
    ounces)

1 cup fresh sage leaves, for garnish

For the lentils:

Bring a pot of water to a boil. Add the lentils and carrots and cook for 20 minutes, adding more water if necessary. Continue to boil until the lentils are tender but still firm, about 15 minutes. Drain and rinse the lentils.

Bring another pot of salted water to a boil. Blanch the cabbage for 3 minutes or until tender. Shock the cabbage in an ice water bath and drain. Mix the cabbage with the lentils and carrots.

To prepare the vinaigrette:

Combine the celery, shallot, chives, and parsley with the vinegar, mustard, and walnut oil. Mix well and season with salt and pepper to taste.

In another pot of water, simmer the sausages for 5 to 7 minutes. Remove the sausages, transfer them to a cloth, and pat dry. Heat a large sauté pan over medium heat and add the blended oil. Add the sausage and cook until browned on all sides, about 2 to 3 minutes per side. Remove the sausages and keep warm. In the pan over medium heat add the lentil mixture along with the pancetta, toss with the vinaigrette, and heat through, about 3 minutes.

Heat a small amount of blended oil to 300°F and fry the sage leaves until crispy. Transfer the sage leaves to paper towels to drain and cool.

To serve:

Divide the lentils equally among the plates, top with a garlic sausage, and garnish with a few fried sage leaves.

Serves 6

Syrah Poached Pears

Loxton Cellars Syrah Port, Sonoma Valley, California
Krupp Brothers Black Bart Syrah Port, Napa Valley, California

This dessert is a nice alternative to a heavy chocolate or custard dessert. Autumn's perfect pears are just waiting to be slowly simmered in spiced wine. To add some depth and flavor contrast, include a wedge of Fourme d'Ambert or Rogue River Blue cheese.

1 teaspoon yellow mustard seeds, toasted

1 tablespoon whole cloves

1 tablespoon allspice

6 pieces star anise

½ teaspoon black peppercorns

4½ cups red wine

1 cup orange juice

¼ cup fresh lemon juice

2 cups sugar

8 firm pears, such as Bosc or Seckel, peeled

2 cinnamon sticks

Mix the mustard seeds, cloves, allspice, star anise, and black peppercorns together. Set half of the spice mixture aside to use for garnish.

In a medium saucepan, heat the red wine, orange juice, lemon juice, and sugar over high heat and bring to a boil. Add the pears, cinnamon, and half of the spice mixture and reduce to a simmer. Cook the pears slowly for about 25 to 30 minutes or until the pears are knife tender but not mushy. Remove the pears from the liquid and chill in the refrigerator for at least 1 hour and up to overnight.

Strain the liquid through a fine-mesh sieve into a saucepot and bring to a boil over high heat. Reduce the heat and simmer until the liquid is reduced to a thick syrupy consistency, about 10 minutes.

To serve:

Serve the pears warm or at room temperature. Slice two of the pears into 9 lengthwise slices and set aside. Place one whole pear in the center of each bowl. Garnish each bowl with 3 pear slices and an equal portion of the remaining spices. Drizzle the syrup in each bowl and serve.

Serves 6

ROQUEFORT

REGION:	Rouerge, France
MILK:	sheep
PROCESS:	raw
PRODUCTION:	cooked, unpressed
AFFINAGE:	minimum of 90 days
FLAVOR:	distinctive sweet flavor, butter, salt, caramel
AROMA:	special bouquet, lightly mildew
TEXTURE:	soft, crumbly, slightly moist
SIMILAR CHEESES:	Fourme d'Ambert, Bleu d'Auvergne
PAIRINGS:	Fastachi Hazelnut Butter
	Savannah Bee Tupelo Honey
	B & R Farms Blenheim Sun-dried Apricots
	Panevino No. 6 Grissini
	dried fruits, greens
NOTES:	Roquefort is turned five times a day during affinage. For optimum flavor, let Roquefort sit at room temperature for at least 1 hour before serving.

HelloCello
FigCello di Sonoma
Sonoma

We're always looking for local purveyors that will enhance our restaurants and promote the region, whether they're winemakers, farmers, or artisans. So, when we met Fred and Amy Groth, our neighbors and founders of HelloCello, a certified organic limoncello made in Sonoma, we were intrigued.

Limoncello, a lemon liqueur originally from Italy, is a difficult spirit because, outside of Italy, it's often too sweet and syrupy. Fred and Amy's Limoncello di Sonoma tastes light and fresh—like it actually comes from real lemons (which it does!). It was the perfect fit for ESTATE, where we serve it as a digestivo, or after-dinner drink, and have incorporated it into cocktails.

The story behind HelloCello is a testament to the entrepreneurial spirit that seems to flourish in Sonoma. Fred and Amy moved to Sonoma from Colorado in 2008 after visiting Sonoma and basically falling in love with the town. "We wanted to do something fun and different and wanted a lifestyle change," recalls Fred. "Sonoma was perfect because it has a European feel to it and there are so many artisan products here, like cheese and wine." The Groths packed up their three kids and moved to Sonoma. They had always loved limoncello and made it as a hobby, but they realized there was no one in the U.S. making artisan limoncello. "The limoncello here in the U.S. is pasteurized and shelf stabilized," says Fred. "We wanted to make a small-batch, artisan product."

Fred went to Italy for a month to learn the techniques of making limoncello. They built a distilled spirits plant in Sonoma, and one year later they started production with 80 cases. Production is now 100 to 150 cases made four to five times a year. "We want it really fresh," says Fred. Everything is done by hand and the only full-time employees are Fred and Amy. "My wife and I do everything," says Fred. "We make it, bottle it, and deliver it."

What makes HelloCello Limoncello di Sonoma different from mass-market limoncello are the ingredients and the freshness. They start with organic Eureka and Sorrento lemons, which grow year-round in California. The Sorrento lemon, grown in the town of Sorrento, Italy, is the original lemon used in Italian limoncello. Instead of cane sugar Fred and Amy decided to use agave, for both taste and health reasons; it gives the limoncello a deeper flavor and doesn't spike blood glucose levels like other sweeteners do. Instead of a high-proof grain alcohol, HelloCello is made with distilled grapes, or brandy. (Fred and Amy found someone to make brandy to their specifications.) "Everything except for the agave is from within 60 to 80 miles of our plant," notes Fred. All of the ingredients are 100 percent certified organic.

The Groths use the traditional limoncello process and the most important ingredient is the lemon peel. Each batch requires the peels of 4,000 lemons, though the recipe only uses the yellow peel, not the pith or juice. The Groths turned the time-consuming chore of peeling lemons into a festive occasion by throwing lemon-peeling parties. "Our friends come over, we'll get a keg or and have wine, and everyone sits at a big table and peels and zests," says Fred, laughing. There are no machines that could peel the lemons because when working with organic citrus there are imperfections that a machine couldn't work around, notes Fred. The lemon peels then go into a tank with the brandy, where the liquid is filtered, simple syrup is added, and the limoncello is bottled. The whole process takes about one month from start to finish. "It's fresh to market," says Fred. We were so impressed with their product that we asked them to make us a fig liqueur. They agreed and started researching recipes and techniques.

"It was an interesting and fun process," says Fred. "We made 30 samples with various botanical and flavor elements (such as orange peel, tarragon, and star anise) to decide which would go well with fig and alcohol." We had an informal tasting panel, and we chose the flavors that worked the best. Production had to start almost immediately to take advantage of the second fig season that was just beginning. Fred and Amy (and their kids!) wild-harvested 400 pounds of fresh figs from around Sonoma Valley. "We chopped them up and threw them in with the alcohol and herbs, let it sit for a month, and then filtered it and added sugar," Fred remarks. Voilà—our fig liqueur! Fred and Amy produced 55 cases and we serve it in the restaurants. It was so delicious that they plan to make it a seasonal product.

Besides the fig liqueur, Fred and Amy's latest product is Bello Cello, an orange-flavored brandy made from navel oranges and damiana, a flower from Baja known for its powers as an aphrodisiac. They have two or three more artisanal spirits in the works that should be appearing soon. Right now HelloCello products are available only in California (see Sources, page 325, for contact information), so pick up a bottle next time you're in Northern California.

It's amazing that two Americans could travel to Italy, fall in love with a beverage, and recreate it here in Sonoma. "We're small producers filling a niche in specialty spirits," says Fred. They are devoted to making the perfect organic limoncello and in our mind they've succeeded.

autumn
Nº 4

Entrée
Mixed Chicory Salad,
White Balsamic Vinaigrette

Plat
Sautéed Pork Chop,
Onion-Apple Ragoût, Mustard Jus

Dessert
Apple & Prune Crisp

Fromage
Bellwether Farms Carmody

Mixed Chicory Salad, White Balsamic Vinaigrette
Stolpman Vineyards "L' Avion" Roussanne, Central Coast, California

Chicory greens make a surprisingly lovely base for a salad. They are not as delicate as lamb's lettuce (mâche) or freshly picked baby mizuna, but the rough texture of the chicory greens works nicely with heartier salad ingredients. For a variation, add some dried pears or apples, or for an entrée salad add grated hard-boiled egg, grilled shrimp, or bacon lardons.

For the vinaigrette:
¼ cup white balsamic vinegar
½ cup extra-virgin olive oil
Salt and pepper to taste

For the salad:
1 bunch mizuna, cleaned and large stems removed
1 head radicchio, cleaned and torn into 3-inch pieces
2 heads endive, leaves removed
2 cups arugula
1 head frisée, cleaned and core removed
½ cup fresh pomegranate seeds
2 blood oranges, cut into supremes or thin slices (see below)
2 navel oranges, cut into supremes or thin slices (see below)

To prepare the vinaigrette:
Whisk together the vinegar and the olive oil. Season with salt and pepper to taste.

To prepare the salad:
In a large mixing bowl combine the mizuna, radicchio, endive, arugula, frisée, pomegranate seeds, and citrus with the vinaigrette. Toss well and season with salt and pepper to taste. Distribute evenly among 6 plates.

Serves 6

Supremes

Supremes, also known as sections or segments, allow for easy removal of citrus fruit from their skin. Using this method you will get most of the fruit without the bitter taste of the white pith.

To cut into supremes start by cutting off the top and bottom of the fruit. Set the fruit on the flat bottom and carefully cut the peel away in strips. Trim away all of the remaining white pith. (The white ribs between each wedge of fruit should become visible.) Scrape the fruit and the interior skin away from the peel. Reserve the peel for another use, such as candied peels, zest, or drink garnishes.

Over a bowl to catch any juice, cut each segment on the left and the right to separate the segment from the membrane, resulting in thin wedges of fruit. Squeeze the remaining center to extract any remaining juice.

Chicory

Chicory, a cousin of the popular endive, is a plant with rosette leaves produced from certain tender-rooted varieties. We love adding chicory to salads to add texture because it doesn't wilt as quickly as other types of lettuce. It can be used either fresh or roasted.

The roasted and ground root of the plant can be added to, or used as a substitute for, coffee. (It gives the coffee a woody, earthy flavor.) The French love chicory and use it fresh and dried; dried chicory is often added to liquids like milk and made into sauces to accompany meat.

There are many different types of chicory, and they may be more recognizable to you as curly endive, escarole, Belgian endive, Treviso, or radicchio. Fresh chicory is usually eaten raw and is treated as a lettuce or salad green. Its slightly bitter flavor can stand up to assertive ingredients like mustard. It's always nice to have a flavor counterpart to the bitterness, such as a sweet fruit, a nut, or salty fat like bacon. Look for brightly colored, crisp leaves and store it in the refrigerator for up to three days. It's available year-round.

Sautéed Pork Chop, Onion-Apple Ragoût, Mustard Jus

Fess Parker Winery Viognier, Santa Barbara, California
Mounts Family Winery Pink Grenache, Dry Creek Valley, California

This recipe has many flavors that work in perfect harmony. The apples, cabbage, and onions are substantial fall flavors that will stand out against the more mild pork flavor. With the addition of a spicy whole-grain mustard jus and a side of caramelized Yukon Gold potatoes, you will have a wonderful, hearty meal that is perfect on a cool evening. Some apple varieties that pair nicely with pork are Jonathan, Arkansas Black Twig, Rome Beauty, and Gravenstein apples.

For the brine:

3 bay leaves
½ tablespoon black peppercorns
1 whole clove
½ tablespoon crushed red pepper flakes
¾ tablespoon dried thyme
1 tablespoon anise seed
1 cup sugar
¾ cup salt
1 tablespoon minced garlic

For the pork:

6 pork chops (about 10 ounces each and 1-inch thick)
3 tablespoons blended oil

For the vegetables:

4 tablespoons (½ stick) unsalted butter
2 apples, peeled and sliced into ½-inch lengthwise pieces
2 pounds Yukon Gold potatoes, peeled and sliced into ¼-inch pieces
½ pound green or red cabbage, sliced into ¼-inch slices
Salt and pepper to taste

For the sauce:

½ cup Demi-Glace (see Sources, page 318)
2 tablespoons honey
3 tablespoons whole-grain mustard
2 tablespoons unsalted butter

To prepare the brine:

In a spice grinder or a coffee bean grinder, grind the bay leaves, peppercorns, clove, red pepper, thyme, and anise seed to a fine powder.

In a very large, deep bowl, add 1 gallon water along with the sugar and salt. Stir until the sugar and salt are dissolved. Stir in the herb-spice mix and minced garlic. Add the pork to a pan or a large zip-top bag and cover the pork with the brine. Refrigerate for at least 4 hours or overnight.

To prepare the pork:

Preheat the oven to 425°F.
Remove the pork from the brine and pat it dry with paper towels. Heat the blended oil in a large ovenproof sauté pan (large enough to hold the chops) over high heat. Sear the pork chops until golden brown on both sides and place the pan in the oven. Roast until the internal temperature reaches 135°F for medium-rare or 165°F for well-done. Remove the pan from the oven, cover with foil, and set aside.

To prepare the vegetables:

Place the sauté pan back on high heat and add 2 tablespoons butter and the apples. Season with salt and pepper to taste and cook until the apples are caramelized, about 8 to 10 minutes. Remove the apples from the pan and set aside. Sauté the potatoes in the remaining butter for about 8 minutes, add the cabbage, and sauté for an additional 2 minutes until the cabbage is slightly softened.

To prepare the sauce:

Combine the demi-glace, mustard, and honey in a small saucepan over low heat and bring to a simmer. Cook until the mixture thickly coats the back of a spoon, about 8 minutes. Season to taste, whisk in the butter, and set aside.

To serve:

Place a serving of potatoes and cabbage on each plate and cover the potatoes with one pork chop. Drizzle the sauce over the top and garnish with the apples.

Serves 6

Apple & Prune Crisp

Ramos Pinto Tawny Porto, Portugal
Domaine de Durban Muscat de Beaumes-de-Venise, France

This is a perfect fall dessert. It's not too sweet, but is dense with the flavors of harvest fruit. This has the best parts of a tart and a crisp, using our wonderful shortbread dough and walnut crisp topping. You can have the crisps ready to pop in the oven as you are sitting down to dinner, and by the time you're ready for dessert they will be nice and warm and ready for a scoop of gelato.

For the crust:

7 tablespoons unsalted butter
¼ cup sugar
1 large egg yolk
Pinch of salt
½ teaspoon pure vanilla extract
1¼ cups all-purpose flour

For the filling:

2 cups dried prunes, chopped
1 cup verjus blanc (See Sources, page 318)
6 Gala or Fuji apples, peeled, cored, and diced
Juice from 1 lemon
¼ cup sugar
2 tablespoons cornstarch
½ teaspoon freshly grated nutmeg
1 teaspoon ground cinnamon
¼ teaspoon ground cloves
¼ teaspoon ground ginger

For the crisp topping:

¼ cup plus 2 tablespoons walnuts
⅔ cup plus 3 tablespoons sugar
⅔ cup firmly packed brown sugar
¾ teaspoon salt
¾ teaspoon baking powder
2¼ cups all-purpose flour
12 tablespoons (1½ sticks) unsalted butter,
   thinly sliced
1½ teaspoons pure vanilla extract
2 large egg yolks

Gelato, for serving (optional)

To prepare the crust:

In a mixer fitted with a paddle attachment, cream the butter and sugar. Add the egg yolk, salt, and vanilla. Mix to incorporate. Add the flour to the mixture and mix just until the dough comes together. Form the dough into a ball, wrap it in plastic wrap, and refrigerate overnight.

Preheat the oven to 350°F.
Divide the dough into 6 equal portions. On a lightly floured surface, roll the dough out to 4½-inch rounds to fit into 4-inch tart shells. Bake the shells until lightly browned, about 8 to 11 minutes. Set aside.

To prepare the crisp topping:

Grind the walnuts with 3 tablespoons of sugar in a food processor and set aside. In a food processor or a mixer, mix the remaining sugar, brown sugar, salt, baking powder, and flour and process until well combined. Add the butter and mix until the mixture clumps, about 1½ to 2 minutes. Add the vanilla and egg yolks to the butter mixture and process for another 40 seconds.

To prepare the filling:

In a small pot over low heat, add the prunes and the verjus. Bring the prunes to a simmer, remove the pan from the heat, and let the prunes steep for 10 to 15 minutes.

In a medium bowl, combine the apples and lemon juice. In a separate small bowl, combine the sugar, cornstarch, nutmeg, cinnamon, cloves, and ginger. Add the dry mixture to the apples and toss until coated. Pour the prune and sugar mixture into the apples and toss again.

Fill the tart shells generously with the fruit mixture (it will shrink down as it bakes). In a bowl crumble together the crisp topping with the walnut and sugar mixture. Sprinkle the mixture over the fruit filling and bake for 20 to 25 minutes, until the fruit is tender and the topping is golden and crunchy.

To serve:

Add a scoop of your favorite gelato and serve while still warm.

Food for Thought:

You will have some leftover crisp topping, spread it on a baking sheet and bake at 325°F until crisp and brown about 10 to 12 minutes. Let cool and save as an ice cream or yogurt topping.

Serves 6

BELLWETHER FARMS CARMODY

REGION:	Petaluma, California
MILK:	Jersey cows
PROCESS:	pasteurized
PRODUCTION:	uncooked, unpressed, semi-hard, natural rind
AFFINAGE:	two months
FLAVOR:	buttery, creamy, tangy
AROMA:	gentle sweet grass
TEXTURE:	soft, smooth
SIMILAR CHEESES:	Cheddar
PAIRINGS:	the girl & the fig Dried Fig Compote
	Blackberry Farm Apple Butter
	Sarabeth's Kitchen Chunky Apple
	Blue Chair Fruit Co. Early Girl Tomato Jam

NOTES: Carmody was inspired by two Italian cheeses, Bra and Toma. During the aging process the wheels are kept on planks of pine wood since the pine will not impart any additional flavor to the cheese. Carmody is named after the road that runs adjacent to the farm.

Bohemian Creamery
Sebastopol
California

While we love cheeses from France, Italy, and Spain, we're always looking for local cheeses that will fit our flavor profile and show off the terroir of the region. Cheese is just another avenue that shows how incredible Sonoma County is. Each one has a personality, flavor, and texture you'll find nowhere else. Artisan American cheeses have flooded the market in the past ten years, using goat's, sheep's, or cow's milk, which has left us with a lot of choices.

One of our favorite discoveries in 2009 was Bohemian Creamery, a two-woman operation in Sebastopol, near the coast of Sonoma County. The women behind this delicious cheese are Lisa Gottreich and Miriam Block. Relying on their head of 40-plus Alpine goats, supplemented by locally milked goats, sheep's, and Jersey cow's milk, Lisa and Miriam make nine different Italian-influenced cheeses.

Lisa lived in Italy for seven years and then started making cheese from animals she kept on her property. After making cheese in her home for 15 years for friends and family, she met Miriam. They decided to combine her palate and knowledge with Miriam's biology background and start a cheese company. They found property with an old creamery and barn just off Highway 116 just minutes from their houses. They renovated the creamery, brought the goats to their new home, and started making cheese.

Lisa's Italian influence becomes clear in the salt levels of the cheese, which Lisa likes to keep low—something she learned in Italy. "When Italy was occupied during World War I, the Italians were taxed heavily on salt, so it was a precious commodity, especially in the inland areas," she says. "In the region of Umbria, they still make bread without salt, which is left over from the days when salt was too expensive to use." Lisa wants salt to be just one component of the flavor profile rather than the dominant one.

Miriam & Lisa

The cheesemaking process is straightforward; it's the aging that gives Lisa and Miriam a chance to personalize the product. They start with milk (goat, sheep, or cow), and gravity-feed it into the pasteurization vat. They can make cheese in the vat or separate it into other vats for different types of cheese. They test the pH levels before culturing and renneting the cheese, and then test the pH levels again. The curds are then moved to the stainless-steel tables where the cheese is hooped and shaped. The cheese may be drained at this point, depending on the cheese. Some cheeses will also be dipped in a brine before aging, while the soft cheeses are dry-salted before being moved to the aging rooms.

The cheese then enters the affinage, or aging, stage: it will sit in the aging rooms from anywhere from two to ten months. "This is where the real process happens," says Lisa. With the changes in weather and humidity, "you have to deal with what nature hands you," she adds. "While some cheesemakers try to battle the molds, we try to make the best of it." These molds that exist naturally in the air are what give the cheese its character. Lisa notes the wild blue mold in Sonoma County that flourishes in the warm summer months "doesn't like the humidity. It comes back in the spring." Some cheesemakers spray their cheese with certain bacteria, but Lisa and Miriam use mostly wild molds. The aging process is essentially waiting for the cheese to break down; flavor in cheese develops from the breakdown of fatty acids, "and the flavor can change in 24 hours," Miriam explains. It's a waiting game: waiting for the cheese to age and evolve into their vision, but also dealing with challenges that come up every day. "Change is the constant in cheesemaking," according to Miriam. "Every day is like a dance. You think you've figured it out, but then the milk supply changes and the weather changes."

While the cheese ages it's turned once or twice a week and the mold is scraped off, depending on the type of cheese. Lisa watches the cheese, using instinct and experience to determine how the aging process is coming along, while Miriam takes samples and monitors the numbers in the lab. Both processes are needed to determine when the cheese will be ready.

At that perfect stage of maturity, it's cleaned (sometimes the mold is scraped with a knife to give it a more desirable appearance) and delivered to the customer. The result is nine types of cheese, all with their own personalities (and tongue-in-cheek names), but all clearly from Bohemian Creamery: Capriago, Boho Bel, Caproncino, Bo Poisse, Boviago, Bovoncino, Bo Peep, Romeo, and Bodacious. They range in color from creamy white to buttery yellow, depending on the milk used. Lisa's tip for identifying cheeses made from different animals: goat's milk cheese is always pure white, while sheep's and cow's milk cheeses are more yellow.

What most people don't realize is that cheesemaking is more about cleaning than making cheese! "We make cheese 20 percent of the time and we clean 80 percent of the time," says Miriam. A clean facility is crucial to managing bacteria.

Not content with just a handful of cheeses, Lisa is constantly thinking up new types of cheese. She "listens to chefs and their flavor suggestions" and incorporates their ideas into her brainstorming. Her newest creation is a Robiola-style cheese pressed with cacao nibs called Holy Mole. Naming the new cheeses is the most fun part, according to Lisa.

Lisa is in charge of sales and marketing, and visits restaurants and talks to chefs almost every day. Chefs can come to the creamery to learn about cheesemaking, with a group visiting every month. "I love working with chefs," says Lisa. "They're using our cheeses in such interesting and creative ways, especially how they're cooking with them." Lisa and Miriam don't eat much cheese themselves, given the amount they sample each day. "I love giving our cheese away to friends, and then when they serve it to me it's like a new thing," says Miriam.

Bohemian Creamery makes less than 20,000 pounds of cheese each year, and the cheeses are only available wholesale and in a few local retail markets. Lisa and Miriam plan to keep it that way. "I just want to be able to pay myself and my bills," says Lisa. "We don't want to become so popular that we can't keep up with the supply." Miriam feels similarly: "We don't want to get so big that we're not touching the cheese."

Lisa and Miriam's passion as well as the amazing quality is what keep their cheeses on our menus. Our chefs take Lisa's advice as to when the different cheeses are best consumed, and we are always willing to be cheese tasters when it comes to trying her new creations. We serve it on a cheese plate, rather than combining it with other ingredients, to really show off the subtle flavors. For more on Bohemian Creamery, the goats, and Lisa and Miriam, check out their website at www.bohemiancreamery.com.

Entrée
*Ricotta Gnocchi, Arugula Pesto,
Olive Oil Tomatoes*

Plat
*Sautéed Alaskan Salmon,
Roasted Root Vegetables, Tarragon Cream*

Dessert
*Brioche-Fig Bread Pudding,
Caramel Sauce*

Fromage
Fontina Val d'Aosta

Ricotta Gnocchi, Arugula Pesto, Olive Oil Tomatoes

Qupé Winery Marsanne, Santa Ynez Valley, California
The Ojai Vineyard Viognier, Roll Ranch, Central Coast, California

We prepare ricotta gnocchi at ESTATE. It is one dish that I was not planning to include in this book, but on a recent trip to the Rhône Valley, I saw more Italian-influenced menu items on Plats du Jour menus than ever before. When properly prepared, gnocchi should be light and airy—a bit lighter than a typical gnocchi but with some heft. The spicy arugula pesto and the olive oil from the poached tomatoes will lightly coat the gnocchi and make this a wonderful starter. Feel free to double the recipe if you prefer to serve it as an entrée. Both the tomatoes and the pesto can be made a day ahead.

For the gnocchi:

2 pounds ricotta cheese, (drained overnight
   in cheesecloth or strainer over a bowl)
2 tablespoons grated Pecorino cheese
4 large egg yolks
2 tablespoons chopped fresh flat-leaf parsley
2 tablespoons chopped fresh oregano
¾ cup "00" flour (see Sources, page 318)

For tomatoes:

30 cherry tomatoes (about 1½ pints, depending
   on size)
2 cups extra-virgin olive oil
2 sprigs fresh thyme
½ teaspoon whole peppercorns
1 teaspoon salt

For the pesto:

2 cups arugula
½ cup tomato oil (from the oil-poached
   tomatoes)
2 garlic cloves
3 tablespoons pine nuts, toasted
3 tablespoons grated Pecorino cheese
Salt and pepper to taste

¼ cup shaved Pecorino cheese, for garnish
6 red pearl onions, blanched and thinly sliced,
   for garnish

To prepare the gnocchi:

In a bowl combine the ricotta, Pecorino, egg yolks, and herbs. Slowly add the flour a little at a time; the dough should be slightly sticky. Add more flour if mixture is still wet. (You may not use all the flour.) Refrigerate the dough for 1 hour. Lightly sprinkle some flour on a work surface and working in three batches, roll the gnocchi into 1-inch thick ropes. Use a sharp knife to cut the dough into 1-inch pieces. Repeat with the remaining dough. Transfer the gnocchi to a lightly floured baking sheet. Lightly dust the gnocchi with flour and freeze for 1 hour.

To prepare the tomatoes:

Place the tomatoes, olive oil, thyme, peppercorns, and salt in a small saucepan and bring to a simmer. Remove the pan from the heat and let the tomatoes soak in the oil for 15 minutes. Remove the tomatoes with a slotted spoon and set aside. Reserve ½ cup of the tomato oil for the pesto; the remaining oil can be strained and set aside for another use. (The oil will keep for two weeks in the refrigerator.)

To make the pesto:

Place the arugula, tomato oil, and garlic in the bowl of a food processor and pulse until smooth. Add the pine nuts and Pecorino and pulse just until the mixture comes together. Season with salt and pepper to taste and set aside.

To serve:

Heat a large pot of salted water (it should taste salty like the ocean) to a rolling boil and cook the gnocchi in two batches for 3 to 5 minutes or about 1 minute after they float to the surface.

Place the hot gnocchi in a large bowl and gently toss them with the pesto and the tomatoes. Divide the gnocchi into 6 serving bowls and garnish with the shaved Pecorino and onions.

Serves 6

Sautéed Alaskan Salmon, Roasted Root Vegetables, Tarragon Cream

Wellington Vineyards Marsanne, Sonoma Valley, California
Krupp Brothers "Black Bart" Marsanne, Stagecoach Vineyard, Napa Valley, California
Château de Beaucastel Châteauneuf-du-Pape Blanc, Rhône Valley, France

When perusing a menu, most guests are comfortable ordering salmon before they try fish such as Arctic Char, Corvina, or Opah. Salmon is neither too fishy nor too mild and has a great texture that will hold up to many cooking methods, including grilling, poaching, smoking, and sautéing. Get a nice crispy sear on the outside of the salmon for textural contrast as well as to keep the fish moist on the inside. As we move further into fall, root vegetables take the main stage in the garden. When preparing root vegetables, dice all the vegetables the same size so they will cook evenly. Choose your favorites but if you add red beets to the mixture you may want to roast them separately so the entire medley does not turn red.

For the root vegetables:

1 large carrot, cut into ½-inch dice
1 parsnip, cut into ½-inch dice
2 small turnips, cut into ½-inch dice
½ rutabaga, cut into ½-inch dice
½ celery root, cut into ½-inch dice
2 tablespoons extra-virgin olive oil
Salt and white pepper to taste

For the Tarragon Cream:

⅔ cup dry white wine
2 tablespoons minced shallots
2 whole black peppercorns
1 sprig fresh thyme
1 cup heavy cream
4 tablespoons unsalted butter, at room temperature
2 tablespoons chopped fresh tarragon

For the salmon:

3 tablespoons blended oil
6 pieces Alaskan salmon (5 ounces each, skin on)

To prepare the vegetables:

Preheat the oven to 350°F.
In a large bowl toss the carrots, parsnips, turnips, rutabaga, and celery root with the olive oil and season with salt and white pepper to taste. Transfer the mixture to a baking sheet and roast until the vegetables are just tender, about 15 to 18 minutes. Set aside.

To prepare the Tarragon Cream:

Place the white wine, shallots, peppercorns, and thyme in a small saucepan and bring to a simmer over medium heat. Simmer until the liquid has evaporated but the ingredients are still wet, about 3 minutes. Add the cream and reduce by one third. Remove the pan from the heat and whisk in the butter to emulsify. Strain the sauce and add the tarragon. Set aside.

To prepare the salmon:

Preheat the oven to 425°F.
Heat the blended oil in a large ovenproof sauté pan over high heat. Sear the salmon, skin side down, until the skin has browned, about 3 minutes. Turn the salmon over, place the pan in the oven, and roast for an additional 5 to 7 minutes.

To serve:

Divide the cream sauce equally among the plates and top with a piece of salmon and a spoonful of vegetables.

Serves 6

Brioche-Fig Bread Pudding, Caramel Sauce

Truchard Vineyards Late Harvest Roussanne, Carneros, California
d'Arenberg "Daddy Long Legs" Tawny Port, McLaren Vale, Australia

When we first opened the restaurant, bread pudding recipes became important to us as a way to use leftover bread. Besides bread crumbs and croutons, bread pudding is a perfect way to use day-old bread. We make many versions, sometimes in a loaf pan and sometimes in a ramekin. Some bread puddings are topped with simple dessert sauces and others have dollops of fresh macerated fruits and ice cream on top. Once you master the custard part of the recipe you will be able to make just about any version you want.

For the caramel:

½ cup sugar
¼ cup heavy cream
1 tablespoon unsalted butter
½ teaspoon sea salt

For the bread pudding:

10 ounces brioche, cut into 1-inch cubes,
     (about 1 loaf)
6 large eggs
2 cups heavy cream
2 cups whole milk
1 cup sugar
1 teaspoon pure vanilla extract
1½ cups dried Black Mission figs, cut in
     ¼-inch dice
Pinch of salt

To prepare the caramel:

Heat the sugar with 2 tablespoons of water in a non-reactive pan until the sugar is well caramelized, about 8 to 10 minutes. Remove the sugar from the heat and add the cream, butter, and salt. Stir until incorporated.

To prepare the bread pudding:

Preheat the oven to 350°F. Lightly grease a 8 x 8-inch baking pan.
Place the brioche on a baking sheet and bake for 6 to 8 minutes or until the brioche just starts to toast. In a large bowl whisk the eggs, cream, and milk together until light and pale. Add the sugar and vanilla and whisk until smooth. Add the toasted bread, figs, and salt and gently mix together.

Pour the mixture into the baking pan and let it sit for 15 minutes. Bake the bread pudding for 45 to 60 minutes or until set. Test for doneness by inserting a knife in the center of the pudding to see if the custard is still loose. Once it's set, remove the pudding from the oven and let it rest for 20 minutes.

To serve:

Cut the bread pudding into 6 pieces. Place a piece of bread pudding on each plate, drizzle with caramel, and serve.

Serves 6 to 8

FONTINA VAL D'AOSTA

REGION:	Aosta Valley, Italy
MILK:	cow
PROCESS:	raw
PRODUCTION:	uncooked, pressed, semi-hard, natural rind
AFFINAGE:	at least 90 days, salt-rubbed in a humid cellar
FLAVOR:	mild, nutty aftertaste, sweet, rustic
AROMA:	floral, hay, mushrooms
TEXTURE:	gentle, smooth
SIMILAR CHEESES:	Raclette, Comté, Beaufort
PAIRINGS:	the girl & the fig Apricot Fig Chutney Blackberry Farm Blackberry Jam Queener Fruit Farm Black Cherry Jam Orchard Choice Dried Mission Figs
NOTES:	There are only 400 producers in Italy that make authentic Fontina. This is important because commercial Fontina tastes very different from the real thing. It takes 1¼ gallons of milk to produce just 1 pound of Fontina.

Entrée
Sweet Gem Romaine, Vella Dry Jack,
Caper Vinaigrette

Plat
Duck & Sausage Cassoulet

Dessert
Chocolate Pots du Crème

Fromage
Vella Dry Jack

Sweet Gem Romaine, Vella Dry Jack, Caper Vinaigrette

Atmosphere "Dos Burros" Marsanne/Roussanne, La Prenda Vineyard, Sonoma Valley, California
Truchard Roussanne Carneros, Napa Valley, California

Sweet Gem Romaine became popular in markets a couple of years ago. This variety seems to be the perfect size for a salad without losing layers of the bitter, hard outer romaine leaves, and this salty, tangy vinaigrette works beautifully with the lettuce. Sweet Gem Romaine can be prepared the same way as grilled endive: lightly coated with olive oil, sprinkled with salt and pepper, and thrown on the grill for a few minutes. It makes a flavorful—and unusual—side dish.

6 tablespoons capers, drained and patted dry
¼ cup blended oil

6 heads Sweet Gem Romaine, cut in half and washed
¾ cup Caper Vinaigrette (page 312)
Salt and freshly cracked black pepper
30 slices Vella Dry Jack, sliced with a vegetable peeler
   (about ¼ pound)
¼ cup caperberries
½ medium red onion, sliced thin
12 white Spanish anchovies, drained (optional)

Heat the blended oil in a small sauté pan over medium heat. Add the capers to the hot oil and fry until they are crispy. Strain the capers and place them on a paper towel to drain. Set aside.

Place the lettuce in a bowl and toss with the vinaigrette, salt, and pepper. Place two halves of the Sweet Gem lettuce onto each chilled plate. Sprinkle the fried capers, 5 slices of Vella Dry Jack, and caperberries over each portion. Add the red onion slices and anchovies on top and garnish with the remaining vinaigrette around the plate to taste.

Food for thought:
If you can't locate Sweet Gem Romaine, you can substitute another romaine or a chicory type green.

Serves 6

Duck & Sausage Cassoulet

kunin wines "pape star" Red Rhône Blend, Central Coast, California
Tablas Creek Vineyard "Côte du Tablas" Paso Robles, California
Mathilde et Yves Gangloff "La Sereine," Côte Rôtie, France

This recipe hasn't changed from the last book, and I don't think it ever will! Since it's a time-consuming dish to prepare, I recommend opening a bottle of Tavel to enjoy while cooking. Even though I am quite satisfied with this version, there is no reason not to experiment by substituting a different sausage, type of meat, or beans. My love affair with cassoulet continued in the small town of Paradou, France. One of my favorite restaurants in the world, called Bistrot du Paradou, is the town's hidden gem. My good fortune has brought me there several times, but I've never had a better meal than the night of my friend Howie's birthday. The perfect cassoulet was served, with wonderful friends and, of course, yummy wine and cheese!

2 cups white beans, soaked overnight in water to cover and drained (see Food for Thought)

8 cups Chicken Stock (page 313)

3 tablespoons Pernod

2 bay leaves

4 garlic cloves, crushed

1 pound bacon, diced

2 pounds mild pork sausage links, cut into ½-inch pieces

2 large carrots, cut into ½-inch dice

1 fennel head, cut into ½-inch dice

2 celery stalks, cut into ½-inch dice

¼ cup chopped fresh flat-leaf parsley

2 tablespoons chopped fresh thyme

2 tablespoons chopped fresh sage

6 confit duck legs, meat removed from the bone and skin removed (page 316)

2 tablespoons unsalted butter

2 tablespoons fennel seeds

2 cups plain bread crumbs (preferably from French bread)

Preheat the oven to 350°F.

In a large saucepan, simmer the soaked beans in 7 cups of the chicken stock along with the Pernod, bay leaves, and garlic for 1 hour or until the beans are soft.

Meanwhile, in a sauté pan, cook the bacon and sausage over high heat until browned. Remove and set aside. Sauté the carrots, fennel, celery, and fresh herbs in the bacon fat. Combine the beans and duck with the bacon, sausage, and vegetable mixture in a large stainless-steel bowl.

In a large pan, melt the butter with the fennel seeds and toss with the bread crumbs. Set aside.

Fill a large casserole dish with the cassoulet mixture, cover with the bread crumbs, and drizzle the remaining 1 cup chicken stock over the bread crumbs. Cover and bake for 1 hour.

Remove the cassoulet from the oven and remove the lid. Return the pan to the oven and bake until the bread crumbs are golden brown, about 5 to 8 minutes. Serve hot.

Food for Thought:
Common white beans are widely available. If you like to cook with beans, you may want to check out Rancho Gordo, a local company that specializes in heirloom beans. Rancho Gordo grows a large assortment of varieties in limited quantities in order to offer the best and freshest beans possible (see Sources, page 319).

Serves 6

Method: Confit

Confit (pronounced "kon-FEE") is a French cooking method and one of the oldest ways to preserve food. The food is salted, immersed in a substance (fat or olive oil), and slowly cooked. The result is tender, moist, and extremely flavorful meat. Sealed and stored in a cool place, confit can last for up to 6 months. This method is a specialty of southwestern France where goose, duck, and pork are most often used.

We're known for our Duck Confit, a staple we keep on our menu year-round. Our guests are crazy for the flavorful, tender duck meat, but we've also tried confit of rabbit, which adds extra flavor and moisture to the rabbit meat. (See page 88 for the recipe.)

Chocolate Pots du Crème

Wind Gap Wines Syrah, Griffin's Lair Vineyard, Sonoma Coast, California
Wellington Vineyards Old Vine Port, Sonoma Valley, California
Domaine Madeloc Pierre Gaillard, Banyuls, France

Chocolate Pots du Crème can be made up to a few days ahead, however, if you lack self-control you may want to double this recipe so that you have enough when it comes time to serve your guests! Delicious warm or cold, our Chocolate Pots du Crème will cheer up any rainy day. For a quick variation, drizzle some Italian cherry juice over the whipped cream.

1 cup whole milk
¾ cup heavy cream
7 ounces bittersweet chocolate, roughly chopped
1 teaspoon pure vanilla extract
6 large egg yolks
⅓ cup sugar

Preheat the oven to 350°F.

Place the milk and cream in a saucepan and bring to a boil. Remove from the heat. Add the chocolate and vanilla, cover, and allow the chocolate to melt. In a large bowl, whisk the egg yolks and sugar. Remove any foam. Stir the chocolate mixture until smooth and slowly whisk it into the egg mixture. Strain the mixture and chill it in the refrigerator until cool, about 1 hour.

Place six 4-ounce ramekins in a baking pan. Fill the ramekins with the chocolate mixture and pour boiling water into the baking pan, about two thirds up the side. Cover the pan with foil and bake for about 1 hour or until just set. Eat the pots du crème straight from the oven or refrigerate for at least 2 hours and then serve.

Food for Thought:
Serve with a dollop of crème fraîche or whipped cream.

Serves 6

VELLA CHEESE COMPANY, SPECIAL SELECT DRY JACK

AUTUMN № 6

REGION:	Sonoma Valley, California
MILK:	cow
PROCESS:	pasteurized
PRODUCTION:	cooked, pressed, hard, rubbed
AFFINAGE:	minimum of 1 year
FLAVOR:	rich, sweet, balance of salt & acidity, hay
AROMA:	subtle, nutty
TEXTURE:	firm, grainy, brittle
SIMILAR CHEESES:	Pecorino, Parmigiano-Reggiano
PAIRINGS:	California Olive Ranch Extra-Virgin Olive Oil
	Matiz Fig & Walnut cake
	San Giacomo Saba
	June Taylor Pear & Fennel Butter
	Candied Pumpkin Seeds (page 315)
NOTES:	This is a special cheese that has been rubbed with vegetable oil, cocoa, and black pepper to protect the cheese during aging. Visitor's love to visit the Vella Cheese Company which is just a couple of blocks off the Sonoma Plaza.

Entrée
Mushroom Soup, Madeira Cream

Plat
Braised Breast of Veal, Chickpea Fries

Dessert
*Heirloom Apple Galette,
Fennel Caramel*

Fromage
Morbier

Mushroom Soup, Madeira Cream

Bonny Doon Vineyard DEWN Cinsault, California
Yalumba Viognier, Eden Valley, Australia

When the fall wild mushrooms hit the stores and markets, we immediately want to incorporate mushrooms into every dish. The wonderful variety and earthy flavors add their own personality to everything from omelettes and risotto to pizza and pasta. We use some everyday mushroom varieties in this recipe, but if you can't resist the beautiful seasonal fungi then substitute accordingly. Mix it up a bit and add some wild mushroom trimmings as a soup garnish or to other dishes such as Pot Roast or Braised Short Ribs. Just remember that mushrooms cook down significantly, so while you may think you have too many, you probably don't.

For the soup:
½ cup dried porcinis

4 tablespoons (½ stick) unsalted butter
1 small yellow onion, chopped
3 celery stalks, heart leaves reserved, chopped
1 small carrot, chopped
1 large leek, white part only, cleaned and chopped
2 shallots, diced
4 garlic cloves, crushed
½ pound shiitake mushrooms, cleaned and chopped
1 pound crimini mushrooms, cleaned and chopped
4 tablespoons blended oil
1 cup dry white wine
Herb sachet (dried thyme, bay leaves, and black
    peppercorns)
½ cup heavy cream
Salt and white pepper to taste

For the Madeira Cream:
1 tablespoon unsalted butter
1 shallot, diced
1 garlic clove, diced
1 cup Madeira
1 sprig fresh thyme
½ cup heavy cream
Salt and white pepper to taste
Chopped fresh herbs, for garnish (optional)

To prepare the soup:
Soak the dried porcinis in a bowl filled with 1 cup of hot water for about 10 minutes. Melt the butter in a medium saucepan over medium-low heat. Add the onion, celery, carrot, leek, shallots, and garlic and sauté until the vegetables are soft, about 7 minutes. Stir the vegetables occasionally to prevent browning.

In another sauté pan cook the mushrooms in the blended oil over high heat until browned. Combine the mushrooms and the reconstituted porcinis (with their liquid) to the other vegetables. Add the white wine and reduce until the liquid has almost completely evaporated, about 3 to 4 minutes. Add 6 cups of water and the herb sachet and season with salt and pepper to taste. Bring to a boil. Reduce the heat and cook until the mushrooms are tender. Take the pan off the heat and remove the sachet. Add the cream and purée the mixture in a food processor or a blender. Strain the mixture through a fine-mesh sieve. Adjust the seasoning with salt and pepper to taste.

To prepare the Madeira Cream:
In a small saucepan heat 1 tablespoon of butter and sauté the shallots and garlic over medium heat. Add the Madeira and thyme and reduce the liquid until the liquid has almost completely evaporated, about 3 to 4 minutes. Add the cream and reduce by half. Season with salt and pepper to taste. Remove the pan from the heat, remove the thyme sprig, and purée the mixture in a food processor or a blender. Strain the mixture through a fine-mesh sieve.

To serve:
Garnish each serving of soup with a spoonful of the Madeira Cream and a few mushroom trimmings or a pinch of chopped fresh herbs, if desired.

Serves 6

Braised Breast of Veal, Chickpea Fries

Lasseter Family Winery "Chemin de Fer" Red Rhône Blend, Sonoma Valley, California
Peay Vineyards "La Bruma" Syrah, Sonoma Coast, California
Grey Stack Cellars "The Folly," Red Rhône Blend, Greywacke Vineyard, Bennett Valley, California

Our chickpea fries are amazing. They're not difficult to make, but timing will prove critical. Make sure you have your pans close at hand when it comes time to spread out the mixture; you will have a short window. This recipe calls for cumin, which gives the fries an unexpected flavor. Other spices and herbs you could try include smoked paprika, garlic, fennel, and saffron. You can also cut the chickpeas in circles or squares instead of fries if you prefer. The chickpea fries need to set for at least four hours or overnight so you may want to start this ahead.

For the veal:

3 pounds boneless veal breast (in one piece)

2 garlic cloves, minced

3 tablespoons chopped fresh herbs (such as rosemary, thyme, and flat-leaf parsley)

¼ cup extra-virgin olive oil

Salt and pepper to taste

5 tablespoons blended oil

1 medium yellow onion, chopped

1 medium carrot, chopped

1 celery stalk, chopped

¼ cup tomato paste

1 cup sherry

1 gallon Veal Stock (page 313, beef broth can be substituted)

For the fries:

4 cups whole milk

1 tablespoon cumin seeds, toasted and ground

1 tablespoon garlic powder

Salt and pepper to taste

3 cups Garbanzo Bean flour, sifted (see Sources, page 318)

2 tablespoons unsalted butter, for serving

2 heads mâche, washed and dried, for garnish

2 tablespoons extra-virgin olive oil, for garnish

To prepare the veal:

Preheat the oven to 350°F.

Place the veal on a table, rib side up. In a small bowl mix together the garlic, herbs, and olive oil. Spread the mixture evenly over meat and season with salt and pepper. Roll the veal tightly and secure with butcher's string.

Place a large Dutch oven or roasting pan over high heat and add the blended oil. Sear the veal on all sides until golden brown, about 4 to 5 minutes per side. Remove the veal from the pan and set aside. Add the onion, carrot, and celery to the pan and cook until the vegetables have browned, about 10 minutes. Add the tomato paste and cook for 3 more minutes. Add the sherry and using a wooden spoon, scrape all the brown bits off the bottom of the pan. Add the veal stock, return the veal to the pan, and bring to a simmer. Cover the pan and place it in the oven. Roast for 2 to 3 hours, turning the veal occasionally until the veal is knife tender. Remove the pan from the oven and let the veal rest until cool enough to handle, about 1 hour. Lower the oven temperature to 200°F.

Remove the veal from the pan and strain the sauce into a saucepan. Bring the sauce to a simmer, skim off excess fat, and reduce it until it lightly coats the back of a spoon, about 15 minutes. Put the veal back in the pan and return it to the warm oven while you cook the fries.

To prepare the fries:

Place a medium saucepan over low heat and combine the milk, 4 cups water, cumin, and garlic powder and season with salt and pepper. Bring the mixture to a boil and whisk in the flour. Cook for 5 minutes, whisking to work out any lumps.

Strain the chickpea mixture into a greased 8 x 8-inch baking pan and chill overnight. Once the mixture cools it will harden enough to cut into ½-inch x 4-inch fries. Set aside. Place a large pot over high heat and add 3 inches of blended oil. Heat the oil to 375°F. Fry the chickpeas in small batches until golden brown. Remove the fries to a plate lined with paper towels and season lightly with salt. Set aside.

Slice the veal into ½-inch pieces (you should get 12 to 14 pieces).

To serve:

Distribute the fries equally among 6 plates. Remove the veal from the sauce and place 2 pieces on each plate. Heat the sauce to a simmer, whisk in the 2 tablespoons butter, and drizzle the sauce over the veal slices. Toss the mâche in the olive oil and garnish the plates with the mâche.

Serves 6

autumn

Chanterelles

This flute-shaped wild mushroom is the wonder of the mushroom world. If their bright yellow to orange color doesn't woo you, the aroma of apricots and the spicy, nutty flavor of the chanterelle certainly will.

Fresh chanterelles are available September through February on the West Coast, and usually throughout the summer months on the East Coast though they're also imported from Europe. This is a meaty mushroom, so cut it into fairly large pieces to maximize flavor, and be careful not to overcook them, or they will toughen up. The flavor of chanterelles is best cooked; they are not pleasant when raw.

Chanterelles make a fabulous addition to sauces, a vegetarian side dish, or an accompaniment to chicken or other meats. We love them simply sautéed with butter and garlic, in omelets, or even as a pizza topping. (They're also loaded with beta carotene, so they're very nutritious.) They're also available dried.

If you're buying fresh chanterelles, look for those that appear plump and feel spongy and ignore any with shriveled or dry caps. As with all mushrooms, don't wash them before use; simply brush them lightly with a cloth to remove any dirt. Store them in a paper bag (not plastic) in the refrigerator for a day or two, but it's better to cook them immediately after purchase.

Mushrooms

We rely on mushrooms for so many things: to add depth to a sauce, to add a meaty flavor to vegetarian dishes, or to add a contrasting texture to a recipe. Their earthy, woodsy flavor is sublime. These edible fungi are truly a wonder of nature. While they were once found only in the wild, many varieties are now cultivated (shiitake, crimini). We use both wild and cultivated mushrooms in our restaurants, but the anticipation of waiting for a certain seasonal variety is one of my favorite parts of seasonal cooking. Certain types remain only in the wild: truffles, cèpes, and chanterelles must be foraged. Each mushroom has its own personality and thrives in a particular environment.

Morels are a favorite spring wild mushroom of ours; they arrive at the restaurant in mid to late March, and we use them as much as we can until they disappear in June. Their earthy, nutty, smoky flavor is unparalleled and their honeycombed cap makes them unforgettable. They thrive in areas that have recently been burned and under oak trees, old elms, and abandoned apple orchards. A few mushroom growers have been successful in cultivating morels, but not in any quantity. Morels don't like wet weather and if it's particularly rainy, we end up paying more for morels because they have absorbed the water and weigh much more than usual! They usually grow singly, rather than in groups, and should not been eaten raw (they're toxic raw).

In our last book we introduced you to Stephen, the Mushroom Man. He was our go-to guy that would show up at the back door selling whatever he had foraged that day. In the years since we started purchasing mushrooms this way, there have been many more mushroom foragers looking to sell their goods. We are very careful to purchase mushrooms only from expert foragers. Because there are so many mushroom species, it's very important to know what you are buying. We also look closely at the water content of the mushrooms—too wet and they will not be as flavorful; if too dry, they could be last year's.

We prefer fresh, but you can find imported canned morels in some specialty stores. Dried morels are widely available and have a more intense flavor than fresh.

Buying local mushrooms is ideal because you'll know the provenance and they will, of course, be fresh. Choose mushrooms that are plump and avoid any bruised or soggy specimens. Gently brush off any excess dirt (never wash them; they will absorb the water) and trim the very end of the stalk. Store mushrooms in a paper bag (never plastic) in the refrigerator for a few days. Dried mushrooms stored in an airtight container will last six months.

We use mushrooms in literally hundreds of dishes: sautéed, grilled, braised, and as a pizza topping. The trick is to maximize their flavor and choose complementary flavors. Virtually any herb brings out the flavor of a mushroom (we love thyme and rosemary), and butter or olive oil is always a simple yet delicious choice.

Soup

A bowl of homemade soup is a wonderfully satisfying dish no matter what the season is. We love thick, rich soups in the autumn and winter and bright, light soups (often chilled) in spring and summer. Most of our soups are simply vegetable purées using the freshest vegetables we can find. Soup is such an easy way to highlight fresh produce and use up any veggies in your refrigerator. Because of this, it's essential to use the best vegetables and ingredients you can find. Armed with a good, heavy-bottomed soup pot, it's easy to create your own homemade soups.

The starting point for any soup is the liquid, from water, broth, or stock to milk and cream. The flavor base almost always includes onions, celery, and carrots, and sometimes leeks and garlic are thrown in there, too. (Make sure to chop everything in a uniform size to ensure even cooking.) This creates the second layer of flavor, so it's important to sauté them slowly to soften the texture and blend the flavors. Cook, stirring occasionally, until the vegetables are soft but not browning, about 5 minutes. Salt soup as our chefs do, in layers. Add some salt to the onion mixture and other vegetables as you cook them. If you're preparing a soup with meat, cook the meat separately and make sure it is well seasoned before it goes into the pot. And, most importantly, taste it before serving and add salt as needed. Finishing salts are a wonderful final layer of flavor.

We love the texture of a puréed soup, particularly for many of our vegetable soups. Use a good blender or immersion blender and purée in batches. You can purée half the soup and add it back to the pot if you want to preserve some of the texture.

It's a nice touch to add a bit of something fresh right before serving, including fresh herbs, fresh citrus juice, or a dollop of heavy cream or yogurt. To add texture, we love topping our soups with croutons, crispy bacon or prosciutto, or minced fresh apples.

Heirloom Apple Galette, Fennel Caramel

Warre's 10 Year Premium Tawny Port, Portugal
Blandy's "Alvada," 5 Year Old Madeira, Portugal

Several varieties of apples work brilliantly in this galette: Rome Beauty, William's Pride, Crispin, and Gravenstein are our favorites. Many apples are interchangeable, but some are just right for eating while others are better suited for baking. For a savory twist, we added fennel seed to the caramel. To really gild the lily, serve the galette with caramel gelato and a pinch of Maldon Sea Salt.

For the galette:
½ cup brandy
1¼ cups sugar
1 lemon, quartered
1 cinnamon stick
1 star anise
3 large apples, peeled, cut in half, and cored
1 sheet puff pastry (10 x 15-inch or sized to make six 3-inch rounds)
1 large egg

For the caramel:
½ cup sugar
½ cup heavy cream
1 tablespoon unsalted butter
¼ teaspoon fennel seed, toasted and ground

6 scoops vanilla ice cream, for serving

To prepare the galette:
Preheat the oven to 375°F. Line a baking sheet with parchment paper and set aside.
Combine the brandy, sugar, and 1½ cups water in a medium saucepan and cook over medium heat until the sugar has dissolved. Add the lemon, cinnamon, star anise, and apples and simmer until the apples are tender, about 5 to 7 minutes. Remove the apples from the sauce and set aside to cool. Strain the mixture and return the liquid to the pan. Reduce the mixture until it heavily coats a spoon, about 5 to 7 minutes.

Place the apples cut side down and slice the apples crosswise halfway into ¼-inch thick slices, keeping the apple intact. Cut six 3-inch rounds out of the puff pastry sheet. Place the puff pastry rounds on the baking sheet. Place the flat side of the apple on top and drizzle the apple with the reduced poaching syrup. In a bowl beat the egg with 2 tablespoons of water until light and pale and lightly brush the pastry edges with the egg wash. Bake until the apples and the pastry are golden brown, about 15 to 18 minutes.

To prepare the caramel:
Heat the sugar and 2 tablespoons of water in a non-reactive pan stirring constantly until the sugar is caramelized (amber colored), about 5 minutes. Remove the sugar from the heat and add the cream, butter, and fennel seed. Stir until well incorporated. The caramel can be made ahead and kept refrigerated for up to 1 week. To reheat, place the caramel in a small saucepan and heat until warm and melted.

To serve:
Place each warm galette on a plate, add a scoop of vanilla ice cream, and drizzle with the Fennel Caramel.

Serves 6

MORBIER

REGION:	Franche Comte, France
MILK:	cow
PROCESS:	raw or pasteurized
PRODUCTION:	uncooked, pressed, semi-hard, natural rind
AFFINAGE:	at least 2 months, salt-rubbed in a humid cellar
FLAVOR:	mild, nutty aftertaste, sweet, supple
AROMA:	floral, hay, mushroom
TEXTURE:	gentle, smooth, supple
SIMILAR CHEESES:	Raclette, Comté, Fontina
PAIRINGS:	the girl & the fig Red Onion Confit Quince & Apple Figs & Black Tea Preserves Sonoma Syrup Black Currant Berry Drizzler
NOTES:	Morbier was originally made for the personal consumption for the Comté cheesemakers. The decorative vegetable ash in the center is tasteless, but stands as a reminder of the traditional methods.

autumn

winter

The end of autumn and the beginning of winter is a seamless transition in Sonoma. The brilliant orange and red leaves cling to the tree branches as the winter rains arrive in mid-December. Towering oaks with fluorescent green moss line the roads. The vineyards seem naked: the brown, gnarled grapevines have shed their last leaves and will remain bare until spring budbreak. People don't think California has seasons, but our winter is very specific—damp and rainy—yet we're often outside enjoying the cold sunshine. The gray clouds over the hills are heavy with rain. The rain can last a day, a week, even a month, keeping the grass an emerald green. Cold nights mean frost the next morning, the green fields shimmering silver in the morning light. Even the animals are bundled up: thick winter coats cover the goats, sheep, and horses that roam the hillsides. The valley slows down after the hectic fall season; harvest is over and everyone can breathe a collective sigh of relief.

The winter chill begs for comfort foods; in winter we like to serve things that warm your soul and your appetite. Before business slows in January, we stay busy through the holidays with festive groups at lunch and celebratory dinners right through New Year's. Stews, roasts, and braises fill the menu and are served with big red wines that sell like crazy on cold winter nights. Winter gives us a chance to use cuts of meats that aren't necessarily well known but that are great in soups and stews. We turn to heartier soups made from root vegetables such as parsnip, kohlrabi that are made daily. The lighter autumn vegetables are replaced with their winter counterparts: leafy Swiss chard, purple-black kale, parsnips, onions, and beets. Fragrant rosemary flourishes, and we snip it off in large bunches for stews and soups. Hazelnuts add a crunch to salads and soups and become the star ingredient in winter desserts. Local pears add a tanginess and texture to salads and are incorporated into sweets like a Pear Hazelnut Tart.

Eating "in season" allows us to draw from very California-specific winter ingredients. Dungeness crab, found only in the Pacific Ocean, starts arriving in mid-November, and we serve the sweet meaty crab in many ways: crab cakes, pastas, and salads. The bright, slightly sweet flavor of Meyer lemons, a cross between an orange and a lemon that is available through the winter months, are transformed into cocktails, desserts, and sauces. As winter starts transitioning into spring, purple lavender buds bloom through the dreary winter months, giving color to the landscape but adding flavor to Lavender Crème Brûlée and Lavender Sorbet.

Last but not least, winter in wine country means olive oil. We use olive oil in virtually every dish and love the flavor and depth it can bring to an ingredient (or just a piece of fresh bread). Depending on the weather, the olives are harvested between late November and mid-December and pressed in December. Local olive presses like The Olive Press and Figone offer a community harvest, where locals can bring their olives to press and bottle. We started pressing our own olives in 2009, and the grassy golden oil was so delicious it inspired us to try it every year. (For more on our olive oil, see page 17.)

We're fortunate to have a winter climate that provides us with so many ingredients and a season that gives us a chance to slow down just a bit before the flurry of spring and summer arrive.

winter cheese

Milk produced in winter is much different than milk from other seasons. It lacks the intensity of fresh spring milk, but winter milk has a higher fat content and a very special richness. While dairies in other parts of the U.S. struggle through the harsh winter months, here in Sonoma we only have rain and mud to contend with. Winter grasses are plentiful and the animals grow thick, shaggy coats to protect themselves from the winter frost.

In other regions, dairy farmers feed their livestock the stored, dried hay and grains harvested earlier in the year, and the animals live inside sheds or barns. Silage is often fed to the animals, which is basically fermented hay. Silage affects the flavor of the milk and produces cheeses that are rich and slightly sweeter. Some cheesemakers feel it has a negative effect, and many European regions prohibit the use of silage as feed. The Consorzio del Formaggio Parmigiano in Italy, a group of about 600 dairies that sets the standards for Parmigiano-Reggiano, forbids the use of silage, as do the Swiss cheesemakers who make true Swiss cheese, and the French in the Comté AOC.

France in particular is known for their winter cheeses, including Pont-l'Evêque, Camembert, and Vacherin Mont d'Or from Haute-Savoie, which are high in fat, runny, and truly spectacular. They appear in stores in late November or early December and are usually available through February.

Some cheeses are best in winter even though they are made with summer milk. For example, the famous blue cheese Stilton from England is made in summer but ages for about nine weeks, so it is best to eat it in late autumn and early winter. Europe has a tradition of winter cheeses, using spring and summer milk to make cheese that would sustain the locals through the long, harsh winters.

(Clockwise from top left; Le Brebiou, Winchester Gouda, Point Reyes Original Blue, Fiscalini Cheddar, Camellia, St. George).

MINI CROQUE MONSIEUR

Our Croque Monsieur has been on the menu since the day we opened. About a year ago, we started making bite-sized versions for our catering events. Who doesn't like a combination of French Toast and the best grilled cheese and ham sandwich ever? Experiment with different cheeses or add mustard or a dipping sauce for variety.

8 slices brioche (½-inch thick slices)

8 ounces Joe Matos St. George cheese, thinly sliced (see Sources, page 318, cheddar cheese can be substituted)

8 ounces thinly sliced jambon ham (country ham can be substituted)

3 large eggs

1 cup heavy cream

Pinch of nutmeg

Pinch of salt and white pepper

4 tablespoons unsalted butter

Chopped chives, for garnish
Pickled Shallots (page 313), for garnish

Preheat the oven to 350°F.

Assemble 4 sandwiches with the brioche, cheese, and ham. Beat the eggs, cream, nutmeg, salt, and pepper together in a bowl. Heat a large ovenproof sauté pan over medium heat. Melt 2 tablespoons of the butter in the pan.

Soak the sandwiches in the egg mixture. Place the sandwiches face down and cook them on one side until well browned, about 4 minutes. Add the remaining butter to the pan, turn the sandwiches over, and place the pan in the oven for 8 to 10 minutes or until the cheese has melted completely and the sandwiches are well browned on both sides. Remove the sandwiches from the oven and cut each sandwich into 4 to 6 pieces. To serve, garnish each sandwich with a sprinkling of chives and a spoonful of Pickled Shallots.

Makes 16 to 20 nibbles

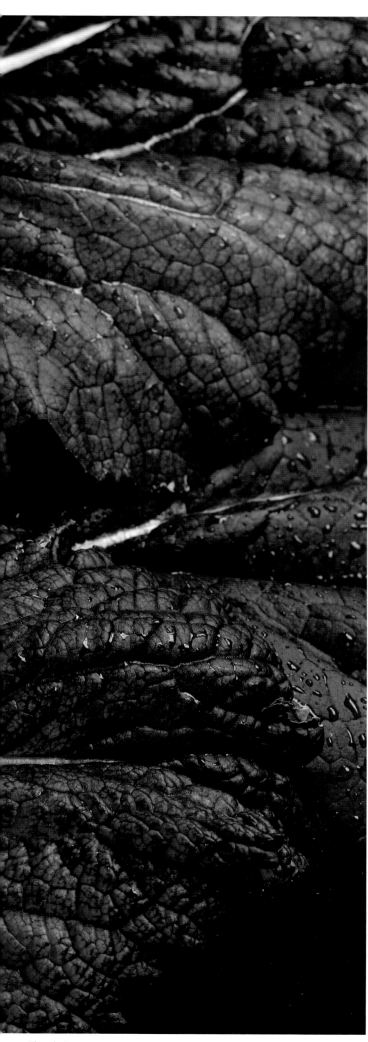

winter menus

Entrée
Honey-Glazed Winter Squash

Plat
Wild Boar Ragoût, Polenta Cakes

Dessert
Espresso Cheesecake

Fromage
Point Reyes Original Blue

Honey-Glazed Winter Squash

Cyril Mares Mas des Bressades, Costières de Nîmes, France
Monte Oton Garnacha, Campo de Borja, Spain

We originally created this recipe for the girl & the gaucho, our Latin/tapas restaurant that was open in early 2000. We've revised the recipe a bit, removing the dried chili and adding bourbon (a great idea from our friend Merrilee). At ESTATE, we prepare this dish in the wood-fired oven. We have edited the instructions to use the broiler, however, feel free to use your wood-fired oven; you'll get an incredible layer of flavor from the wood and the fire. Winter squash comes in different varieties and sizes. For this recipe, about 3 to 4 pounds of squash should suffice.

1 Delicata squash, sliced in half and seeds removed

1 medium Acorn squash, sliced in half and seeds removed

1 small Butternut squash, peeled, sliced in half and seeds removed

2 tablespoons extra-virgin olive oil

Salt and pepper to taste

2 tablespoons unsalted butter

¼ cup honey

2 tablespoons brandy or bourbon (optional)

¼ cup grated ricotta salata cheese

3 tablespoons fresh marjoram leaves

3 tablespoons Candied Pumpkin Seeds (page 315), for garnish

2 teaspoons Maldon Sea Salt, for garnish

Preheat the oven to 350°F.

Slice the Delicata and Acorn squash into ½-inch-thick quarter rounds. Cut the butternut squash into ½-inch pieces.

Toss the squash with the olive oil, salt and pepper and roast for 15 minutes or until just soft. Let cool to room temperature.

Set the broiler to high.

Place a large sauté pan over medium heat and melt the butter with the honey and brandy. Add the squash, mix well, and cook until the honey begins to thicken. Place the pan under the broiler until squash begin to caramelize, about 5 to 8 minutes.

Remove the squash, place it on a serving platter and sprinkle with the grated cheese, marjoram, pumpkin seeds, and sea salt.

Serves 6

Honey

Rich, golden honey is a true gift from nature. Bees produce the naturally sweet substance in a beehive after collecting nectar from local flowers. The color and flavor of honey depends on the flower blossom, and there are more than 300 types in the U.S. alone. Just as with wine, each different honey varietal is distinctive and certain types of honey are only available in certain areas—it all depends on where the flowers grow. The most common types of honey are alfalfa, clover, and orange blossom.

We use honey in an array of dishes at the restaurants, including cocktails and desserts (as a substitute for sugar) or simply drizzled over cheese. One of our most prized local honeys comes from an amazing local farm called Hector's Honey, where Hector Alvarez has been keeping bees for years. He first places the beehives in the apple and almond orchards to pollinate the trees, and then moves them to his flower garden to gather the nectar. His honey has an unmistakable gentle flavor. Hector's honey can be found at the Sonoma farmers markets on Tuesdays and Fridays. He does not have an online retail outlet, so you will need to come visit the farmers market to get your supply!

Wild Boar Ragoût, Polenta Cakes

Loxton Cellars Syrah, Archer Vineyard, Russian River, California
d'Arenberg "The Dead Arm" Shiraz, McLaren Vale, Australia
Tallulah Wines Syrah, Del Rio Vineyard, Rogue Valley, Oregon

With the recent pig craze, boar has taken a step up the food chain. Gamier than most of the other commercially available pigs, braised boar has a rich, intricate flavor. Boar is so popular that one January we were unable to get it from any of our reliable suppliers. Even though we recommend braised pork shoulder as a substitute, it's still not the same! In the winter, the variety of rich greens are abundant and a side of Wilted Greens (page 314) would be a nice addition to this dish. Boar can be pre-ordered from your butcher. Give them as much time as you can so they can find the best product available in your area.

For the boar:

½ cup olive oil

3 pounds wild boar shoulder, divided into 3
    large pieces (pork shoulder can be substituted)

1 leek, white part only, sliced

4 celery stalks, roughly chopped

2 large carrots, roughly chopped

1 medium yellow onion, quartered

1 head garlic, cut in half

2 tablespoons all-purpose flour

4 cups red wine

2 cups Chicken Stock (page 313)

1 bay leaf

4 sprigs fresh thyme

Salt and freshly cracked black pepper to taste

For the polenta cakes:

2 cups whole milk

4 tablespoons (½ stick) unsalted butter

Salt and white pepper to taste

1 cup polenta

½ cup grated Parmigiano-Reggiano cheese

To prepare the boar:

Preheat the oven to 350°F.

Heat the ¼ cup olive oil in a large casserole dish or braising pan and sear the meat on medium heat until well caramelized, about 5 to 7 minutes per side. Remove the boar from the pan and set aside. Add the leek, celery, carrots, onion, and garlic and cook for another 5 to 7 minutes until browned. Add the flour and mix well to incorporate. Return the boar to the pan. Add the red wine, chicken stock, bay leaf, and thyme. Increase the heat and bring the mixture to a boil. Turn off the heat and cover the pan. Place the pan in the oven and braise for 2 hours.

Remove the pan from the oven and let the boar cool for 20 minutes. Remove the boar from the pan, cover it with foil, and set aside. Strain the stock using a fine-mesh sieve. Pour the stock back into the pan, return it to the stove, and reduce by half over high heat, about 8 to 10 minutes.

Meanwhile, cut the boar into ½-inch cubes and add them to the sauce. Return the pan to the oven and cook for 1 more hour. Remove the pan from the oven, place it back on the stove over low heat, and simmer for about 5 minutes. Turn off the heat and season with salt and pepper to taste.

To prepare the polenta cakes:

Line a 9 x 12-inch baking pan with parchment paper and set aside.
Combine 2 cups of water, the milk, and butter together in a large saucepot. Season with the salt and bring to a simmer over medium heat. While stirring with a wire whisk, slowly add the polenta and beat it into the liquid. Simmer and continue to stir until the polenta has thickened, about 10 minutes. Add the cheese, stir to combine, and adjust the seasoning if necessary. Pour the polenta into the baking pan, let it stand at room temperature until cool, and then refrigerate for at least 2 hours or overnight. Cut the cold polenta into 6 rounds using a 3- to 4-inch ring mold or cookie cutter and set aside.

To serve:

Heat the remaining olive oil in a sauté pan over medium heat and sauté the polenta cakes until browned on both sides, about 5 minutes. Place a polenta cake in the middle of each plate. Spoon some of the braised boar shoulder and the gravy over the top and serve.

Serves 6

Method: Braising

We are very fond of braising at our restaurants; it works for a wide range of meat and vegetables, helps retain flavor, and creates a very tender dish. Certain types of fish, such as swordfish and halibut, are suitable for braising, too. Braising is a moist-heat cooking method in which the ingredient is first seared in fat and then slowly cooked in a closed vessel with a small amount of liquid, either on the stove or in the oven.

The best equipment for braising is a Dutch oven, a large sauté pan with a lid, a slow cooker, or pressure cooker. (Le Creuset makes a line of enameled pots and pans that can go from the stove to the oven, and they are great for braising.)

Tough cuts of meat such as brisket, short ribs, and pork shoulder are particularly suited for braising because the long, slow cooking breaks down the tough connective tissue into collagen.

Over time, the moisture and heat build and the collagen dissolves into gelatin. Eventually, the fibers relax and absorb the melted fat and melted gelatin, resulting in very tender meat. Don't bother braising a lean cut from the loin area; the meat is already tender and has little fat or connective tissue. With vegetables, braising breaks down the cellulose and stretches the starches, resulting in tender veggies.

The best vegetables for braising are heartier veggies such as winter squashes, onions, carrots, turnips, Brussels sprouts, and cabbage. Because vegetables usually take less time to cook, add any vegetables to the braising pot after the meat has started to cook.

Braising is a great method for home cooks because after searing, you don't have to babysit your food—the oven or stove does all the work. The cozy feeling it creates, with the delicious aromas wafting through the house, is an added bonus.

Boar

We've added boar to our menu in the last few years, and it always surprises our guests with its rich, earthy flavor. Wild boar used to be eaten by game hunters and it's now farmed in Texas; the farmers capture the young boar and raise them on farms. (Both male and female boar are raised; the males are castrated, so there is no flavor difference between them.) When we can't get boar, we substitute pork shoulder. It's not as gamey as boar but has a similar texture.

The age of the boar affects the appearance of the meat: young boars provide pinker meat while meat from older animals will be darker in color. Boar is a lean meat, so ask your butcher for a cut that still has fat on it. Roasting and braising are the best ways to prepare boar. Only the tougher cuts, such as the leg, loin, and flank, need to be marinated before cooking.

Espresso Cheesecake

Buena Vista Winery Syrah Port, Ramal Vineyards, Carneros, California

If you have an affinity for coffee this may become your favorite cheesecake. The bitter flavor of the coffee combined with the rich and creamy cake is almost like having a cafè latte on a plate!

1 cup plus 2 tablespoons graham cracker crumbs

3 tablespoons unsalted butter, melted

1 cup sugar

1 pound cream cheese, softened

2 large eggs

1½ tablespoons cornstarch

1 vanilla bean, scraped

⅓ cup crème fraîche

⅓ cup heavy cream

¼ cup brewed espresso, at room temperature

2 tablespoons ground instant espresso

1 teaspoon salt

Whipped cream, for serving (optional)

To prepare the crusts:

Preheat the oven 350°F.

In a large bowl combine 1 cup of the graham cracker crumbs with the butter. Distribute the graham cracker crumbs equally among six greased 4 x 2-inch ring molds. Place the ring molds on a baking sheet. Tamp down the crust, using the bottom of a glass, until firm and bake for 5 to 7 minutes until browned on the edges. Remove the crusts from the oven and let them cool to room temperature. Lower the oven temperature to 325°F.

To prepare the filling:

Place the sugar and cream cheese in the mixing bowl of a mixer fitted with a paddle attachment. Mix until smooth on medium speed and add the eggs, cornstarch, vanilla bean, crème fraîche, cream, brewed espresso, instant espresso, and salt. Mix until smooth.

Pour the mixture into the ring molds and bake for 15 to 20 minutes or until set. Refrigerate for at least 1 hour or overnight. The filling can be made up to 1 day ahead.

To serve:

Set each cheesecake on a plate and sprinkle 1 teaspoon of graham cracker crumbs around and on top each of the cakes. Add a dollop of whipped cream, if desired.

Serves 6

POINT REYES FARMSTEAD CHEESE COMPANY ORIGINAL BLUE

WINTER № 1

REGION:	Point Reyes, California
MILK:	Holstein cow
PROCESS:	raw
PRODUCTION:	homogenized, uncooked, unpressed, soft cheese with veins of blue mold
AFFINAGE:	5 to 6 months
FLAVOR:	robust, buttermilk tang, sharp, elegant
AROMA:	medium, fruity
TEXTURE:	moist, dense, creamy, soft
SIMILAR CHEESES:	Maytag Blue, Roquefort, Bleu d'Auvergne
PAIRINGS:	Sonoma Syrup Meyer Lemon Drizzler LouLou's Garden Pickled Cherries Panevino No. 6 Grissini Muscat grapes, Chestnut Honey
NOTES:	The production facility is fueled entirely by the methane gas that rises from the farm's collected cow manure, showing another example of the Giacomini Family's commitment to sustainability.

winter

MANO FORMATE *Coppa*

Variety of MANO FORMATE salumi

MANO FORMATE
Salumi

One of our newest projects at the restaurant is MANO FORMATE, our housemade salumi. What the French call charcuterie, the Italians call salumi, which means cured meat. Ten years ago, the only salumi you could get was from a specialty supplier, usually imported, but cured meats have taken off in the past three years; many chefs and restaurants around the U.S. are making their own. With the opening of ESTATE, we increased our cured meat production as part of our menu concept. With the success and quality of the few items we started to make, we realized that we could produce all of our cured meats for the company.

Now we make our own pancetta, prosciutto, sausage, salame, and bacon. "My first attempt to make salumi was in 1998 when I tried to cure my own prosciutto leg," says John. "I cured it for a year in the walk-in, and no one would try it but me. Their loss; it was delicious." After that first successful foray into cured meats, and lots of studying, experimenting, and trial and error, we've perfected our salumi process. John, along with our chefs Dustin and Uriel, devote one day each week to salumi production and we go through between 100 and 200 pounds of pork (10 to 20 bellies) each week based on the level of business.

Salumi is air-dried, salted, cooked, smoked, or processed with a combination of methods. John has developed recipes and ratios for each type of salumi, though "salumi is essentially controlled spoilage," says John, "but you spoil it your way."

Chef John checking on salumi fermentation.

There are four elements that are crucial in making any type of salumi. The quality of the meat is the most important factor. Using the right temperatures at the right time is the next key component; if it's too hot the risk of bacteria skyrockets, and the fat literally melts. Fat is like butter—once it melts you can't put it back together and it's useless. (If you're grinding your own meat and it starts to smear like butter, the meat has gotten too warm and you should start over.) Because of this, we keep everything extremely cold; we even freeze the grinder attachment. Our favorite time to make salumi is on cold winter days; that should tell you how important the temperature is!

Balancing the pH (acidity) levels is also critical, because this is what prevents spoilage. Fat is another critical ingredient. We use back fat, and the fat ratio changes according to the type of salumi. The fat should be fresh. If you're making your own salumi, you can buy fat from any reputable butcher. John age-cures the fat (called lardo) and uses it to top pizzas and salads. A high-quality lardo should melt in your mouth.

Finally, the use of nitrates and nitrites are important to prevent botulism, spoilage, and to enhance color and flavor. These are chemical compounds that are frequently used in salumi products. They come in synthetic form but they also occur naturally in vegetables like carrots and spinach. (Celery has the highest level of naturally occurring nitrates, and celery juice is the most common ingredient in nitrate-free meat products.)

We believe that to get a premium product you have to start with good meat. We use primarily Niman Ranch beef and pork as well as pork from Devil's Gulch Ranch, about an hour away from the restaurants in Marin County. We use a variety of breeds, knowing that the breed will change the flavor the same way the feed might. Flavorings are where the salumi maker can get creative. We only use dried herbs and stay fairly traditional in the Italian sense, selecting fennel and anise seeds, black pepper, and pimentón, depending on the recipe. Fresh herbs are never used because of their moisture content, which increases the risk of bacteria.

Here's an abbreviated step-by-step guide to our salumi products:

Applewood Smoked Bacon: Bacon is seasoned and smoked pork belly. Before we smoke the bacon, we season the pork belly with salt, brown sugar, and spices for four days. On the fifth day, we remove the bacon from the cure, wash it, and then hang it for another day. We use a home smoker loaded with applewood to smoke our bacon. The bellies hang in the smoker for two hours, and we make sure the temperature doesn't get too high or the fat will melt and make a mess. The bacon is then transferred to a 275°F oven for about two

Samples of our salumi.

and a half hours until the internal temperature reaches 130°F. Then it's ready to eat! Fresh bacon, wrapped tightly in plastic wrap, freezes nicely for up to four months.

Pancetta: Pancetta is a salt-cured salumi made from a pig's belly. It's essentially the Italian answer to bacon, except that it isn't smoked. We make our pancetta both in slabs and rolled. We rub the bellies with the cure mix (which includes sugar and dried spices such as coriander, mace, nutmeg, thyme, and anise seed) and place them in a plastic bag in the refrigerator for five days. We remove the pancetta from the bag, rub the bellies again, put them back in plastic bags, and refrigerate for another five days. We scrape off the salt mixture, wipe the bellies clean, and lay the bellies in the refrigerator for two more days, uncovered. Then they're ready to be rolled and hung. They will hang for at least three weeks before they are usable.

The salt rub draws out moisture and the result is a sliceable, somewhat moist, and very flavorful meat. You can eat pancetta raw because it's cured, but we dice it and sauté it for salads and pizzas. Pancetta stays fresh in the freezer, so you can keep it on hand to add to salads, soups, stews, or simply a pan of roasted vegetables.

Salami: Salami is an Italian dried sausage, a generic term for pork that is encased and fermented (salami is the plural form of salame). Making salami takes many steps. Among the many steps in making salami include: grinding the meat, stuffing the meat in casings, inoculating, fermenting, and then aging.

We start by measuring the ingredients with a keen eye for accuracy. Trimming the meat is crucial to a high-quality product; you have to cut out the silver skin to get beautiful textured salami. The trimmed meat is transferred to a meat grinder and ground to the size and texture for the particular salami that is being made. The meat is than transferred to a work surface where we add the seasonings (pimentón, saba, oregano) and than we use our hands to work the meat. It's similar to making bread: you have to work it enough but not too much. Certain meats bind more than others, which affects the texture.

The ground meat is then fed into casings. We use a combination of collagen and natural casings (we get ours from butcherandpacker.com; see Sources, page 318). The key with casing salami is eliminating any air pockets. The air pockets will create imperfections, which can affect fermentation, taste, and texture. We always save a small amount of the mixture from each batch as a "test case" to monitor fermentation and pH levels, which we enter into our Salumi logbook for quality control.

Salami production relies on bacteria, just like in cheese, and the white film on the outside of salami

Chef Dustin butchering a Devil's Gulch pig for salumi.

***MANO FORMATE** Lonzo*

is actually a thin layer of mold (like the bloom on cheese). The mold can be white or blue-green and both are completely harmless. "It's all about the bacteria and mold cultures," says John. The bacteria is essential for transforming the meat and creating the texture and flavor notes, while the mold assists as a flavor enhancer and acts as a natural regulator for the outside of the salami. As John notes, the Italians never inoculated their meat; they relied on wild bacteria and mold that was naturally found in their meat cellars, much like wine.

We converted an old baking proof box into our salami fermenter. The temperature is set to 75 to 85°F; (depending on the type of salami), the perfect environment for what John calls "controlled spoilage." Temperature is crucial; too hot and the fat will melt, and the salami will cook. If it's too cold, the fermentation process won't begin. After three to five days in the fermenter, we move the salami to the aging room, a 10- by 10-foot converted walk-in refrigerator. Monitoring temperature, humidity, and air movement are crucial to the production of slow-aged, traditional-type salami. From beginning to end, the process can take as long as six months to develop the flavors and texture we desire.

Salami can last up to ten years at room temperature; it just gets drier as it ages. Just be sure to store it in a breathable material like paper or cheesecloth, not plastic wrap.

Prosciutto: Prosciutto is air-cured ham. (Most people are familiar with Prosciutto di Parma from Italy.) The leg is rubbed with salt and then hung to dry for about a year. We rub it only with salt to draw out the moisture and the finished product has a silky texture with a subtle salty flavor. The saltiness is a perfect match with sweet fruit as well as just-picked tomatoes, and we also use it on pizzas. We make the traditional style as well as prosciutto cotto, a cooked prosciutto. While traditionally prosciutto is made from pork, last year we made lamb prosciutto from lamb raised on the Benziger property in Sonoma.

If this hasn't satisfied your curiosity, we also teach salumi classes; come join us for a morning of salumi-making in Sonoma!

Chef John in the meat locker

MANO FORMATE Prosciutto

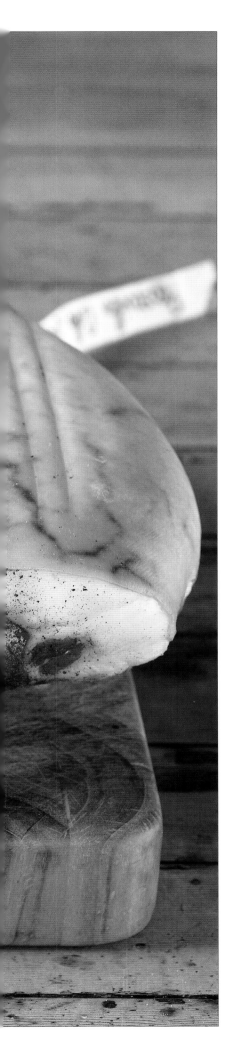

Chocolate

It's hard to know where to start with chocolate; this beguiling ingredient has captivated humanity since the 6th century, when the Mayans began cultivating cacao. The word chocolate comes from the Aztec word xocolatl, meaning "bitter water".

Being from Pennsylvania, I've been to the Hershey chocolate factory. It's not quite like the Willy Wonka version, but it did have an intoxicating smell of milk chocolate that stayed with me for years. As chocolate purists and fanatics of single-origin chocolate keep popping up, I'll admit I have a weakness when it comes to milk chocolate. I have, however, traded my Hershey bar in for milk chocolate from Valrhona in the Rhône Valley, Gianduja from Italy, or the perfect chocolates from Lindt, the famous Swiss chocolate company.

People are passionate about chocolate—they know what they like, and it's hard to get them to experiment. Chocolate appears almost solely in desserts in our restaurants, with the exception of an occasional cocktail or a decadent hot cocoa for brunch. There are wonderful chocolates being produced around the world, including France, Venezuela, and the U.S., and we have experimented with many chocolates over the years. For a long time, we only used Callebaut from France, but now we also use El Rey Gran Saman from Venezuela, Guayaquil Extra Bitter from France, and San Francisco's E. Guittard at the espresso station.

All chocolate goes through the same basic process to get from bean to bar. The cacao beans are removed from their shell and then fermented, dried, roasted, and cracked. The nibs are separated from the shells and ground to release the cocoa butter. The resulting thick, brown paste is called chocolate liquor. Then, either cocoa butter is extracted from the chocolate liquor and ground to make cocoa powder, or other ingredients are added. The last step is called conching, when machines blend the chocolate liquor, removing volatile acids and excess moisture. Small amounts of cocoa butter and sometimes lecithin are added to achieve a smooth texture.

The rows of chocolate on store shelves can be overwhelming, but here's a basic guide to get you started:

Unsweetened: This is the purest form of chocolate available, often called baking or bitter chocolate. By law, it must contain between 50 and 58 percent cocoa butter. It's too bitter to eat straight.

Bittersweet: Made by adding sugar, lecithin, and vanilla to the chocolate liquor. By law, it must contain at least 35 percent chocolate liquor.

Semisweet: This variety contains sugar, lecithin, and vanilla and has more sugar than bittersweet. By law, it must contain between 15 and 35 percent chocolate liquor. It contains less fat than bittersweet, averaging about 30 and 35 percent.

Sweet: This variety contains sugar, lecithin, and vanilla and more sugar than semisweet. It must contain at least 15 percent chocolate liquor.

Milk: Milk chocolate is made by adding dried milk to sweetened chocolate. Law dictates that it must contain 12 percent milk solids and 10 percent chocolate liquor. It's the type of chocolate most often consumed in the U.S.

White: This actually isn't chocolate—it's made from sugar, milk solids, cocoa butter, lecithin, and vanilla.

Cook's Tip: You can use bittersweet and semisweet chocolate interchangeably in recipes, but don't substitute milk or white chocolate; they contain milk protein, which will completely alter the texture and flavor of the dish.

Chocolate will keep for some time if you avoid two things: air and light. Store chocolate in an airtight container in a cool, dark place and it will stay fresh for 9 to 12 months for milk chocolate, and 12 to 18 months for dark chocolate; after that the flavors begin to fade.

Entrée
Cauliflower & Romanesco Gratin,
Cauliflower Cream

Plat
Braised Pork Cheeks,
Three Onion Ragoût

Dessert
Apple & Raisin Bread Pudding

Fromage
Matos Cheese Factory St. George

Cauliflower & Romanesco Gratin, Cauliflower Cream

Eberle Winery Viognier, Mill Road Vineyard, Paso Robles, California
Whetstone Wine Cellars Viognier, Catie's Corner Vineyard, Russian River Valley, California

This recipe started out as a mac & cheese in disguise but it truly stands out on its own. It's a hearty dish that's just perfect for a winter night. You can prepare it in either small ramekins for individual servings or in a casserole dish and serve it family style. Romanesco broccoli, a delicious variety of green cauliflower, may be difficult to find. If you're unable to find it, substitute broccoli instead. Both the cauliflower and the Romanesco can be blanched ahead of time. We've had fun with this dish at ESTATE, finishing it in our wood-fired oven to give it a crispy topping.

1 large head cauliflower, cut into 1-inch florets
1 large head Romanesco, cut into 1-inch florets
¼ cup extra-virgin olive oil
Salt and pepper to taste
1½ cups heavy cream
½ cup whole milk
6 tablespoons grated Parmigiano-Reggiano cheese
Pinch of nutmeg
1 cup Herbed Bread Crumbs (page 311)
1 tablespoon chopped fresh flat-leaf parsley

Cauliflower

This odd-looking veggie has had a renaissance of late. White cauliflower used to be the only option, but orange and purple cauliflowers now share space in stores and farmers markets. (Purple cauliflower is milder and sweeter in flavor than the white variety.)

We use it a lot for sauces and soups, and it's a natural pairing for cheese—even the most reluctant cauliflower lover will inhale a plate of cauliflower au gratin. It also makes a wonderful soup, with fresh apple, a dash of curry, or a drizzle of truffle oil adding another layer of flavor. Small cauliflower florets pickled in vinegar and/or oil are wonderful to snack on.

Look for cauliflower heads (called curds) that are tightly closed, surrounded by bright green leaves. It's available year-round but is most plentiful in autumn.

Gardener's Tip: *Cauliflower is considered one of the most difficult vegetables to grow in a home garden!*

Preheat the oven to 450°F.

To prepare the cauliflower:
Reserve ½ cup of the white florets and the white stems and set aside.

Toss the remaining cauliflower and Romanesco with the olive oil and season with salt and pepper to taste.

Roast the mixture on a baking sheet for 12 to 15 minutes or until the cauliflower has browned on the edges. Remove from the oven and set aside.

To prepare the cream:
Heat the cream, milk, cheese, nutmeg, and the reserved cauliflower in a large saucepan over medium heat. Season with salt and pepper to taste and simmer over low heat until the cauliflower is tender, about 15 to 20 minutes. Place the mixture in a food processor or blender, purée until smooth, and adjust the seasoning as needed.

To finish:
Mix the bread crumbs and parsley together. In a large bowl combine the sauce and the roasted cauliflower and stir until well-coated. Transfer the mixture to a casserole pan or six small ramekins. Distribute the bread crumbs equally over the top(s) and bake until golden brown, about 7 to 9 minutes. Serve hot. The gratins can be made 1 day ahead. Reheat them in a 350°F oven for about 12 to 15 minutes or until heated through.

Serves 6

Braised Pork Cheeks, Three Onion Ragoût

Radio-Coteau Syrah, Las Colinas, Sonoma Coast, California
Michel-Schlumberger Wines "La Source" Syrah, Dry Creek Valley, California
Broc Cellars Mourvèdre, Luna Matta Vineyards, Paso Robles, California

Pork cheeks have been available for many years, just not at the local meat counter. It's worth asking a reputable butcher to find them for you. Traditionally in France, plats du jour were created around less-expensive meats and cuts that were widely available. Cooking these cuts is easy, but be sure to allow enough time; both pork and beef cheeks are not appropriate for quick cooking. For the very best results, a low, slow heat is necessary to break down the fibers of the meat that will allow them to melt in your mouth.

For the ragoût:

3 tablespoons olive oil
1 pound cipollini onions, peeled
3 sweet onions (Walla Walla or Maui), peeled with
 root attached and cut in half
½ pound red pearl onions, peeled and blanched
1 tablespoon unsalted butter
1 tablespoon chopped fresh thyme

For the pork cheeks:

¼ cup olive oil
3 pounds pork cheeks, cleaned (see Note)
1 leek, white part only, sliced
4 celery stalks, roughly chopped
2 medium carrots, roughly chopped
1 medium yellow onion, quartered
1 head garlic, cut in half
3 tablespoons honey
2 cups red wine
1 bay leaf
4 sprigs fresh thyme
6 cups Veal or pork Stock (page 313; beef broth
 can be substituted)
Salt and pepper to taste
2 bunches baby mâche, for garnish

Mâche

Mâche, the delicate lettuce that so often appears in salad mixes, is also known as corn salad, lamb's lettuce, and field lettuce. Originally from Europe, mâche has dark green leaves and a mild, nutty flavor. It's often served raw but can also be cooked and used in soups and stuffings. Mâche is extremely perishable and should be used within 1 day of purchase. Look for nice, evenly shaped bunches with dark green leaves; avoid any with yellow leaves.

To prepare the ragoût:
Preheat the oven to 400°F.
Heat 1 tablespoon of the olive oil on medium heat in an ovenproof pan large enough to hold all of the onions. Add the cipollini onions and caramelize them until golden brown, about 6 to 8 minutes. Place the pan into the oven and roast for an additional 15 minutes or until the onions are soft.

Toss the sweet onions with the remaining 2 tablespoons olive oil and season with salt and pepper to taste. Place the onions face down on a baking sheet and roast until the onions are soft and browned, about 35 minutes. Heat the butter in a large sauté pan and add the onions, butter, and thyme. Adjust the seasoning and cook until hot, about 5 to 7 minutes. Keep warm.

To prepare the pork cheeks:
Preheat the oven to 350°F.
Heat the olive oil in a large casserole dish or braising pan over medium heat. Add the pork cheeks and sear them until they are well caramelized on all sides. Remove the pork from the pan and set aside.

Add the leek, celery, carrots, onion, and garlic and cook until browned. Add the honey and mix well. Return the pork to the pan and stir again. Add the red wine, bay leaf, and thyme and bring to a boil. Reduce the liquid by half. Add the stock and bring to a simmer. Cover the pan, transfer it to the oven, and roast for 2½ hours.

Remove the pan from the oven and let it cool for 20 minutes. Remove the pork from the pan and set aside. Strain the liquid into a medium saucepan and bring to a simmer. Reduce the liquid by a little more than half, skimming the top. Add the pork back to the liquid and adjust the seasoning with salt and pepper to taste.

To serve:
Divide the onion ragoût evenly among 6 plates and top with the braised pork cheeks. Garnish with the mâche.

Note: Before cooking the pork cheeks, they need to be cleaned or trimmed. Use a boning knife to carefully remove the silver skin and any obvious fat. (There may be a hard piece of cartilage that also needs to be removed.) Once you've cleaned the pork cheeks you will have two separate pieces. If you want the butcher to do this for you, ask them at the time you place your order.

Serves 6

Apple & Raisin Bread Pudding

Core Wine Company "Candy Core" Late Harvest Grenache, Santa Barbara, California
Domaine Fontanel Rivesaltes, Ambré, France

Here is another version of bread pudding that will really stand out if you use a soft, buttery bread like brioche or challah. If you can find Northern Spy, Golden Delicious, Stayman Winesap or Gravenstein apples for this bread pudding, you will not be disappointed with the pure apple flavor.

6 large eggs

2 cups heavy cream

2 cups whole milk

1 cup firmly packed brown sugar

½ teaspoon pure vanilla extract

1 teaspoon ground cinnamon

10 ounces soft bread, toasted and cut into 1-inch cubes (about 1 loaf)

3 cups peeled and diced apples (from about 3 to 4 apples or 1 pound of apples)

½ cup golden raisins

Pinch of salt

Preheat the oven to 350°F. Butter a 9 x 12-inch baking pan and set aside.

In a large bowl whisk the eggs, cream, and milk together until light and pale. Add the sugar, vanilla, and cinnamon and whisk until smooth. Add the bread, apples, raisins, and salt and gently mix together.

Pour the mixture into the baking pan and let it sit for 15 minutes.

Bake the bread pudding for 45 to 60 minutes or until set. (Test for doneness by inserting a knife in the center of the pudding to see if the custard is still loose.) Once set, remove the bread pudding from the oven and let it rest for 20 minutes.

Serves 6 to 10

MATOS CHEESE FACTORY ST. GEORGE

REGION:	Santa Rosa, California
MILK:	Holstein and Jersey cows
PROCESS:	heat treated, unpasteurized
PRODUCTION:	uncooked, pressed, semi-hard, natural rind
AFFINAGE:	2 to 7 months
FLAVOR:	tangy, spicy, full lingering flavors, firm acidity
AROMA:	fresh, green
TEXTURE:	dense, cheddar-like
SIMILAR CHEESES:	Havarti, Cheddar
PAIRINGS:	Heirloom Tomato Jam (page 315)
	Fastachi sesame honey crunch
	Mendocino Mustard seeds & suds
	cornbread
NOTES:	St. George is made using the traditional Portugese recipe, except for the shape. This cheese melts and grates nicely and we have been using the St. George on our grilled cheese sandwiches and croques monsieurs since we opened.

Entrée
Celery Root Soup, Toasted Walnuts

Plat
Braised Lamb, Root Vegetable Sugo

Dessert
Meyer Lemon Tart

Fromage
Laguiole

Celery Root Soup, Toasted Walnuts

Carica Wines Grenache Rosé, Bennett Valley, California
Frick Winery Cinsaut, Dry Creek Valley, California

In winter, we transform celery root into comforting soups and purées. Sometimes, we add celery root to our mashed potatoes and other times we dice it small to serve with a medley of roasted root vegetables. In a soup, celery root has a rich earthy flavor and the addition of the chopped walnuts adds a nice textural element and highlights the nutty flavor of the celery root. We don't overlook celery root in summer. In warm months, we julienne it for a simple, light side salad to accompany charcuterie and sandwiches.

8 tablespoons (1 stick) unsalted butter
1 small yellow onion, chopped
3 celery stalks, heart leaves reserved, chopped
1 large leek, white part only, cleaned and chopped
2 shallots, diced
4 garlic cloves, crushed
2 pounds celery root, peeled and chopped (about 3 to 4 celery root depending on size)
Salt and white pepper to taste
½ cup heavy cream

½ cup walnuts, toasted and crushed, for garnish
Extra-virgin olive oil, for garnish

To prepare the soup:
Melt 4 tablespoons of the butter in a medium stockpot over medium-low heat. Add the onion, celery, leek, shallots, and garlic and sauté until the vegetables are soft, about 5 to 7 minutes. Stir the vegetables occasionally to prevent browning. Add the celery root to the vegetable mixture and stir. Add 1½ quarts water, season with salt and pepper to taste, and bring to a boil. Reduce the mixture to a simmer and cook until the celery root is just tender, about 20 to 25 minutes. Add the cream and the remaining 4 tablespoons of butter.

Remove the pot from the heat and immediately purée it in a food processor or a blender. Strain the soup through a fine-mesh sieve and adjust the seasoning if necessary.

To prepare the garnish:
In a small bowl toss the reserved celery heart leaves and crushed walnuts with 1 to 2 tablespoons of olive oil.

To serve:
Ladle the soup into 6 bowls and garnish each bowl with 1 teaspoon of the walnut mixture and a drizzle of olive oil.

Serves 6

Braised Lamb, Root Vegetable Sugo

Arrowood Vineyards & Winery "Côte de Lune Rouge" Lasseter Vineyards, Sonoma, California
Scribe Winery Syrah, Napa Valley, California
Domaine La Barroche PURE, Châteauneuf-du-Pape, France

Our guests absolutely love when we offer our tender braised lamb. No matter how we put lamb on the menu, it is sure to be popular (some days we prepare over fifty portions—and will completely sell out). We slow-cook the lamb until the meat is practically in shreds, and the flavor becomes mellow and rich. The Root Vegetable Sugo is a nice complement to the dish. When you prepare this dish you may want to make extra lamb to use in the Polenta, Braised Lamb, and Gremolata Small Bite (page 183).

For the lamb:

2½ pounds boneless lamb breast
2 garlic cloves, minced
2 tablespoons chopped fresh rosemary
¼ cup extra-virgin olive oil
Salt and pepper to taste
5 tablespoons blended oil
1 medium yellow onion, chopped
1 medium carrot, chopped
1 celery stalk, chopped
¼ cup tomato paste
2 tablespoons all-purpose flour
1 cup red wine
1 gallon Veal Stock (page 313; beef broth can be substituted)

For the vegetables:

2 medium carrots, cut into ½-inch dice and blanched
1 medium parsnip, cut into ½-inch dice and blanched
¼ medium rutabaga, cut into ½-inch dice and blanched
1 medium turnip, cut into ½-inch dice and blanched
¼ cup garlic cloves, peeled and roasted
1 cup pearl onions, cleaned and blanched
4 tablespoons unsalted butter
Salt and white pepper to taste
2 tablespoons unsalted butter, for serving
1 tablespoon fresh oregano leaves, for serving

Ragoût, Ragu, Sugo, or Gravy?

You say ragoût, I say ragu—we love these slow-cooked stews with layers of flavors. While a ragoût (pronounced "ra-GOO") is traditionally a thick French stew, we use the word to convey any meat or vegetable stew. It can refer to any vegetable or meat dish that is slow-cooked over low heat. (A French ragoût is not the same as the Italian ragu; the Northern Italian dish is made from beef, tomatoes, onions, celery, and carrots and served over pasta.) And a sugo (or sugo all'Amatriciana) is generally a combination of sautéed celery and onion with seared meat that's simmered for hours in wine or broth. They are all essentially gravy. And gravy really isn't gravy unless it tastes twice as good the next day!

To prepare the lamb:

Preheat the oven to 350°F.
Place the lamb, rib side up, on a cutting board. In a bowl combine the garlic, rosemary, and olive oil. Spread the mixture evenly on the meat and season with salt and pepper. Roll the lamb tightly and secure with butcher's twine.

Heat the blended oil in a large Dutch oven or roasting pan over high heat. Sear the lamb on all sides until golden brown, about 5 to 8 minutes. Remove the lamb from the pan and set aside. Add the onion, carrot, and celery to the pan and cook until the vegetables have browned. Add the tomato paste and red wine and cook for an additional 3 minutes, using a wooden spoon to scrape the brown bits off the bottom and sides of the pan. Add the veal stock, place the lamb breast back in the pan, and bring to a simmer. Cover the pan and transfer it to the oven.

Roast for 2½ to 3 hours, turning the lamb every so often, until the lamb is knife tender. Remove the lamb from the oven and let it rest on the stovetop until it becomes cool enough to handle, about 1 hour. Remove the lamb from the pan, cover with foil, and keep warm.

Strain the liquid into a saucepan and bring it to a simmer. Skim off any excess fat and reduce the sauce until it lightly coats the back of a spoon, about 12 to 15 minutes.

Slice the lamb into ½-inch slices (you should get 12 to 14 pieces) and gently place them back in the sauce to reheat.

To prepare the vegetables:

While the lamb is resting, place the carrots, parsnips, rutabaga, turnip, garlic, and pearl onions in a saucepot with 1½ cups water and the butter. Season with salt and pepper to taste and simmer over low heat until the vegetables are very soft and most of the liquid has evaporated, about 15 to 20 minutes. (The vegetables should have a brilliant color but will be very soft.)

To serve:

Distribute the root vegetables equally among 6 plates. Remove the lamb from the sauce and place 2 to 3 pieces of lamb on each plate. Heat the sauce to a simmer, whisk in the butter, and drizzle the sauce equally over the lamb. Garnish with the oregano leaves.

Serves 6

Meyer Lemon Tart
Champagne, Prosecco or Sparkling Wine

My only problem with lemon tarts is that I eat the lemon curd while I'm baking and don't have enough to fill my tart shells! Regular lemons or other citrus can be substituted, but the Meyer lemons add a sweeter, more complex citrus flavor. These tarts are often requested from our wedding catering menu for special dessert buffets. The bite-sized tarts are a nice light sweet that won't fill you up before the dancing begins. The shortbread dough recipe is one of our tried-and-true tart shell recipes. Easy to prepare and quite tasty, it works well with a variety of flavors including cocoa powder, nuts, and other spices. This recipe makes enough for two 11-inch tarts. If you're only making one tart, simply freeze the remaining dough. If you intend to use all the dough, you will need to double the filling.

For the tart shell:
Lemon Shortbread Dough (page 317)

For the filling:
6 large eggs
1 cup powdered sugar
¾ cup granulated sugar
½ cup fresh Meyer lemon juice (fresh lemon juice can be substituted)
¼ cup fresh lime juice
1 cup heavy cream
Zest of 2 Meyer lemons (regular lemons can be substituted)

Whipped cream, for garnish

To prepare the filling:
Preheat the oven to 350°F. Bake the Lemon Shortbread Dough.

Whisk the eggs and sugars together in a large bowl until light and pale. Add the lemon and the lime juice. Whisk in the cream and strain the mixture. Add the lemon zest and mix well. Pour the filling in the baked Lemon Shortbread tart shell(s). Bake for about 20 minutes for a large tart and about 5 to 7 minutes for the miniature tarts or until set; be careful not to jiggle them. Let the tart(s) cool.

To serve:
Slice the large tart into 6 to 8 slices. Add a dollop of whipped cream on top, if desired, and serve.

Serves 6 to 8 with an 11-inch tart or makes 24 miniature tartlets

---

LAGUIOLE

REGION:	Midi-Pyrénées, France
MILK:	cow
PROCESS:	raw
PRODUCTION:	uncooked, pressed, semi-hard, natural rind
AFFINAGE:	6 to 18 months
FLAVOR:	complex, grassy, tangy, intense, nutty
AROMA:	powerful, cheddar-like
TEXTURE:	moist when young, brittle, gritty, crumbly as it ages
SIMILAR CHEESES:	Cantal, Salers, Monterey Jack
PAIRINGS:	Frog Hollow Farm Peach Chutney Fastachi Walnut Butter Harvest Song Quince Preserves American Spoon Pumpkin Butter
NOTES:	Each wheel of Laguiole requires 90 gallons of milk to produce a 100 pound wheel.

Jeff Cohn
JC Cellars
Oakland, California

As longtime Rhône wine lovers, for our tenth year anniversary of the girl & the fig we decided to make our own wine. It just seemed like a natural extension of our menu and our philosophy. We had always loved the Syrah and other red wines from Jeff Cohn of JC Cellars in Oakland, California, so we asked him to make a wine for us. We wanted a Syrah from Sonoma, and Jeff was able to find local Syrah grapes and made 50 cases (two barrels). We named it Très Bonnes Années for our "very good years."

Five years later, we're still making wine with Jeff. We had intended to try new wineries every year but we loved the wine so much the first year that we never switched. We know how committed he is to making the best possible wine and to Rhône varietals, and he is hands-on with everything. Though we don't pick the grapes, we do sit down with Jeff and taste the blends he presents every January. The blend changes every year. Last year's blend was Syrah from the famed Rockpile Vineyard in Sonoma County, with a bit of Viognier. For each vintage, we use a different piece of "fig" art on the label from artist Julie Higgins (see Sources, page 318). Every year, the wine arrives in July and we sell it in the restaurants, and it always sells out very quickly. We hold back a few cases, because one year I want to sit and open ten vintages at once!

His laid-back, smiling demeanor doesn't reveal Jeff's dedication to winemaking. A native of Maryland, his background is in restaurant and hospitality management. During a wine class in college, Jeff tasted his first Châteauneuf-du-Pape, a wine memory that stayed with him. After working in restaurants and in a gourmet store that specialized in wines, Jeff decided to go back to school for winemaking. He moved to California and spent three years getting his master's degree from Fresno State University. During his summer breaks Jeff worked at a small winery in Maryland, his first direct experience making wine.

With his master's degree in hand, Jeff applied for a job at Rosenblum Cellars in Alameda, California, about an hour south of the famed Sonoma and Napa wine regions. Rosenblum was known for its Zinfandel, and in 1996 Jeff

started as an intern but was quickly promoted to the Enologist. He was then put in charge of the white wines and then the reds, until eventually he was in charge of all Rosenblum wines. During his time at Rosenblum, the 2003 Rockpile Zinfandel was rated the number three wine in the world by Wine Spectator magazine in 2005, which at that time was the highest rated Zinfandel. Jeff also oversaw the Rhône program at Rosenblum, using varietals that until then were not part of their portfolio. When Jeff first started at Rosenblum, Kent asked Jeff if he wanted to start his own label. Jeff said yes, and after 10 years of juggling both jobs he left Rosenblum to focus on his own winery, JC Cellars.

Jeff points to French winemakers when describing his influences. As a young winemaker, he connected with a group of Rhône Valley winemakers and wine aficionados at what was then the Viognier Guild. This is now the annual Hospice du Rhône event held each May in Paso Robles, California. He made lasting friendships, visiting the winemakers at their wineries in France. "After connecting with the French winemakers, I thought, 'I am going to make my wines as incredibly rich, powerful, and intense as these wines,'" says Jeff. "That was the first step in my winemaking style, being influenced by the French. Not just their style, but their philosophy as well. It led to a big jump in quality for me." JC Cellars is flourishing, producing 18 wines (including Syrah and Grenache), and getting great reviews from the wine critics.

Jeff spends his time driving to the various vineyards around California that he contracts with, working with vineyard managers and checking on the fruit. Back at the winery, he works on blends and oversees the entire production. "I feel like when you make wine you're in charge but really not," he observes. "You can only guide it, but you can't control it. It's kind of like raising a child."

Luckily Jeff still finds time to work with us. "The [girl & the fig] wine goes with the philosophy that two personalities together is better than one of us alone," Jeff feels. "Sondra is coming to me because she knows I will be as passionate about it as she is."

If you're visiting Northern California, take time to stop by the JC Cellars tasting room in Oakland. It's a wonderful way to sample his wines, and Jeff loves to talk Rhône! (For contact information, see Sources, page 318.) "Being able to share your passions with someone is so important," says Jeff. We couldn't agree more.

Entrée
Watercress, Shaved Fennel & Winter
Citrus Salad

Plat
Coq au Vin

Dessert
Pear & Hazelnut Tart

Fromage
Le Brebiou

Watercress, Shaved Fennel & Winter Citrus Salad

JC Cellars "The First Date" Roussanne/Marsanne, California
Domaine Marc Sorrel "Les Rocoules" Hermitage Blanc, Hermitage, France

This salad is meant to be a quick, flavorful, easy dish, and it is all of those things. These winter ingredients are perfect together and yet pair wonderfully with the hearty Coq au Vin. At this time of year, your local market should have a large variety of citrus fruits so simply choose your favorites. I would recommend using a bit of the same citrus in the salad dressing to tie the flavors together.

For the vinaigrette:
¼ cup white balsamic vinegar
½ cup extra-virgin olive oil
Salt and pepper to taste

For the salad:
1 bunch watercress, cleaned and large stems removed
1 head escarole, cleaned and torn into 3-inch pieces
1 large fennel bulb, shaved thinly
1 large ruby grapefruit, segmented
2 medium navel oranges, segmented
1 Meyer lemon, segmented (regular lemon can be substituted)

To prepare the vinaigrette:
Whisk together the vinegar and olive oil. Season with salt and pepper to taste.

To prepare the salad:
In a large mixing bowl combine the watercress, escarole, fennel, and citrus with the vinaigrette. Toss well and season with salt and pepper to taste. Distribute evenly among 6 plates.

Serves 6

Coq au Vin

Nicholson Ranch Syrah, Las Madres, Carneros, California
Enkidu Wines Syrah, Kick Ranch, Sonoma County, California
Domaine de Marcoux, Châteauneuf-du-Pape, Vielles Vignes, Châteauneuf-du-Pape, France

Here is another tried-and-true favorite from our first cookbook. Over the years, we have received so many notes, emails, and even Facebook mentions of how well this recipe turned out. That is the highest compliment for a cookbook author, recipe developer, or chef: that the recipe is easy to understand and will come together to create a perfect meal and food memory! Coq au Vin is a typical Plats du Jour dish, and though it takes a while for the flavors to meld the preparation is not difficult and the results are superb. This is a recipe that must be started at least one day ahead.

For the marinade:

1½ cups red wine
½ tablespoon chopped fresh flat-leaf parsley
3 garlic cloves, chopped
½ cup blended oil
2 teaspoons salt
2 bay leaves
2 tablespoons soy sauce

6 chicken legs
6 chicken thighs

2 pounds Yukon Gold potatoes, quartered
2 tablespoons olive oil
Salt and pepper to taste

For the braising liquid:

1 large carrot, chopped
1 medium onion, chopped
½ bunch celery, chopped
2 tablespoons blended oil
½ tablespoon whole peppercorns
2 tablespoons tomato paste
1 tablespoon unsweetened cocoa powder
½ teaspoon ground cinnamon
4 cups red wine
Bouquet garni (4 sprigs fresh thyme, 4 sprigs fresh
    flat-leaf parsley, and 2 bay leaves)
6 cups Chicken Stock (page 313)

For the chicken:

2 cups all-purpose flour
Salt and pepper to taste
½ pound pancetta, diced
1 pound button mushrooms, trimmed and cleaned
2 tablespoons blended oil
3 tablespoons Cognac or brandy
2 cups red wine
30 pearl onions, blanched and peeled

To prepare the marinade:

Mix the red wine, parsley, garlic, oil, salt, bay leaves, and soy sauce together in a large bowl big enough to accommodate the chicken. Add the chicken and marinate for at least 8 hours and up to 24 hours.

To prepare the potatoes:

Preheat the oven to 400°F. In a roasting pan, toss the potatoes with the olive oil, salt, and pepper and roast for about 35 minutes or until soft. Set aside and turn off the oven.

To prepare the braising liquid:

In a stock pot slowly sauté the carrot, onions, and celery in the blended oil until the onion is lightly browned and soft, about 5 to 7 minutes. Add the peppercorns and tomato paste and cook until soft. Add the cocoa powder and the cinnamon. Deglaze the pan with the red wine and reduce by half. Add the bouquet garni and chicken stock. Simmer for 1 hour and strain the liquid. (There should be 1 quart of liquid remaining.)

To prepare the chicken:

Preheat the oven to 350°F.
Remove the chicken from the marinade and pat it dry. Discard the marinade. In a bowl, combine the flour, salt, and pepper and dredge the chicken in it. Set aside.

Cook the pancetta until crisp in a heavy-bottomed ovenproof pan large enough to hold all of the chicken. Remove the pancetta and set aside, keeping the fat in the pan. Sauté the mushrooms in the pancetta fat until well browned and remove. In the same pan, sauté the chicken until well browned on both sides, about 5 minutes per side. (Add more oil if necessary.)

Deglaze the pan with Cognac and then with the red wine. Reduce the liquid by half. Add the reduced chicken stock, pancetta, mushrooms, and pearl onions and place the pan in the oven for about 20 minutes. Transfer the chicken to a platter and keep warm. Reduce the wine sauce by one third.

To serve:

Add the potatoes to the wine sauce and pour over the chicken.

Serves 6 to 8

Pear & Hazelnut Tart

Cambria Late Harvest Viognier, Tepusquet Vineyard, Santa Maria, California
Graham's 20 Year Tawny Port, Portugal
Yalumba Antique Tawny Port, Australia

My friend Laura can't stop talking about this nutty, fruity pear tart. I keep promising her the recipe, which she will eventually get before you do! Knowing that she is such a great chef on her own, I think she will probably add a new and wonderful touch to it. We use Bosc pears in this recipe, but you can use any thick-skinned pear available. This is a recipe with a lot of little steps. Each component can be made in advance, and although it's not a difficult recipe it will take a bit of time to complete. We recommend that you make the dough the day before and let the dough firm up in the refrigerator overnight.

For the tart shell:

9 tablespoons cold, unsalted butter, cut into
    ½-inch pieces
1½ cups all-purpose flour
¼ teaspoon salt
2½ tablespoons sugar
⅛ teaspoon baking powder
1 large egg yolk

For the filling:

6 tablespoons unsalted butter
2 large eggs
½ cup sugar
1 cup all-purpose flour
Pinch of salt
1 vanilla bean, scraped
¼ cup hazelnuts, toasted and crushed

For the pears:

2 pears, peeled, cored, and halved
½ cup sugar
1 tablespoon fresh lemon juice
1 cinnamon stick

For the currants:

½ cup dried currants
½ cup red verjus (see Sources, page 318)
¼ cup sugar

2 tablespoons toasted hazelnuts, for serving
½ cup whipped cream, for serving

To prepare the tart shell:

In a mixer fitted with a dough hook, add the butter, flour, salt, sugar, and baking powder and mix on medium speed until the dough is the size of pebbles. In a separate bowl, mix together 3 tablespoons of ice water and the egg. Add the egg mixture to the dough and continue to mix until the dough just comes together. Wrap the dough in plastic wrap and refrigerate 2 hours or overnight.

Preheat the oven to 350°F.
Roll out the dough on a lightly floured surface to a ¼-inch thickness and press it into 6 individual 3½-inch tart molds. Bake until just golden brown, about 10 to 15 minutes. Remove the tart shells from the oven and set aside to cool.

To prepare the filling:

In a small saucepan over medium heat cook the butter until it begins to brown slightly. Remove the pan from the heat and set aside. In a bowl whisk the eggs and sugar together until light and pale. Add the flour, salt, and vanilla and mix until smooth. Slowly add the brown butter and then the hazelnuts.

To prepare the pears:

In a small saucepan combine the pears with 1 cup of water, the sugar, lemon, and cinnamon and simmer on low heat for 10 to 15 minutes or until the pears are soft. Remove the pears from the pan and let them cool. Slice the cooled pears into ½-inch lengthwise pieces.

To prepare the currants:

In a small saucepan combine the currants with ½ cup water, the verjus, and sugar and cook over low heat until the mixture thickens to a syrup, about 10 to 15 minutes. Set aside.

Preheat the oven to 350°F.
Scoop the brown butter filling into each tart shell. Arrange the pear slices as desired, overlapping them slightly. Bake for 25 to 30 minutes or until set.

To serve:

Place each tart on a plate, top with a spoonful of toasted hazelnuts, a dollop of whipped cream, and a drizzle of currant sauce.

Serves 6

LE BREBIOU

REGION:	Pyrénées, France
MILK:	sheep
PROCESS:	pasteurized
PRODUCTION:	uncooked, unpressed, soft, natural mold, sometimes ash
AFFINAGE:	matures within two weeks
FLAVOR:	sweet, tangy, mildly salty, short finish
AROMA:	grassy, pungent, strong
TEXTURE:	creamy, velvety rind
SIMILAR CHEESES:	Brin d'Amour (no herbs), Port Salut, Brie
PAIRINGS:	Hector's Honeycomb Sonoma Syrup Meyer Lemon Drizzler Jimtown Store Fig & Olive Spread Made in Napa Fig & Roasted Shallot Tapenade nut bread, roasted pistachios nuts
NOTES:	Even though Le Brebiou tastes like a triple cream cheese, it is only a single cream at 45% fat.

Entrée
Winter Vegetable Salad,
Creamy Black Pepper Dressing

Plat
Pan Roasted Chicken, Gnocchi,
Sherry Jus

Dessert
Butterscotch Pots du Crème

Fromage
Fiscalini Bandaged Cheddar

Winter Vegetable Salad, Creamy Black Pepper Dressing

Acacia Vineyard Estate Viognier, Carneros, California
Imagery Estate Winery Viognier, Sonoma County, California

This salad is a great way to use up some of your winter vegetables. This is a beautiful salad, particularly if you slice the vegetables in a variety of ways. Blending some of the roasted vegetables with fine slivers of fresh veggies will add both flavor and texture to the finished dish. For variety, add a handful of toasted pine nuts or chopped walnuts to the salad. What makes this dressing so creamy is the addition of crème fraîche.

For the dressing:
½ cup heavy cream
¼ cup grated white Cheddar cheese
1 teaspoon fresh finely ground pepper
1 teaspoon Dijon mustard
½ cup crème fraîche
½ tablespoon fresh lemon juice
Salt to taste

For the vegetables:
1 celery root, peeled and cut into 1-inch diamonds
    (see photo page 292)
3 heads baby fennel, cut into quarters lengthwise
2 to 3 medium turnips, peeled and cut into 1-inch
    diamonds (see photo page 292)
1 bunch white radishes, sliced in quarters lengthwise
2 tablespoons extra-virgin olive oil

For serving:
2 bunches baby carrots, peeled, blanched, and
    cut in half lengthwise
1 parsnip, peeled and shaved into long strips using a
    vegetable peeler

To prepare the dressing:
Place a small saucepan over low heat, add the cream, and bring it to a simmer. Add the cheese and pepper and whisk until smooth. Transfer the mixture to a bowl and let it cool to room temperature. Whisk in the mustard, crème fraîche, and lemon juice and season to taste. The dressing can be made ahead and refrigerated for up to 5 days; just be sure to whisk the dressing before using.

To prepare the vegetables:
Preheat the oven to 350°F.
In a large bowl toss the celery root, fennel, turnips, and radishes with the olive oil and salt and pepper to taste. Lay the vegetables on a baking sheet and roast them until the edges are browned, about 15 to 20 minutes. Remove the pan from the oven and let the vegetables cool to room temperature.

To serve:
Toss all of the roasted vegetables with the carrots and the parsnip strips. Add a small amount of the vinaigrette and toss to coat. Place a dollop of the dressing on each of the 6 plates and spread the vinaigrette with a spoon. Place the vegetables alongside and serve.

Serves 6

Pepper, the spice

Like salt, pepper appears in most of our recipes. Freshly ground pepper adds a bite and a textural element that you don't get with pre-ground pepper. There is a depth of flavor that grinding whole peppercorns provides. Peppercorns are the fruit of the peppercorn plant (Piper nigrum), a flowering vine that flourishes in tropical climates. (Most of the world's peppercorns are grown in India, Brazil, and Indonesia.)

They are picked when they aren't quite ripe and then dried, and the drying process turns the outer layer of the green peppercorn to black.

Black peppercorns are often named for the place where they were produced, such as Tellicherry, Malabar, and Singapore.

White pepper comes from the same plant as black peppercorns, but the fruit has been allowed to ripen fully and the darker colored skin of the fruit has been removed. White pepper tends to be slightly milder than black pepper and has a musky flavor, and it's often used in light-colored sauces where black peppercorns would stand out.

Pan Roasted-Chicken, Gnocchi, Sherry Jus

Miner Family Vineyards Viognier, Simpson Vineyard, California
Beckmen Vineyards Grenache Blanc, Purisima Mountain Vineyard, Central Coast, California
Chateau d'Aqueria Rosé, Tavel, France

This recipe makes the best winter chicken breast entrée and we use an airline breast cut, available from most butchers and meat departments. The light and airy gnocchi, tossed with roasted stalks of winter vegetables, make the perfect base. Don't forget to season the chicken before searing it. A quick sear on either side before roasting will keep the chicken breasts nice and juicy. Deglazing is also very important; be sure to scrape all of the hardened bits from the pan to release every bit of flavor.

For the vegetables:

3 tablespoons blended oil
2 bunches baby carrots, trimmed
1 head fennel, cut into ½-inch strips
2 large parsnips, peeled and cut into ½-inch
   batons
Salt and pepper to taste

For the gnocchi:

1 pound ricotta cheese, drained overnight in
   cheesecloth or strainer over a bowl
1 tablespoon grated pecorino cheese
2 large egg yolks
½ tablespoon chopped fresh flat-leaf parsley
½ tablespoon chopped fresh thyme
½ tablespoon chopped chives
½ cup "00" flour (see Sources, page 320)

For the chicken:

6 airline chicken breasts (10 ounces each)
3 tablespoons blended oil

For the sauce:

½ cup dark sherry
1 cup Chicken Stock (page 313)
2 tablespoons unsalted butter

3 tablespoons unsalted butter, to finish

To prepare the vegetables:

Heat the blended oil in a large sauté pan over high heat. Sear the carrots, fennel, and parsnips until golden brown on all sides, season with salt and pepper to taste, and set aside.

To prepare the gnocchi:

In a bowl, combine the ricotta, pecorino, egg yolks, and herbs. Slowly add the flour a little at a time; the dough should be slightly sticky. Add more flour if the mixture is still wet (you may or may not use all of the flour). Wrap in plastic and refrigerate the dough for 1 hour. Lightly sprinkle some flour on a work surface and working in 2 batches, roll the gnocchi into 1-inch thick ropes. Use a sharp knife to cut the dough into 1-inch pieces. Repeat with the remaining dough. Transfer the gnocchi to a lightly floured baking sheet. Lightly dust the gnocchi with flour and freeze for 1 hour. Heat a large pot of salted water (it should taste salty like the ocean) to a rolling boil and cook the gnocchi in two batches for 3 to 5 minutes or about 1 minute after they float to the surface. After cooking, immediately submerge the gnocchi into an ice water bath, remove, and gently pat dry.

To prepare the chicken:

Preheat the oven to 350°F.
Pat the chicken with paper towels and season it generously with salt and pepper. Heat the blended oil in a large sauté pan over high heat and add the chicken. Cook the chicken, skin side down, until the skin has browned, about 4 to 6 minutes. Turn the chicken over and place the pan in the oven for 10 to 12 minutes or until the chicken has cooked through. Remove the chicken from the pan and set aside to rest.

To prepare the sauce:

Place the saucepan used to cook the chicken back on high heat and add the sherry. Using a wooden spoon, scrape off the browned bits on the bottom of the pan and reduce the sherry by two thirds. Add the stock and reduce the liquid until the mixture lightly coats the back of a spoon, about 10 to 12 minutes. Remove the pan from the heat and whisk in the 2 tablespoons butter.

To serve:

Place a large sauté pan over high heat and add the 3 tablespoons butter. Sear the gnocchi until golden brown on all sides and warmed through, about 2 to 3 minutes. Gently add the vegetables and toss together. Divide them equally among the 6 plates. Top with a piece of chicken and drizzle the sauce over the top.

Serves 6

Butterscotch Pots du Crème

Salamandre Wine Cellars Late Harvest Viognier, Arroyo Seco, California
Graham's 20 Year Old Tawny Port, Portugal

This dish brings me right back to my childhood. I was quite familiar with butterscotch pudding from a box so I was surprised how different it was made from scratch! Pots du Crème is just a fancy word for pudding. We started making this dessert at the fig café & winebar, and it has been off and on the menu ever since. When my office was in Glen Ellen, I would sneak in the walk-in and have a secret snack of Butterscotch Pots du Crème! The method for making this pots du crème is similar to the one used in our other custard desserts, but the richness of the butter and brown sugar is unbelievable.

⅔ cup granulated sugar
¼ cup firmly packed brown sugar
4 tablespoons unsalted butter
1 tablespoon pure vanilla extract
Pinch of ground cinnamon
Pinch of salt
2½ cups heavy cream
6 large egg yolks

In a medium saucepot over medium heat cook the granulated sugar until it caramelizes to dark brown, about 7 to 9 minutes. Remove the pot from the heat and whisk in the brown sugar. Whisk in the butter, vanilla, cinnamon, and salt. Meanwhile, scald the cream in a separate pot. Combine the cream with the caramelized sugar mixture.

In a stainless-steel bowl, beat the egg yolks until light and pale. Slowly add one quarter of the cream and sugar mixture to the yolks. Continue adding the remaining cream mixture in a slow stream until completely mixed. Skim off any foam. Chill the mixture in an ice-water bath for 15 minutes.

Preheat the oven to 325°F.

Pour the custard mixture into six 4-ounce ramekins and place them in a large baking dish. Add enough hot water to the dish to reach halfway up the sides of the ramekins. Cover the dish with foil and bake for 45 minutes or until the custards are set around edges but still slightly wiggly in the centers.

Remove the custards from the baking dish and transfer to a rack. Cool for about 45 minutes or until they come to room temperature. Cover with plastic wrap and refrigerate until chilled, at least 2 hours or overnight.

Serves 6

FISCALINI FARMS/FISCALINI CHEESE CO. BANDAGED WRAPPED CHEDDAR   WINTER № 5

REGION:	Modesto, California
MILK:	cow
PROCESS:	raw
PRODUCTION:	uncooked, pressed, hard, bandaged wrapped
AFFINAGE:	extra mature: 14 - 17 months
	vintage: 17 -26 months
FLAVOR:	clean, nutty, earthy, slightly salty, rich, complex
AROMA:	sharp
TEXTURE:	dense, solid, brittle
SIMILAR CHEESES:	English Cheddar
PAIRINGS:	Harvest Song Quince Preserves
	Happy Girl Kitchen Honeyed Pears
	A Perfect Pear Tomato Pear Chutney
	Blue Chair Fruit East Coast Blueberry Jam
NOTES:	Each wheel of Bandaged Wrapped Cheddar are 60 pounds each. During the first 2 months of aging the cheese is hand turned two times a day.

Entrée
Chicken Livers, Warm Bacon Vinaigrette

Plat
Pan-Seared Duck Breast,
Red Wine Gastrique

Dessert
Pumpkin Cheesecake

Fromage
Winchester Aged Gouda

Chicken Livers, Warm Bacon Vinaigrette

Spann Vineyards Mourvèdre, Lodi, California
Broc Cellars "Carbonic" Carignane, Alexander Valley, California
Deerfield Ranch Winery Syrah, Sonoma Valley, California

I am always a willing taster when the chefs create new recipes with chicken livers. At ESTATE, we like to serve them as a salad over farm greens, but I also enjoy chicken livers with sautéed mushrooms, a poached egg, and grilled bread. The Bacon Vinaigrette creates a salty contrast to the tender livers.

For the livers:
¾ pound chicken livers, cleaned
2 cups whole milk
½ cup Wondra flour (see Sources, page 319)
5 tablespoons blended oil
Salt and pepper to taste

For the vinaigrette:
2 tablespoons extra-virgin olive oil
3 strips thick-sliced bacon, cut into ¼ inch strips
2 tablespoons minced shallots
½ cup champagne vinegar
1 tablespoon whole-grain mustard
1 tablespoon chopped fresh tarragon
Salt and pepper to taste

For serving:
¼ cup currants, rehydrated in warm water
1 bunch frisée, cleaned
2 heads endive, cleaned and leaves separated
2 medium Chiogga beets, cooked and sliced into
   6 wedges each
¼ head radicchio, cleaned and leaves separated

To prepare the livers:
Place the chicken livers in 1 cup of milk and let them soak for 1 hour. Strain the livers and discard the milk. Place the chicken livers in the remaining 1 cup of milk and let them soak for 4 hours.

To prepare the vinaigrette:
Heat the olive oil in a medium sauté pan over medium heat, add the bacon, and cook until browned, tossing occasionally, about 6 to 8 minutes. Using tongs or a slotted spoon transfer the bacon to a paper towel-lined plate to drain and set aside.

Pour off all but 2 tablespoons of the bacon fat from the sauté pan and return the pan to the heat. Add the shallots, vinegar, and mustard to the pan and stir, scraping up any browned bits until the dressing is combined. Add the tarragon and season to taste. Keep warm.

To prepare the chicken livers:
Remove the chicken livers from the milk and lightly pat them dry with a paper towel. (The chicken livers should not be dry, but should not contain excess moisture.)

Season the livers with salt and pepper and dredge them in the flour. Place a large saucepan over high heat and add the blended oil. Add the chicken livers and cook until golden brown, about 2 to 3 minutes. Flip the livers over and cook for another 2 to 3 minutes.

To serve:
In a large bowl toss the currants, frisée, endive, beets, radicchio, and vinaigrette together and season to taste. Divide the mixture evenly among six plates, top with the warm chicken livers, and serve.

Serves 6

Pan-Seared Duck Breast, Honey-Roasted Root Vegetables, Red Wine Gastrique

Torbreck Vintners "The Pict" Mourvèdre, Barossa Valley, Australia
Domaine Tempier "La Tourtine," Bandol, France

Sonoma County is known for its wonderful free-range ducks. Although we usually make confit with our duck, a perfectly cooked duck breast is a real treat. The ducks we use in the restaurant have a nice mellow flavor and are not as gamey as wild ducks or other game birds. The dark pink meat is sometimes surprising compared to chicken and is a reminder that duck can be cooked like some cuts of beef. Most of us are familiar with the commercial version of gastrique, which is basically sweet and sour sauce. The difference here is that using good-quality vinegars in the reduction will give you endless flavor options.

For the vegetables:

7 tablespoons blended oil
2 small celery root, peeled and cut into ¼-inch batons
2 small rutabagas, peeled and cut into ¼-inch batons
2 small parsnips, peeled and cut into ¼-inch batons
6 tablespoons honey
2 tablespoons unsalted butter

For the gastrique:

½ medium yellow onion, cut in small dice
1 celery stalk, cut in small dice
1 large carrot, cut in small dice
6 garlic cloves, peeled
1 bay leaf
4 sprigs fresh thyme
6 whole black peppercorns
¼ cup sugar
¼ cup red wine vinegar
4 cups duck stock (Chicken Stock can be substituted, page 313)
1 cup Veal Demi-Glace (see Sources, page 320)
2 tablespoons unsalted butter

6 duck breasts

To prepare the vegetables:

Preheat the oven to 400°F.

In a medium ovenproof sauté pan heat 3 tablespoons of blended oil over high heat and sauté the celery root, rutabagas, and parsnips for about 6 to 8 minutes until they start to turn golden brown. Add the honey and toss the vegetables well to coat. Place the vegetables in the oven and roast until they are soft and caramelized, about 5 minutes. Add the butter and stir to combine. Cover the vegetables with foil and keep warm.

To prepare the gastrique:

In a medium sauté pan heat 2 tablespoons blended oil and sauté the onion, celery, carrot, and garlic over medium-high for about 5 to 7 minutes or until the vegetables are caramelized. Spread the sugar evenly over the vegetables. Stir constantly to make a dark caramel, about 5 to 7 minutes. Deglaze the pan with the red wine vinegar. (The sugar will seize up but will melt again after a few minutes.) Add the bay leaf, thyme, and peppercorns. Let the vinegar reduce until almost dry, about 3 to 5 minutes, and add the duck stock. Bring to a boil and reduce by half. Add the demi-glace and reduce until the sauce holds a nice line on a plate, about 5 to 7 minutes. Strain the gastrique through a fine-mesh sieve, whisk in the butter, and set aside in a warm spot.

To prepare the duck:

Score the fat side of the duck breasts, making criss-cross marks with a paring knife and being careful not to cut all the way through to the flesh. Lightly coat a sauté pan with the remaining 2 tablespoons blended oil and on low heat, place the duck breasts skin side down to render out the fat. (Do not overcrowd the pan; you may have to render the duck in two separate batches.) Continue to render until the skin is golden and crispy, about 10 to 15 minutes.

Flip the duck breasts over and sear the flesh side, increasing the heat to medium-high and basting the skin using a spoon and the rendered duck fat. Cook the duck to desired doneness (135°F for medium rare). Remove the duck breasts from the pan and let them rest for about 5 minutes.

To serve:

Arrange the root vegetables in the center of 6 large, warm plates. Spoon the gastrique around the vegetables. Slice the duck breasts into 4 slices lengthwise, place the slices on top of the vegetables, and serve.

Serves 6

Root Vegetables

Root vegetables take over our kitchens all winter long. These are the hearty vegetables that flourish in the winter months, including carrots, salsify, turnips, rutabagas, beets, and parsnips. They taste particularly sweet during winter because the cold encourages the conversion of starch to sugar.

Beets: Many confessed beet haters change their tune when they taste a roasted beet. Their sweet flavor explodes when cooked properly. Yellow or red, the skin has a deep color that doesn't change with cooking; just be sure to peel them after cooking. (The leafy green tops are also edible, and taste wonderful when sautéed or stuffed into ravioli.) They are particularly delicious with goat's cheese or Puy lentils. Store beets in a plastic bag in the refrigerator for up to three weeks.

Salsify: This root is virtually unknown in the U.S., but the creamy white flesh is delicious boiled, mashed, or used in soups and stews. It has an oyster-like taste when cooked and is sometimes known as "the oyster plant." Peel the thick skin and cut it into short lengths. Salsify discolors very quickly, so plunge immediately into acidulated water after slicing. Simmer for 30 minutes until soft, drain, and sauté in butter. It's in season June through February.

Parsnips: The sweet, earthy parsnip is under appreciated in the U.S. It can be eaten raw or cooked, but we love to mash it and serve it alongside roasted meats. It's also wonderful in soups and stews. Available year-round, parsnips are at their peak in autumn and winter.

Turnips: This vegetable is often ignored by American foodies, but one bite of a perfectly roasted turnip will turn you into a believer. They have a wonderful sweet, earthy flavor that comes alive when cooked. You can also substitute them for potatoes for a flavorful mash—just peel them, cook them, and mash them with butter and milk. Peak turnip season is October through February. They can be refrigerated for up to two weeks or kept in a cool, dark place for up to two months. Choose those that smell sweet and have fresh green tops.

Pumpkin Cheesecake

Anaba Wines Late Harvest Viognier, Nelson Vineyards, Mendocino, California
Noval LB Finest Reserve Porto, Portugal

Over the years, pumpkin desserts have moved beyond Grandma's Thanksgiving pumpkin pie, and we created a delectable spiced pumpkin cheesecake to celebrate autumn. In the restaurant, we like to prepare individual cheesecakes because they're easier to handle than slicing a whole cake in our hot kitchen, but at home you can choose either size based on the occasion. We use canned pumpkin purée for this recipe rather than roasted fresh pumpkin; the texture and flavor are much more consistent. For an alternative garnish, try Candied Walnuts (page 315) or Hazelnut Praline (page 317).

For the crust:
¾ cup graham cracker crumbs
1 tablespoon sugar
4 tablespoons unsalted butter, melted

For the spice mix:
¼ teaspoon ground cloves
¼ teaspoon white pepper
¼ teaspoon nutmeg
¼ teaspoon ground ginger
1 teaspoon ground cinnamon

For the filling:
2 teaspoons Spice Mix
⅔ cup sugar
1 pound cream cheese, softened
2 cups heavy cream
2 large eggs plus 2 large egg yolks
1 vanilla bean, scraped
¼ cup fresh lemon juice
1½ cups pumpkin purée (from one 15-ounce can)
½ cup firmly packed brown sugar

½ cup Candied Pumpkin Seeds, for garnish (page 315)

To prepare the crust:
Preheat the oven to 350°F.

Mix the graham cracker crumbs and sugar together in a stainless-steel bowl. Add the butter and mix well. Distribute the graham cracker crumbs equally among six 4 x 2-inch ring molds. Place the molds on a baking sheet. Tamp down the crumbs with the bottom of a glass and bake for 5 to 7 minutes or until browned on the edges. Remove the crusts from the oven and let them cool to room temperature.

To prepare the spice mix:
Thoroughly combine all of the ingredients in a small bowl and set aside.

To prepare the filling:
Lower the oven temperature to 325°F.
Place the sugar and cream cheese in the bowl of a mixer fitted with a paddle attachment. Mix on medium speed until light and smooth. Add the cream, eggs, egg yolks, vanilla, and lemon and mix until soft peaks form. Add the pumpkin, brown sugar, and the Spice Mix. Mix well to incorporate all the ingredients. Pour the mixture into the ring molds and bake for 15 to 20 minutes or until set. Refrigerate for at least 1 hour or until chilled before serving. The filling can be prepared ahead and refrigerated up to 1 day ahead.

To serve:
Set each cheesecake on a plate and sprinkle the Candied Pumpkin Seeds on top.

Serves 6

WINCHESTER CHEESE COMPANY, SUPER AGED GOUDA

REGION:	Winchester, California
MILK:	Holstein cows
PROCESS:	raw
PRODUCTION:	uncooked, pressed, semi-hard
AFFINAGE:	minimum of 12 months
FLAVOR:	sharp, toasted nuts, caramel, butterscotch
AROMA:	nutty
TEXTURE:	crumbly, grainy, robust, firm
SIMILAR CHEESES:	Gouda, Boerenkaas
CONDIMENTS:	the girl & the fig Raisin-Fig Mostarda
	Happy Girl Kitchen Honeyed Pears
	L'Epicurien Cider Confit with Calvados
	Harvest Song Walnut Preserves

Entrée
Brussels Sprouts & Bacon

Plat
Pan-Roasted Black Cod, Sunchokes

Dessert
Dried Plum Clafouti

Fromage
Redwood Hill Farm Camellia

Brussels Sprouts & Bacon

Terre Rouge Wines "Enigma" White Rhône Blend, Sierra Foothills, California
Arrowood Vineyards & Winery "Côte de Lune Rouge," Lasseter Vineyards, Sonoma, California

This dish is an example of a recipe that is quite simple and uses very few ingredients while offering incredible flavors. It's also a dish that will work with most proteins throughout fall and winter. For those that don't care for Brussels sprouts, I guarantee this recipe will change your mind! The caramelized Brussels sprouts and the salty bacon create an earthy, satisfying vegetable side dish.

4 tablespoons olive oil
½ pound pancetta, diced
6 shallots, halved
2 pounds Brussels sprouts, trimmed, blanched and halved
Salt and pepper to taste
2 tablespoons unsalted butter

Preheat the oven to 425°F.

Heat the olive oil in an ovenproof roasting pan over medium heat. Add the pancetta and cook until golden brown and crisp. Remove the pancetta to a plate lined with paper towels. Add the shallots to the pan and cook until soft. Add the Brussels sprouts and toss to combine. Lightly season with salt and pepper.

Roast the Brussels sprouts and shallots until they are cooked all the way through and golden brown, about 25 minutes, or until the sprouts are crisp on the outside and tender on the inside. Remove the pan from the oven. Add the pancetta and butter and stir well.

Serve the Brussels sprouts on individual plates or family style in a bowl.

Serves 6

Brussels Sprouts

I never liked Brussels sprouts until I moved to California and a friend prepared them for a dinner party. She didn't know that I didn't like them, and I did not want to hurt her feelings, but tasting her Brussels sprouts made me understand their aggressive, bitter sweetness. Cooked properly, Brussels sprouts are one of the most delicious vegetables, releasing their sweetness in a glaze of olive oil. The key is not to overcook them. (Culinary trivia: they are originally from an area outside Brussels, Belgium.) By popular demand, we serve them all season long when they are available, and they are a natural partner for bacon, pancetta, and prosciutto—any salty pork product will be happy with this sprout.

I also love spotting Brussels sprouts in the garden. They grow on stalks in bunches (about 40 per stalk) that can get quite big, up to 3 feet tall! Only in the last few years have markets displayed the whole stalk, and I think it's a wonderful thing. As people continue to learn where their food comes from, the visual image of vegetables can't help but educate and delight.

Younger Brussels sprouts are sweeter. Available year-round, they are at their peak from September through February. Before cooking, remove the first layer of leaves and trim the bottoms. They are perishable, so store unwashed sprouts in a plastic bag in the refrigerator for no more than two days.

Pan-Roasted Black Cod, Sunchokes

Zaca Mesa Winery & Vineyards "Z Blanc," Santa Ynez Valley, California
Sans Liege Wines "Call to Arms," Alta Colina Vineyard, Paso Robles, California

Sunchokes, also known as Jerusalem artichokes, are an unfamiliar and underutilized root vegetable. Interestingly enough, sunchokes are not artichokes at all but are related to the sunflower. We recently planted sunchokes at the farm for the dual purpose of having a beautiful row of flowers and using the tubers in the kitchen. They taste great roasted as well as sliced into thin strips and fried.

For the sunchokes:

2 pounds sunchokes

2½ tablespoons extra-virgin olive oil

Salt and white pepper to taste

10 tablespoons (1¼ sticks) unsalted butter

⅓ cup hazelnuts, toasted and roughly chopped

2 tablespoons saba (Balsamic Reduction, page 311, or maple syrup can be substituted)

For the fish:

6 cod filets (5 ounces each), skin on

2 tablespoons blended oil

2 tablespoons chopped fresh flat-leaf parsley, for garnish

Sunchokes

Don't be put off by their odd appearance: the bumpy, whitish pink skin of the sunchoke actually has a sweet nutty flavor, similar to a water chestnut. This tuber, a member of the sunflower family, is also known as a Jerusalem artichoke but has nothing to do with artichokes! (It's thought that the name is related to the Italian word for sunflower, girasole.) We've been cooking with sunchokes for years, making mashes, purées and soups. (You can eat them raw or cooked, with or without the skins.)

Sunchokes are in season from October through March, and they'll keep in a plastic bag in the refrigerator for up to one week.

To prepare the sunchokes:

Set aside one sunchoke to be used as a garnish. Slice the remaining sunchokes into ¼-inch slices.

Preheat the oven to 425°F.

Heat 2 tablespoons olive oil in a medium roasting pan over medium heat. Add the sunchokes, season with salt and pepper, and sauté until browned, about 20 minutes. Set aside. Place the butter in a large sauté pan and cook over medium-high heat until the butter has browned, about 2 to 3 minutes. Let the butter cool slightly and add the hazelnuts and saba. Toss well and adjust the seasoning if necessary.

To prepare the fish:

Season the fish with salt and white pepper. Heat the blended oil over high heat in an ovenproof pan large enough to hold all the fish. Place the fish in the pan, skin side down, and cook for 3 to 4 minutes. Turn the fish over, place the pan in the oven, and roast for an additional 5 minutes.

To serve:

Thinly slice the reserved sunchoke and toss it with the remaining olive oil and parsley. Divide the roasted sunchokes evenly among 6 plates. Place a piece of fish on top, skin side up, and drizzle it with the brown butter. Garnish each plate with the sunchoke-parsley mixture.

Serves 6

Dried Plum Clafouti

M. Chapoutier Banyuls, Languedoc-Roussillon, France
Cline Cellars Late Harvest Mourvédre, Contra Costa, California

Is it wrong for me to call a prune a dried plum? Dried plum sounds more appealing than prune. Over the years, the prune has become better known for its digestive properties rather than a luscious dessert fruit. Forget everything you know about prunes and try this recipe—you will love it!

2 cups pitted prunes, cut in half
½ cup Armagnac or brandy
1⅓ cups all-purpose flour
1⅓ cups sugar
Pinch of salt
2½ cups whole milk
½ cup plus 1 tablespoon unsalted butter, melted
8 large eggs

Sifted powdered sugar, for garnish

Preheat the oven to 350°F. Butter a 9-inch cake pan and set aside.

In a bowl, cover the prunes with the Armagnac and let them soak for about 15 minutes. If the prunes do not absorb all the liquid, strain the prunes and reserve the liquid.

Sift together the flour, sugar, and salt in a large bowl. Form a well and using a fork, mix in the milk, butter, reserved Armagnac, and eggs. Beat the batter until smooth and strain it through a fine-mesh sieve.

Place the prunes in the pan and cover them with the batter. Bake for 45 minutes or until a toothpick inserted into the middle of the clafouti comes out clean.

Slice the clafouti into 6 slices, place each slice on a plate, and dust with powdered sugar. (You can also warm the clafouti in a 200°F oven for about 10 minutes before serving.)

Serves 6 to 8

REDWOOD HILL FARM CAMELLIA

REGION:	Sebastopol, California
MILK:	goat
PROCESS:	pasteurized
PRODUCTION:	uncooked, unpressed, soft, white mold ripened
AFFINAGE:	3 to 4 weeks
FLAVOR:	mild, uncomplicated, nutty, buttery
AROMA:	mild, tart
TEXTURE:	pale paste, soft and runny when ripe
SIMILAR CHEESES:	Camembert, Saint-Maure de Touraine
PAIRINGS:	Rustic Bakery Walnut & 3-Seed Pan Forte
	Matiz Apricot & Almond Bread
	INNA jam seascape strawberry jam
	Candied Walnuts (page 315)
	Blackberry Farm Pure Honey
NOTES:	Redwood Hill Farm has been family owned and operated for over 40 years.

winter

larder recipes

Balsamic Reduction

1 (500 ml) bottle balsamic vinegar (the better the vinegar,
   the better the reduction will be)

Pour the vinegar into a medium saucepot and bring to a boil
over high heat. Reduce the heat to medium and stir until all
of the sugar has dissolved. Continue to simmer, uncovered,
until three quarters of the vinegar has evaporated. Remove
the vinegar from the heat and let it cool. This will keep in the
refrigerator for at least 6 weeks.

Makes ¾ cup

Crème Fraîche

1 cup heavy cream
2 tablespoons buttermilk

Mix the cream and the buttermilk together in a plastic container.
Cover the container with a layer of cheesecloth and secure
with a string or a rubber band. Leave the container out at room
temperature for approximately 3 days or until the consistency
becomes similar to that of sour cream. Cover and refrigerate for
up to 3 weeks.

Makes 1¼ cups

Peperonata

¼ cup extra-virgin olive oil
2 garlic cloves, sliced
½ red onion, diced (should yield ¼ cup)
3 large bell peppers (color and peppers of your choice), cut in
   ¼-inch dice
Salt and pepper to taste
1 tablespoon red wine vinegar

In a medium size pan, heat the olive oil. Sauté the garlic and
onion until they become soft and lightly browned. Add the
peppers and season generously with salt and pepper. Cook until
the peppers start to brown. Add the vinegar and cook until the
vinegar has evaporated. Adjust the seasoning. Keep refrigerated
for up to 4 days.

Makes 2 cups

Herbed Bread Crumbs

6 slices day old bread, cut in small cubes
2 tablespoons extra-virgin olive oil
Salt and pepper to taste
2 tablespoons chopped garlic
2 tablespoons chopped fresh flat-leaf parsley

Preheat the oven to 350°F.
Toss the cubed bread in a bowl with the olive oil and season with
salt and pepper to taste. Transfer the bread to a sheet pan and
bake until golden brown, about 10 minutes. Remove the bread
from the oven and let it cool. Place the bread in a food processor
and process until they are small, coarse crumbs.

In a medium sauté pan, heat 2 tablespoons olive oil. Add the
garlic and sauté until the garlic becomes fragrant, about 5
minutes (be careful not to burn it). Place the bread crumbs in
the pan and continue to toast until golden brown. Transfer the
bread crumbs to a sheet pan to cool and mix in the chopped
parsley. The bread crumbs will keep for up to 3 weeks in a sealed
container.

Makes 1 cup

Herb-Marinated Olives

1 cup Lucques olives
1 cup Niçoise olives
1 cup Lyons olives
1 cup Picholine olives
½ cup caperberries
¼ cup lemon zest (zested in thin strands)
1 bunch fresh thyme, leaves removed and stems discarded
¼ cup extra-virgin olive oil

Toss all of the ingredients together in a large bowl. Keep
refrigerated for up to 6 weeks.

Makes 4½ cups

Roasted Red Peppers

4 red bell peppers
1 tablespoon olive oil

Roast the peppers on all sides on a grill or under a broiler until
the skin is well charred, about 3 minutes. Put the peppers in a
container, cover with plastic wrap, and refrigerate until cool.
Peel and seed the peppers and slice them lengthwise. Toss the
peppers with olive oil and refrigerate until needed, up to 1 week.

Makes 1½ cups

Vinaigrettes

We make so many different vinaigrettes at our restaurants, changing the flavors to reflect the season or the salad we're preparing. There are several ways to prepare a vinaigrette but the classic recipe is to slowly add 3 parts oil to 1 part vinegar or lemon juice along with salt and pepper, whisking until it emulsifies into a creamy sauce. (You can also use a blender or just shake all of the ingredients together in a jar.)

The options are endless: you can add chopped herbs, garlic, mustard, honey, or egg yolk for flavor and texture. Try using different oils—walnut oil or hazelnut oil adds a wonderful depth of flavor—or different vinegars (balsamic and red wine are two favorites, but rice wine and sherry vinegar are other delicious options).

Mustard Vinaigrette

2 tablespoons orange juice
2 tablespoons minced shallots
2 tablespoons chopped fresh tarragon
1 tablespoon Dijon mustard
2 tablespoons whole-grain mustard
1½ tablespoons honey
¼ cup champagne vinegar
½ cup blended oil
Salt and pepper to taste

Mix the orange juice, shallots, and tarragon together in a small bowl. Whisk in the mustards, honey, and vinegar and slowly whisk in the oil. Season with salt and pepper to taste. The vinaigrette will keep in a sealed container in the refrigerator for up to 1 week. Whisk before using.

Makes 1 cup

Champagne Vinaigrette

¼ cup plus 1 tablespoon champagne vinegar
2 teaspoons minced shallots
2 teaspoons Dijon mustard
1 tablespoon plus 1 teaspoon sugar
½ cup plus 1 tablespoon extra-virgin olive oil
Salt and pepper to taste

Combine the vinegar, shallots, mustard, and sugar in a bowl. Slowly whisk in the olive oil. Season with salt and pepper to taste. The vinaigrette will keep in a sealed container in the refrigerator for up to 1 week. Whisk before using.

Makes 1 cup

Caper Vinaigrette

¼ cup champagne vinegar
¾ cup blended oil
2 tablespoons diced shallots
2 tablespoons fresh thyme leaves
2 tablespoons chopped capers
Salt and freshly ground white pepper
Pinch of sugar
Juice of 1 lemon

Whisk the vinegar, oil, shallots, thyme, and capers together in a bowl. Season to taste with the salt, pepper, sugar, and lemon juice. The vinaigrette will keep in a sealed container in the refrigerator for up to 1 week. Whisk before using.

Makes 1½ cups

Meyer Lemon Vinaigrette

¼ cup plus 2 tablespoons Meyer lemon juice
2 tablespoons chopped Meyer lemon zest
½ medium red onion, finely diced
2 tablespoons chopped fresh parsley
¾ cup extra-virgin olive oil
1 tablespoon canola oil
Salt and white pepper to taste

Combine lemon juice, zest, onion, and parsley in bowl. Slowly whisk in the oil. Season with salt and pepper to taste. The vinaigrette will keep in a sealed container in the refrigerator for up to 1 week. Whisk before using.

Makes 1¾ cups

Fig & Olive Vinaigrette

1 tablespoon Fig Balsamic Vinegar (see Sources, page 320)
¼ cup plus 1 tablespoon balsamic vinegar
2 tablespoons chopped mixed olives, such as Picholine or Niçoise
1 teaspoon chopped fresh thyme
1 teaspoon minced garlic
1½ teaspoons minced shallots
1 cup plus 2 tablespoons extra-virgin olive oil
Salt and pepper to taste

Combine the vinegars, olives, thyme, garlic, and shallots in a large mixing bowl. While whisking, slowly pour in the olive oil. Season with salt and pepper to taste. The vinaigrette will keep in a sealed container in the refrigerator for up to 1 week. Whisk before using.

Makes 1½ Cups

Chicken Stock

1½ pounds chicken feet
5 pounds chicken necks
1 large carrot, roughly chopped
2 large onions, roughly chopped
3 celery stalks, roughly chopped
2 cups dry white wine
1 bay leaf
2 teaspoons whole black peppercorns
5 sprigs fresh thyme
4 sprigs fresh flat-leaf parsley
1 teaspoon minced garlic

Preheat the oven to 450°F.
Roast the chicken parts in a roasting pan until brown, about 1 hour. In a separate roasting pan, roast the vegetables until slightly browned, about 1 hour. Combine the chicken and the vegetables in a large, heavy-bottomed stockpot.

Heat both roasting pans on the stovetop and deglaze each pan with 1 cup wine. Add the wine to the stockpot. Add the bay leaf, peppercorns, thyme, parsley, and garlic with 1½ gallons of water. Bring to a boil and then reduce to a simmer. Cook on low heat for about 4 hours. Strain the stock, let it cool completely, and refrigerate for up to 5 days. You can also freeze the stock for up to 1 month.

Makes about 4 quarts

Shelling Beans

½ small onion, finely diced
1 garlic clove, slivered
1 tablespoon olive oil
¼ large carrot, diced
¼ celery stalk, diced
2 pounds fresh shelling beans, removed from pod (we prefer cranberry beans)
1 tablespoon fresh marjoram leaves
Salt to taste

In a saucepot, slowly cook the onions, garlic, carrots, and celery in the olive oil on medium heat until soft. Add the shelling beans and marjoram and add water to cover. Bring to a simmer and cook over low heat for 10 to 20 minutes (taste the beans to make sure they're cooked through and creamy). Add salt to taste.

Serves 6

Veal Stock

3 large onions, roughly chopped
2 celery stalks, roughly chopped
2 large carrots, peeled and roughly chopped
¼ cup whole garlic cloves, peeled
10 pounds veal bones
½ cup tomato paste
1 cup red wine
4 bay leaves
2 teaspoons whole black peppercorns
6 sprigs fresh thyme
8 sprigs fresh flat-leaf parsley

Preheat the oven to 350°F.
In a heavy-bottomed stockpot on medium heat cook the onions, celery, carrots, and garlic until caramelized, about 4 to 5 minutes.

Place the bones in a roasting pan and roast until brown, about 1 hour. Remove the bones, smear them with tomato paste, and roast for another 10 minutes. Remove the bones and place the roasting pan on the stovetop over medium heat. Deglaze with the red wine. Add the bones to the stockpot along with the wine, bay leaves, peppercorns, thyme, parsley, and 10 quarts of water.

Bring to a boil, reduce the heat, and simmer for at least 6 hours, skimming every 20 minutes. Strain, let cool completely, and refrigerate for up to 5 days. You can also freeze the stock for up to 1 month.

Makes about 6 quarts

Pickled Shallots

2 cups shallots, sliced
1½ cups red wine vinegar
½ cup sugar
½ tablespoon salt
1 sprig fresh thyme
1 bay leaf

In a saucepan, combine the wine vinegar, sugar, and salt. Bring to a boil, stirring to dissolve the sugar. Add the thyme, bay leaf and shallots and stir to coat evenly. Cook briskly for exactly 1 minute over high heat and remove from the heat. Allow the mixture to stand until it cools to room temperature. Transfer to a sealed container and refrigerate for up to 2 days.

Makes 1½ cups

Roasted Potatoes

3 pounds potatoes (such as Yukon Gold or Fingerlings)
2 tablespoons extra-virgin olive oil
Salt and pepper to taste
2 teaspoons minced garlic
1 tablespoon chopped fresh thyme
1 tablespoon chopped fresh flat-leaf parsley
1 teaspoon chopped fresh rosemary

Preheat the oven to 425°F.
Cut the potatoes in half lengthwise and then cut lengthwise
again into about 1-inch pieces. Toss with the olive oil and
generously season with salt and pepper. Place the potatoes in
a large roasting pan and roast for about 35 minutes. When the
potatoes are just soft, toss them with the garlic, thyme, parsley,
and rosemary and roast for another 5 minutes. Adjust the
seasoning and serve.

Serves 6

Fingerling Potato Confit

2 pounds Fingerling potatoes, cut in half
4 cups extra-virgin olive oil
5 garlic cloves
3 sprigs fresh thyme
1½ tablespoons salt
1 teaspoon pepper

Place the potatoes in a deep cooking pot along with the olive
oil, garlic, thyme, salt, and pepper. Make sure the potatoes are
completely covered by the oil (add more oil if necessary).

Heat the oil and cook the potatoes until soft, about 15 minutes.
Remove from the heat and allow the potatoes to rest in the oil
for at least 10 minutes.

Serves 6

Tarragon Aioli

3 large egg yolks
1 teaspoon minced garlic
3 tablespoons chopped fresh tarragon
4 teaspoons fresh lemon juice
1 teaspoon champagne vinegar
¾ cup blended oil
Salt and pepper to taste

Combine the egg yolks, garlic, tarragon, lemon juice, and
vinegar in a food processor. Pulse to combine. Slowly add the
blended oil and season with salt and pepper to taste. The aioli
will keep for 7 days in the refrigerator.

Makes 1 cup

Mashed Potatoes

4 russet potatoes, peeled and cubed
⅔ cup heavy cream
4 tablespoons unsalted butter, at room temperature
1 tablespoon salt
¼ teaspoon white pepper

Place the potatoes in a pot, cover them with cold water, and
cook on medium heat until soft, about 15 to 20 minutes. Drain
the potatoes and run them through a food mill or potato ricer.

Place the cream, butter, salt, and pepper in a saucepan and heat
until the butter has melted completely.

Place the potatoes in a large bowl and slowly work in the cream
mixture with a whisk. Once all the liquid has been added, whisk
the potatoes until they have a light and fluffy texture.
(Be careful not to overwhip or the potatoes will have a glue-like
texture.) Adjust the seasoning and serve immediately.

Serves 6

Wilted Greens

2 pounds greens, such as chard or kale, stemmed and
    well cleaned
2 tablespoons olive oil
1 tablespoon minced garlic
2 tablespoons minced shallots
¼ cup white wine
1 tablespoon unsalted butter
Salt and pepper to taste

Tear the greens into large pieces. Heat the oil in a large pan
and sauté the garlic and shallots until translucent, about 2 to 4
minutes. Add the greens and cook until they begin to wilt, about
1 to 2 minutes. Add the white wine, stir, and cook until most of
the liquid has evaporated. Add the butter and season with salt
and pepper to taste.

Serves 6

Brown Butter

2½ sticks unsalted butter

In a medium saucepan, melt the butter over medium heat. Cook
until the butter is lightly brown, about 10 to 12 minutes. Remove
from heat and strain through a fine-mesh sieve.

Makes ½ cup

Dried Fig Compote

¼ cup olive oil
3 tablespoons minced shallots
2 cups dried figs, quartered
¼ cup mustard seeds
½ cup sugar
1 cup Fig Balsamic Vinegar (see Sources, page 320)
2 tablespoons whole-grain mustard
Pinch of black pepper

Heat the olive oil in a medium saucepan over medium-high heat and sauté the shallots until translucent, about 2 minutes. Add the figs, mustard seeds, sugar, vinegar, mustard, and black pepper. Reduce the heat and simmer until the figs are soft and the compote has thickened to the consistency of fruit preserves, about 20 minutes. Cool and refrigerate for 1 to 2 weeks.

Makes 2½ cups

Apple Compote

2 Fuji apples, cored, peeled, and diced
¼ cup plus 2 tablespoons fresh lime juice
¼ cup quartered dried apricots
¼ cup dried cherries
½ cup Simple Syrup (page 36)
1 cinnamon stick
Pinch of freshly grated nutmeg
1 teaspoon mustard seeds

Toss the apples with 2 tablespoons of lime juice in a bowl. Set aside. Simmer the apricots, cherries, syrup, ½ cup water, the remaining ¼ cup lime juice, cinnamon, nutmeg, and mustard seeds in a saucepan for 10 minutes. Add the apples and simmer for an additional 5 minutes. Remove the pot from the heat and let cool. Remove the cinnamon stick. Let the compote cool and refrigerate for up to 1 to 2 weeks.

Makes 2 cups

Heirloom Tomato Jam

1 pound heirloom tomatoes, seeded and chopped
½ cup sugar
1 tablespoon fresh lemon juice
½ tablespoon lemon zest, chopped
¼ teaspoon ground cumin
¼ teaspoon ground coriander
Pinch of salt
1/8 teaspoon chili flakes

Place a small saucepan over medium heat and add all the ingredients. Stir, bring to a simmer, and cook until the mixture takes on the consistency of thick syrup, about 40 to 50 minutes. Remove from the heat and set aside. The jam will keep in the refrigerator for up to 3 weeks.

Makes 2 cups

Candied Pumpkin Seeds

½ cup sugar
½ cup pumpkin seeds
Salt to taste

Preheat the oven to 350°F.
Combine the sugar and ½ cup water in a small saucepan over medium heat. Stir until the sugar is dissolved and the water begins to boil. Reduce to a simmer and using a fine-mesh strainer dip the pumpkin seeds into the simple syrup for 1 minute.

Remove the pumpkin seeds and place them on a baking sheet. Bake the pumpkin seeds for about 5 minutes or until they have browned. Remove the pumpkin seeds, sprinkle with salt, and cool completely. They will keep in a sealed container for up to 3 weeks.

Makes ½ cup

Candied Walnuts

½ cup sugar
Pinch of salt
½ cup walnuts

In a small saucepan over medium heat, combine the sugar, 2 tablespoons of water, and salt. Stir until the sugar is dissolved. Continue to cook until the mixture is medium brown, occasionally brushing the sides of the pan with a water-dipped pastry brush. Add the walnuts, mix, and then spread the mixture on a marble surface or a parchment-lined baking sheet. Allow the walnuts to cool before breaking them into desired-size pieces. They will keep in a sealed container for up to 3 weeks.

Makes ½ cup

Candied Pecans

½ cup sugar
Pinch of salt
½ cup pecan halves

In a small saucepan over medium heat, combine the sugar, 2 tablespoons of water, and salt. Stir until the sugar is dissolved. Continue to cook until the mixture is medium brown, occasionally brushing the sides of the pan with a water-dipped pastry brush. Add the pecans, mix, and then spread the mixture on a marble surface or a parchment-lined baking sheet. Allow the pecans to cool before breaking them into desired-size pieces. They will keep in a sealed container for up to 3 weeks.

Makes ½ cup

Apricot-Cured Salmon

½ cup dried apricots
½ cup Pernod
¼ cup kosher salt
¼ cup sugar
1 teaspoon whole black peppercorns
2 fennel fronds
1 pound wild salmon, skin on

Place the apricots in a bowl with ½ cup hot water and the Pernod and rehydrate for 20 minutes. Purée the apricots in a food processor. Mix the purée with the salt, sugar, pepper, and fennel fronds.

Cut a piece of cheesecloth large enough to cover the salmon. Place the cheesecloth in a large baking dish and lay the salmon skin-side down on the cheesecloth. Cover the salmon evenly with the apricot-salt mixture and wrap it with the cheesecloth.

Place another baking pan over the cheesecloth and weigh it down with at least 3 pounds of pressure (you can use water jugs, tomato cans, or even books). Refrigerate for 48 to 72 hours.

Remove the weights and unwrap the salmon. Remove the excess salt mixture from the salmon and pat dry. Slice very thin to serve.

Makes 25 to 30 nibbles

Duck Confit

12 duck legs
½ cup coarse salt
15 whole garlic cloves
1 bunch fresh thyme (about 25 sprigs)

For the confit:
3 pounds rendered duck fat (see Sources, page 318)

2 tablespoons blended oil, for searing

Trim the excess fat from the duck and reserve. Salt the duck well on both sides. Layer the duck legs on top of each other with several cloves of garlic and sprigs of thyme between each piece. Refrigerate for 24 hours.

Preheat the oven to 325°F.
Combine the rendered duck fat, duck trimmings, and 1 cup water in a pot and slowly bring to a simmer. Simmer until the water evaporates and the simmering stops, about 12 to 14 minutes.

Rinse the salt from the duck and dry it thoroughly. Place the duck in a hotel pan or deep casserole dish and cover it with the rendered fat. Cover with foil and roast for about 3½ hours. The duck is finished when the meat is easily pulled from the bone.

Chill the duck for at least 4 hours. (The confit must be chilled before cooking it.)

Preheat the oven to 400°F.

Heat the oil over high heat in an ovenproof pan until hot. Place the duck in the hot pan, skin-side down, and cook for 1 minute. Place the duck in the oven and roast for 12 to 15 minutes. Carefully remove the duck from the pan with a spatula so you don't tear the duck skin from the meat.

Serves 6

Chocolate-Dipped Hazelnut Shortbread

1 cup all-purpose flour
¼ teaspoon salt
½ cup plus 1 tablespoon unsalted butter, softened
½ cup sugar
1 large egg, beaten
½ cup finely ground toasted hazelnuts
4 ounces bittersweet chocolate, melted

Preheat the oven to 325°F.

Sift the flour and salt together. Cream the butter and sugar together in a mixer fitted with paddle attachment until smooth and creamy. Gradually beat in the egg. With the mixer on low, add the flour one spoonful at a time, followed by the ground nuts until the mixture clumps together. Lift the dough onto a sheet of plastic wrap and shape it into a 1½-inch diameter roll. Chill the dough for at least 2 hours in the refrigerator. Remove from the refrigerator and shape it into a log. Bake on a baking sheet for 15 to 20 minutes until lightly brown. Remove from the oven and let it cool to room temperature.

Slice the shortbread into ¼-inch slices and arrange them on a nonstick baking pan. Prick them with a fork and bake for 20 minutes until just browned. Cool the shortbread on a wire rack. Dip the cooled shortbread halfway up in the melted chocolate and leave on a piece of baking parchment paper to set. The shortbread will keep in a sealed container for up to 5 days.

Makes 3 dozen

Hazelnut Praline

1 cup sugar
1 cup toasted hazelnuts, chopped
Pinch of salt
Pinch of baking powder

Heat the sugar and 4 tablespoons of water in a saucepan over medium heat. Cook until the mixture is golden brown, about 5 to 7 minutes. Add the hazelnuts, salt, and baking powder and remove from the heat. Mix well. Pour the mixture onto a baking sheet and cool completely.

Once the praline is cool you can either break it into chunks or place it in a food processor and pulse into fine pieces.

This praline is perfect for dessert garnishes, ice cream, or cocktail rims. It will keep in a sealed container for up to 3 weeks.

Makes 1 cup

Hazelnut–Brandy Gelato

½ cup toasted hazelnuts
2 cups whole milk
⅔ cup heavy cream
4 large egg yolks
½ cup sugar
1 tablespoon Frangelico or brandy

Place the hazelnuts, milk, and cream in a saucepot and heat slowly to a simmer over medium heat. Remove from the heat and allow the ingredients to infuse for 1 hour. Strain the mixture and set aside.

In a separate bowl, whisk the egg yolks and sugar together until light and fluffy.

In a saucepan, whisk the milk mixture into the yolks and then add the Frangelico. Cook over low heat, stirring constantly, until the mixture reaches 175°F on a candy thermometer.

Remove the pan from the heat and chill immediately in an ice water bath. When chilled, place the mixture in an ice cream or gelato maker and proceed according to manufacturer's instructions. The gelato can be made 1 day ahead.

Serves 6

Lemon Shortbread Dough

14 tablespoons (1¾ sticks) unsalted butter
½ cup sugar
1 large egg plus 1 large egg yolk
¼ teaspoon salt
Zest of 1 lemon
1 teaspoon pure vanilla extract
2½ cups all-purpose flour

In a food processor, cream the butter and sugar. Add the egg, egg yolk, salt, lemon zest, and vanilla. Add the flour to the butter and egg mixture. Form the dough into a ball, wrap it in plastic, and refrigerate for at least 12 hours.

Preheat the oven to 350°F. Roll the dough out to the desired shape (this depends on the pan size). Prick the dough with a fork and bake for 12 to 15 minutes. If you are making miniature tarts, check them at 8 minutes. Extra dough will keep in the freezer for at least 4 months.

Makes two 11-inch tarts or twelve 3-ounce tarts
or 24 miniature tartlets

sources

A Perfect Pear
www.aperfectpear.com
Pairings - Tomato Pear Chutney, Sun-dried Tomato Tapenade

American Spoon
www.spoon.com
Pairings - Sour Cherry Preserves, Dried Red Tart Cherries, Pumpkin Butter, Bartlett Pear Preserves

Bellwether Farms
www.bellwetherfarms.com
Cheese - Carmody, Crescenza, Pepato

Beltane Ranch
www.beltaneranch.com
Bed & Breakfast, Working Ranch, Grass-fed Beef

Benziger Family Winery
www.benziger.com
Winery

Blackberry Farm
www.blackberryfarm.com
Pairings - Blackberry Jam, Farm Apple Butter, Pure Honey

BLiS
www.blisgourmet.com
Pairings - Bourbon Barrel Matured Pure Maple Syrup

Blue Chair Fruit Company
www.bluechairfruit.com
Pairings - East Coast Blueberry Jam, Apricot-Plum Jam, Bergamot Marmalade, Early Girl Tomato Jam

Bob's Red Mill
www.bobsredmill.com
Pantry - Garbanzo Bean Flour

Bohemian Creamery
www.bohemiancreamery.com
Cheese - Bo Peep, Bo Poisse, Romeo

B & R Farms
www.brfarms.com
Pairings - Blenheim Sun-Dried Apricots

Butcher & Packer
www.butcherandpacker.com
Salumi supplies

California Olive Ranch
www.californiaoliveranch.com
Olive Oil - Arbequina Extra Virgin Olive Oil, Miller's Blend Extra Virgin Olive Oil

Coldani Olive Ranch
www.calivirgin.com
Olive Oil - Premium Extra Virgin Olive Oil, Bountiful Basil Olive Oil

Cowgirl Creamery
www.cowgirlcreamery.com
Cheese - Red Hawk, Mt. Tam

Cypress Grove Chevre
www.cypressgrovechevre.com
Cheese - Humboldt Fog, Midnight Moon

D'Artagnan
www.dartagnan.com
Pantry - Duck Fat

Devil's Gulch Ranch
www.devilsgulchranch.com
Wholesale Only - rabbits, pigs

Ducktrap River Fish Farm
www.ducktrap.com
Pantry - Smoked Fish

ellelle Kitchen
www.ellellekitchen.com
Pairings - Central Coast raspberry, Santa Maria strawberry

Fastachi
www.fastachi.com
Pairings - Hazelnut Butter, Almond Butter, Sesame Honey Crunch, Nuts, Dried Fruit

Firelit Spirits
www.firelitspirits.com
Spirits - Firelit Coffee Liqueur

Fiscalini Cheese Company
www.fiscalinicheese.com
Cheese - Bandaged Wrapped Cheddar

foodzie
www.foodzie.com
Online Specialty Food Marketplace

Frog Hollow Farm
www.froghollowfarm.com
Pairings - Organic Peach Chutney, Organic Asian Pear Chutney, Nectarine-Plum Conserve

Fusion Verjus
www.verjus.com
Pantry - Verjus

GILT Taste
www.gilttaste.com
Online Specialty Food Marketplace

Giusto Flour
www.giustos.com
Pantry - Flour

Gourmet Food
www.gourmet-food.com
Online Specialty Food Marketplace
Pantry - San Giacomo Saba

Graffeo Coffee
www.graffeo.com
Graffeo Coffee

happy girl kitchen co.
www.happygirlkitchen.com
Pairings - Organic Apricot Jam, Strawberry Lavender Jam, Honeyed Pears

Harmony Farm
www.harmonyfarm.com
Farming - Vegetable Transplants

Harvest Song
www.harvestsongventures.com
Pairings - Tea-Rose Petal, Preserves, Quince Preserves, Fresh Walnut Preserves

Hector's Honey Farm
Available at Sonoma Farmer's Markets
Pairings - Honeycomb

HelloCello
www.hellosonoma.com
Spirits - Figcello di Sonoma, Limoncello

INNA jam
www.innajam.com
Pairings - seascape Strawberry Jam, nova Raspberry Jam

JC Cellars
55 4th Street - Oakland, California 94607
www.jccellars.com
Winery, Urban Tasting Room

Jimtown Store
www.jimtown.com
Pairings - Jimtown Fig & Olive Spread, Jimtown Chopped Olive Spread

Julie Higgins
www.artistjuliehiggins.com
Resident Artist at the girl & the fig and the fig café & winebar

June Taylor
www.junetaylorjams.com
Pairings - Red Cloud Apricot Conserves, Summer Sweet Peach & Fennel Conserves, Pear & Vanilla Butter

King Arthur Flour
www.kingarthurflour.com
Pantry - White Coarse Sugar, Pistachio Nut Paste

Laura Chenel's Chevre
www.laurachenel.com
Cheese - Cabecou, Chef's Chévre

L'Epicurien
www.amazon.com (to order)
www.epicurien.com (more information)
Pairings - Cider Confit with Apples & Calvados, Quince Paste, Black Cherry Confit, Sweet Onion Confit

Loulou's Garden
www.loulousgarden.com
Pairings - Rose Petal Jam, Quince Jelly, Almond Butter, Pickled Cherries

Made in Napa Valley
www.madeinnapavalley.com
*Pairings - Fig & Roasted Shallot Tapenade,
Apricot Fig Spread*

Marx Foods
www.marxfoods.com
Online Specialty Food Marketplace
*Pantry - Culinary Lavender, Dried Fruits, Kumquats,
Rabbit, Wild Boar, Carnaroli Rice*

Matiz
www.tienda.com
*Pairings - Savory Olive Oil Crisp Bread, Apricot &
Almond Cake, Fig & Walnut Cake*

Matos Cheese Factory
3669 Llano Road
Santa Rosa, California 95407
707-584-5283
Cheese - St. George

Market Hall Foods
www.markethallfoods.com
Online Specialty Food Marketplace
*Pantry - Maldon Sea Salt, Fennel Pollen, Marcona
Almonds*

McEvoy Ranch
www.mcevoyranch.com
*Olive Oil - Traditional Blend Extra Virgin Olive Oil,
Olio Nuovo Extra Virgin Olive Oil*

Mendocino Mustard
www.mendocinomustard.com
Pairings - Seeds & Suds Mustard

Nana Mae's Organics
www.nanamae.com
*Pairings - Spring Blossom Honey, Autumn Harvest
Honey, Apple Juice*

Nicasio Valley Cheese Company
www.nicasiocheese.com
Cheese - Nicasio Square

Orchard Choice - Valley Fig Growers
www.valleyfig.com
*Pairings - Orchard Choice Mission Figs, Orchard Choice
Golden Figs*

Panevino
www.panevino-napa.com
*Pairings - Original Sea Salt, Fiscalini Cheddar,
Olive & Herbs No. 6 Grissini*

Pasolivo
www.pasolivo.com
*Olive Oil - Tuscan Blend Extra Virgin, California Extra
Virgin, Citrus Blend Olive Oil, Tangerine Olive Oil*

Peaceful Valley Farm Supply
www.groworganic.com
Farming - Seeds

Point Reyes Farmstead Cheese Company
www.pointreyescheese.com
Cheese - Point Reyes Original Blue

Queener Fruit Farm
40385 Queener Drive
Scio, Oregon 97374
Pairings - Black Cherry Jam

Quince & Apple Small Batch Preserves
www.quinceandapple.com
Pairings - Pear with Honey & Ginger Preserves, Orange Marmalade with Lemons, Figs & Black Tea Preserves

Rancho Gordo Heirloom Beans
www.ranchogordo.com
Pantry - Classic Garbanzo Beans, White Tepary Beans

Redwood Hill Farm
www.redwoodhill.com
Cheese - Camellia

Robert Lambert
www.robertlambert.com
Pairings - Salt-Preserved Meyer Lemons, Bergamot Orange Marmalade

Rogue Creamery
www.roguecreamery.com
Cheese - Rogue River Blue

Rustic Bakery
www.rusticbakery.com
Pairings - Kalamata Olive Sourdough Flatbread, Walnut and Three Seed Pan Forte, Whole Grain Sourdough Lavosh

Saltworks
www.saltworks.us
Pantry - Sea Salt

Sarabeth's Kitchen
www.sarabeth.com
Pairings - Strawberry Rhubarb Jam, Chunky Apple

Sausage Maker
www.sausagemaker.com
Salumi supplies

Savannah Bee
www.savannahbee.com
Pairings - Tupelo Honey, Cheese Honey, Orange Blossom Honey

Savor California
www.savorcalifornia.com
Online Specialty Food Marketplace

Sign of the Bear
435 1st Street West
Sonoma, California 95476
707.996.3722
Goods - fine tableware, kitchenware, gadgets & linen ...

Sonoma Country Antiques
23999 Arnold Drive (Hwy 121)
Sonoma, California 95476
www.sonomaantiques.com
Goods - fine tableware, furniture, antiques & linen ...

Sonoma Market & Glen Ellen Market
www.sonoma-glenellenmkt.com
Our Neighborhood Markets - they have practically everything you could ever want!
Pantry - Wild Boar - special order, Rabbit - special order, Wondra flour, Cheese, Pantry ...

Sonoma Syrup Co.
www.sonomasyrup.com
Pairings - Meyer Lemon Cheese/Drizzler, Black Currant Berry Cheese/Drizzler, Hazelnut Syrup

Sparrow Lane
www.sparrowlane.com
Pairings - Blackberry Balsamic Vinegar

Stone Edge Farm
www.stoneedgefarm.com
Olive Oil - Extra Virgin Olive Oil

SummerVine
100 West Spain Street
Sonoma, California 95476
www.summervinesonoma.com
Goods - fine tableware, kitchenware, decors & linen ...

Terra Sonoma Food Company
www.terrasonoma.com
Pantry - Verjus

Territorial Seed Company
www.territorialseed.com
Farming - Lemon Verbena Plants

the girl & the fig
FIGfood

www.thegirlandthefig.com
Pairings - Black Mission Fig Jam, Dried Fig Compote, Apricot Fig Chutney, Raisin - Fig Mostarda, Apple - Fig Mostarda, Red Onion Confit, fig & pistachio cake

The Olive Press
www.theolivepress.com
Olive Oil - Extra Virgin Olive Oil, Citrus Olive Oils

Tumalo Farms
www.tumalofarms.com
Cheese - Classico Reserve, Pondhopper

Uniform Books & Crafts, Inc.
www.unicornbooks.com
1338 Ross Street
Petaluma, California 94954
Distributor for needlework and textile craft books

Valley Fig Growers - Orchard Choice
www.valleyfig.com
Pairings - Orchard Choice Mission Figs, Orchard Choice Golden Figs

Vella Cheese Company
www.vellacheese.com
Cheese - Vella Dry Jack

Whole Food Markets
www.wholefoodsmarket.com
Pantry - Culinary Lavender, Bee Pollen, Castelvetrano Olives, Wild Boar - special order, Rabbit - special order, Garbanzo Bean flour, Carnaroli Rice

Williams-Sonoma
www.williams-sonoma.com
Online Specialty Food Marketplace
Pantry - Demi-Glace (Beef, Chicken, Veal, Mushroom), Duck Fat, Maldon Salt

Winchester Cheese Company
www.winchestercheese.com
Cheese - Winchester Aged Gouda

Zingerman's
www.zingermans.com
Pairings - Saba Balsamic Syrup, Chestnut Honey

Cheese Pairings

Rhône-Alone Friends

Hospice du Rhône

2175 Biddle Ranch Road
San Luis Obispo, California 93401 USA
www.hospicedurhone.org
Hospice du Rhône (HdR), located on the Central Coast of California, operates as a non-profit business league with the specific purpose of improving the business conditions of the grape growers and wine producers of Rhône variety wines and grapes throughout the world. They serve as an international vintners association, providing promotional and educational opportunities through their annual wine event in Paso Robles, California USA.*

Rhône Rangers

www.rhonerangers.org
The Rhône Rangers is a non-profit, 501(c)(6) educational organization, dedicated to promoting the enjoyment of Rhône varietal wines produced in the United States.

In the 1980's, several maverick American winemakers began experimenting with Rhône-style wines and, encouraged by the results and a desire to make something other than Cabernet Sauvignon and Chardonnay, they forged ahead. These brave few soon became known as "The Rhône Rangers." By 1988, eighteen California Rhône wine producers were meeting informally to share information and courage others to follow. In August 1997, 13 wineries established a formal organization under name of "The Rhône Rangers." Today membership consists of nearly 200 wineries from California, Oregon, Washington, Michigan, and Virginia. In order to become a member of the Rhône Rangers, a winery must produce at least one Rhône-style wine, which is comprised of a minimum of 75% of one or more of the twenty-two Rhône grape varieties approved in the Cotes-du-Rhône.

A Note to the Winemakers;
I made a conscious decision not to include vintages and varietal percentages in my suggestions. Knowing that wines change from year to year and some wines may not be available every year.

Sincere apologies if I have failed to mention a wine that should have been included in the book. I wish I could have listed every amazing Rhône varietal wine that I have ever tasted, (and the details of why I enjoyed it), since we opened in 1997. This source list does not even scratch the surface of all the unique, thought-provoking and lovely wines that have come my way. Many of these wines included here jolt my memory back to a special meal, tasting or experience and many others have graced our wine list at one time or another. We have had about five or six wine buyers over the years, each with somewhat of a different palate, all with the desire to learn more about the Rhône varietals, and certainly a passion to find the most interesting selections for our guests.

There are many more wines that I have yet to try and I hope you will all continue to make them over and over again.

Wine Sources by Grape Varietal

Roussanne

Chateau de Beaucastel
Chateuneuf-du-Pape Blanc
Rhône Valley, France
Chemin de Beaucastel
84350 Courthezon, France
www.beaucastel.com   *page 226*

Copain Wine Cellars
Roussanne
James Berry Vineyard, Paso Robles
7800 Eastside Road
Healdsburg, California 95446
www.copainwines.com   *page 128*

Domaine Pierre Gaillard
Saint-Joseph Blanc
Saint-Joseph, France
Lieu-dit, Chez Favier
42520, Malleval, France
www.domainespierregaillard.com   *page 128*

Domiane Quenard Chignin "Les Terrasses"
Roussanne/Bergeron
Savoie, France
73800 Chignan
www.jf-quenard.com   *page 134*

E. Guigal
Saint-Joseph Blanc
Saint-Joseph, France
69420 Ampuis, France
www.guigal.com   *page 154*

Qupé Winery
Roussanne
Bien Nacido Estate, Santa Maria Valley
2963 Grand Avenue - Suite B
Los Olivos, California 93441
www.qupe.com   *page 136*

Sebastiani Vineyards & Winery
Roussanne
Carneros
389 Fourth Street East
Sonoma, California 95476
www.sebastiani.com   *page 166*

Stolpman Vineyards "L'Avion"
Roussanne
Central Coast
2434 Alamo Pintado Avenue
Los Olivos, California 93441
www.stolpmanvineyards.com   *page 214*

Truchard Vineyards
Roussanne
Carneros, Napa Valley
3234 Old Sonoma Road
Napa, California 94559
www.truchardvineyards.com   *page 72, 230*

Wellington Vineyards
Roussanne
Sonoma County
11600 Dunbar Road
Glen Ellen, California 95442
www.wellingtonvineyards.com   *page 44*

Zaca Mesa Winery & Vineyards
Roussanne
Santa Ynez Valley
6905 Foxen Canyon Road
Los Olivos, California 93441
www.zacamesa.com   *page 72, 94*

White Blends

Arrowood Vineyards & Winery
"Côte de Lune Blanc"
Saralee's Vineyard, Russian River Valley
14347 Sonoma Highway
Glen Ellen, California 95442
www.arrowoodwinery.com   *page 50, 304*

Atmosphere
"Dos Burros" Marsanne/Roussanne
La Prenda Vineyard, Sonoma Valley
Hoffman Family Cellars
21481 8th St East, Suite 6
Sonoma, California 95476
www.exclusivefinewines.com   *page 230*

Booker Vineyard
White Blend
Paso Robles
2640 Anderson Rd
Paso Robles, California 93446
www.bookerwines.com   *page 50*

JC Cellars
"The First Date" Roussanne/Marsanne
California
55 4th Street
Oakland, California 94607
www.jccellars.com   *page 286*

Peay Vineyards
Estate Roussanne/Marsanne
Sonoma Coast
207A. N. Cloverdale Blvd. #201
Cloverdale, California 95425
www.peayvineyards.com   *page 94, 196*

Sans Liege
"Call to Arms"
Alta Colina Vineyard, Paso Robles
870 Price St.
Pismo Beach, California 93494
www.sansliege.com   *page 306*

Tablas Creek Vineyard
"Côtes de Tablas Blanc"
Paso Robles
9339 Adelaida Road
Paso Robles California 93446
www.tablascreek.com   *page 64*

Terre Rouge Wines
"Enigma"
Sierra Foothills
PO Box 41
Fiddletown, California 95629
www.terrerougewines.com   *page 304*

Treana Winery
White Rhône Blend
Mer Soleil Vineyard, Central Coast
PO Box 3260
Paso Robles, California 93447
www.treana.com   *page 148*

Très Bonnes Années
Blanc, "the girl & the fig"
Russian River Valley
the girl & the fig
110 West Spain Street
Sonoma, California 95476
www.thegirlandthefig.com   *page 64, 118*

Zaca Mesa Winery & Vineyards
"Z Blanc" Estate
Santa Ynez Valley
6905 Foxen Canyon Road
Los Olivos, California 93441
www.zacamesa.com   *page 306*

Grenache Blanc

Beckmen Vineyards
Grenache Blanc
Purisma Mountain Vineyard, Santa Ynez Valley
2670 Ontiveros Road
Los Olivos, California 93441
www.beckmenvineyards.com   *page 156, 294*

Sans Liege
"Groundwork" Grenache Blanc
Templeton Gap
870 Price St.
Pismo Beach, California 93494
www.sansliege.com   *page 80*

Marsanne

Domaine Marc Sorrel
"Les Rocoules" Hermitage Blanc
Hermitage, France
128 bis avenue Jean-Jaures
26600, Tain-L'Hermitage, France
www.marcsorrel.fr   *page 286*

JC Cellars
Marsanne
Preston Vineyard, Dry Creek Valley
55 4th Street
Oakland, California 94607
www.jccellars.com   *page 80*

Krupp Brothers
"Black Bart" Marsanne
Stagecoach Vineyard, Napa Valley
3267 Soda Canyon Road
Napa, California 94558
www.kruppbrothers.com   *page 226*

La Diligence
Marsanne
Stagecoach Vineyard, Napa Valley
7850 Silverado Trail
Oakville, California 94562
www.minerwines.com   *page 88*

Qupé Winery
Marsanne
Santa Ynez Valley
2963 Grand Avenue - Suite B
Los Olivos, California 93441
www.qupe.com   *page 224*

Wellington Vineyards
Marsanne
Sonoma Valley
11600 Dunbar Road
Glen Ellen, California 95442
www.wellingtonvineyards.com   *page 226*

Viognier

Acacia Vineyard
Estate Viognier
Carneros, Napa Valley
2750 Las Amigas Road
Napa, California 94559
www.acaciavineyard.com   *page 292*

Alban Vineyards
Viognier
Edna Valley
8575 Orcutt Road
Arroyo Grande, California 93420
www.albanvineyards.com   *page 96*

Anaba Wines
Viognier
Landa Vineyard, Sonoma Valley
60 Bonneau Rd
Sonoma, California 95476
www.anabawines.com   *page 166*

Cave Yves Cuilleron
"Les Chaillets" Condrieu
Condrieu, France
58, RN 86 - Verlieu
42410 Chavanay
www.cuilleron.com   *page 136*

Cline Cellars
Viognier
Sonoma Coast
24737 Arnold Drive/Highway 121
Sonoma, California 95476
www.clinecellars.com   *page 186*

Domaine François Villard
Condrieu de Poncins
Condrieu, France
Montjoux 42410 Saint Michel sur Rhône
rhone.vignobles.free.fr/pagesgb/villard   *page 78*

Eberle Winery
Viognier
Mill Road Vineyard, Paso Robles
3810 East Highway 46
Paso Robles, California 93447
www.eberlewinery.com

Failla Wines
Viognier
Alban Vineyard, Edna Valley
3530 Silverado Trail
St. Helena, California 94574
www.faillawines.com

Fess Parker Winery
Viognier
Santa Barbara
6200 Foxen Canyon Road
Los Olivos, California 93441
www.fessparker.com

Graff Family Vineyards
"Chalone" Viognier
Monterey
PO Box 1753
Sonoma, California 95476
www.woodward-graffwinefoundation.org

Imagery Estate Winery
Viognier
Sonoma County
14335 Hwy 12
Glen Ellen, California 95442
www.imagerywinery.com

Kamen Estate Wines
Viognier
Sonoma Valley
PO Box 1404
Sonoma, California 95476
www.kamenwines.com

Kunde Family Estate
Viognier
Sonoma Valley
9825 Sonoma Hwy
Kenwood, California 95452
www.kunde.com

Miner Family Vineyards
Viognier
Simpson Vineyard, California
7850 Silverado Trail
Oakville, California 94562
www.minerwines.com

Stag's Leap Winery
Viognier
Napa Valley
6150 Silverado Trail
Napa, California 94558
www.stagsleap.com

Starlite Vineyards
Viognier
Sonoma County
5511 Highway 128
Geyserville, California 95441
www.starlitevineyards.com

The Ojai Vineyard
Viognier
Roll Ranch Vineyard, Ojai Valley
109 S Montgomery Street
Ojai, California 93023
www.ojaivineyard.com

Whetstone Wine Cellars
Viognier
Catie's Corner Vineyard, Russian River Valley
1075 Atlas Peak Road
Napa, California 94581
www.whetstonewinecellars.com

Yalumba
Viognier
Eden Valley, Australia
Eden Valley Road
Angaston SA 5353 Australia
www.yalumba.com

Rosé

Bedrock Wine Co.
"Ode to Lulu" Rosé of Mourvèdre
Sonoma Valley
PO Box 1826
Sonoma, California 95476
www.bedrockwineco.com

Carica Wines
Grenache Rosé
Bennett Valley
www.caricawines.com

Chateau d'Aqueria
Rosé
Tavel, France
Route Roquemaure
30126 Tavel, France
www.aqueria.com

Domaine de Nizas
Rosé
Coteaux du Languedoc
Languedoc, France
Hameau de Sallèles
34720 Caux - France
www.domainedenizas.com

Domaine Ott
Côtes de Provence Rosé
Provence
Route du Fort-de-Brégançon
83250 La Londe-les-Maures, France
www.domaines-ott.com

Domaine Tempier
Rosé
Bandol, France
1082, Chemin des Fanges
83330 Le Plan du Castellet, France
www.domainetempier.com

Les Jamelles
Cinsault Rosé
France
www.les-jamelles.com

Maison Bouachon
"La Rouviere"
Tavel, France
www.maisonbouachon.com

Mounts Family Winery
Pink Grenache
Dry Creek Valley
3901 Wine Creek Road
Healdsburg, California 95448
www.mountswinery.com

Shane Wine Cellars
"Ma Fille" Rosé
Sonoma County
www.shanewines.com

Cinsault

Black Sheep Winery
Cinsault
Dusty Lane Vineyard, California
221 Main Street
Murphys, California 95247
www.blacksheepwinery.com

Bonny Doon Vineyard
DEWN Cinsault
California
328 Ingalls Street
Santa Cruz, California 95060
www.bonnydoonvineyard.com

Frick Winery
Cinsaut
Dry Creek Valley
23072 Walling Road
Geyserville, California 95441
www.frickwinery.com

Carignane

Broc Cellars
'Carbonic' Carignane
Alexander Valley
805 Camelia St
Berkeley, California 94710
www.broccellars.com

Preston of Dry Creek
Carignane
Dry Creek Valley
9282 Dry Creek Road
Healdsburg, California 95448
www.prestonvineyards.com

Ranchero Cellars
Carignan
Redwood Valley
www.rancherocellars.com *page 98*

Mourvèdre

Broc Cellars
Mourvèdre
Luna Matta Vineyards, Paso Robles
805 Camelia St
Berkeley, California 94710
www.broccellars.com *page 272*

Cline Cellars
"Ancient Vines" Mourvèdre
Contra Costa
24737 Arnold Drive/Highway 121
Sonoma, California 95476
www.clinecellars.com *page 188*

Domaine Tempier
Mourvèdre
Bandol, France
1082, Chemin des Fanges
83330 Le Plan du Castellet, France
www.domainetempier.com *page 300*

Spann Vineyards
Mourvèdre
Lodi
12900 Maple Glen Road
Kenwood, California 95442
www.spannvineyards.com *page 298*

Torbreck Vintners
"The Pict" Mourvèdre
Barossa Valley, Australia
Lot 51, Roennfeldt Road
Marananga, SA, 5355
www.torbreck.com *page 300*

Villa Creek Cellars
"Damas Noir" Mourvèdre
Paso Robles
5995 Peachy Canyon Road
Paso Robles, California 93446
www.villacreekwine.com *page 150*

Grenache

Alban Vineyards
Grenache
Edna Valley
8575 Orcutt Road
Arroyo Grande, California 93420
www.albanvineyards.com *page 198*

Beckmen Vineyards
Grenache
Purisma Mountain, Santa Ynez Valley
2670 Ontiveros Road,
Los Olivos, California 93441
www.beckmenvineyards.com *page 150*

Broc Cellars
Grenache
Dry Stack Vineyard, Sonoma Valley
805 Camelia St
Berkeley, California 94710
www.broccellars.com *page 152*

Domaine La Barroche
"PURE"
Châteauneuf-du-Pape, France
19, avenues des Bosquets
84230 Châteauneuf du Pape, France
www.domainelabarroche.com *page 278*

Elyse Winery
"Les Corbeau" Grenache
Hudson Vineyard, Carneros
2100 Hoffman Lane
Napa, California 94558
www.elysewinery.com *page 120*

Leojami Wines
Grenache
Pierce Ranch Vineyard, Monterey County
PO Box 221062
Carmel, California 93922
www.leojamiwines.com *page 206*

Monte Oton
Garnacha
Campo de Borja, Spain
Bodegas Borsao
C/Capuchinos, 10
50540 BORJA (Zaragoza) ESPAÑA
www.bodegasborsao.com *page 256*

Peter Mathis Wines
Grenache
Sonoma Valley
287 First Street West
Sonoma, California 95476
www.mathiswine.com *page 118*

Prospect 772 Wine Company
"The Brat" Grenache
Sierra Foothills
772 Appaloosa Road
Angels Camp, California
www.prospect772.com *page 88*

Quivira Vineyards & Winery
Grenache
Wine Creek Ranch, Dry Creek Valley
4900 West Dry Creek Road
Healdsburg, California 95448
www.quivirawine.com *page 74*

Skylark Wine Company
Grenache
Mendocino County
129 Lunado Way
San Francisco, California 94127
www.skylarkwine.com *page 88*

Unti Vineyards
Grenache
Dry Creek Valley
4202 Dry Creek Road
Healdsburg, California 95448
www.untivineyards.com *page 206*

Red Rhône Blends

Arrowood Vineyards & Winery
"Côte de Lune Rouge"
Lasseter Vineyards, Sonoma
14347 Sonoma Highway
Glen Ellen, California 95442
www.arrowoodwinery.com *page 278*

Bonny Doon Vineyard
"Le Cigare Volant"
Central Coast
328 Ingalls Street
Santa Cruz, California 95060
www.bonnydoonvineyard.com *page 188*

Cyril Mares
"Mas des Bressades"
Costières de Nîmes
Mas des Bressades
à Manduel 30129, France
www.masdesbressades.com *page 256*

Domaine de Marcoux
Châteauneuf-du-Papes, Vielles Vignes
Châteauneuf-du-Papes, France
Chemin de la Gironde
84100 Chateauneuf du Pape, France
www.châteauneuf.dk/en/cdpen81.htm *page 288*

Domaine le Sang des Cailloux
Vacqueyras, France
Route de Vacqueyras
84260 Sarrians, France
www.sangdescailloux.com *page 168*

Epoch Estate Wines
"Veracity"
Paderewski Vineyard, Paso Robles
7505 York Mountain Road
Templeton, California 93465
www.epochwines.com *page 168*

Grey Stack Cellars
"The Folly"
Greywacke Vineyard, Russian River Valley
4100 Grange Road
Santa Rosa, California 95404
www.greystackcellars.com *page 238*

kunin wines
"pape star"
Central Coast
28 Anacapa Street
Santa Barbara, California 93101
www.kuninwines.com *page 232*

Cambria Winery & Vineyard
Late Harvest Viognier
Tepusquet Vineyard, Santa Maria
5475 Chardonnay Lane
Santa Maria, California 93454
www.cambriawine.com *page 48, 290*

Cave de Rasteau
Vin Doux Naturel
Rasteau, France
Route des Princes d'Orange
84110 Rasteau, France
www.rasteau.com *page 132*

Cline Cellars
Late Harvest Mourvèdre
Contra Costa
24737 Arnold Drive/Highway 121
Sonoma, California 95476
www.clinecellars.com *page 308*

Core Wine Company
"Candy Core" Late Harvest Grenache
Santa Barbara Highland
145 S. Gray St., Suite 103
Orcutt, California 93455
www.corewine.com *page 274*

d'Arenberg
"Daddy Long Legs" Tawny Port
McLaren Vale, Australia
Osborn Road
McLaren Vale SA 5171
www.darenberg.com.au *page 228*

Domaine de Durban
Muscat
Beaumes-de-Venise, France
84190 Beaumes-de-Venise, France
www.domainedurban.com *page 90, 218*

Domaine Fontanel
Rivesaltes Ambre
France
25, Avenue Jean Jaurès
66720 Tautavel
www.domainefontanel.fr *age 54, 274*

Domaine Madeloc, Pierre Gaillard
Banyuls
Banyuls, France
1 bis Avenue du Général-de-Gaulle
66650 Banyuls-Sur-Mer
www.domainespierregaillard.com *page 152*

Domaine Paul Jaboulet Aine
Muscat
Beaumes-de-Venise, France
RN 7 - Les Jalets
B.P. 46 - La Roche de Glun
26600 Tain l'Hermitage
www.jaboulet.com *page 122*

Germain-Robin
Viognier Grappa
P O Box 1059
Ukiah, California 95482
www.germain-robin.com *page 200*

Graham's, 20 Year Tawny Port
W & J Graham's
Rua Rei Ramiro 514
4400 Vila Nova de Gaia, Portugal
www.grahams-port.com *page 82, 290, 296*

Holly's Hill Vineyards
Late Harvest Roussanne
El Dorado
3680 Leisure Lane
Placerville, California 95667
www.hollyshill.com *page 48*

JC Cellars
Late Harvest Viognier
Ripken Vineyards, Lodi
55 4th Street
Oakland, California 94607
www.jccellars.com *page 54, 158*

Krupp Brothers
'Black Bart' Syrah Port
Napa Valley
3267 Soda Canyon Road
Napa, California 94558
www.kruppbrothers.com *page 208*

Loxton Cellars
Syrah Port
Sonoma Valley
11466 Dunbar Road
Glen Ellen, California 95442
www.loxtonwines.com *page 208*

M. Chapoutier
Banyuls
Languedoc-Roussillon

M. Chapoutier
Rasteau
Côtes du Rhônes
18, av Dr Paul Durand - B.P.38
26601 Tain, France
www.chapoutier.com *page 158, 308*

McCrea Cellars
Late Harvest Roussanne
Yakima Valley, Washington
11515 Eagleview Lane
Rainier, Washington 98576
www.mccreacellars.com *page 138*

Noval LB Finest Reserve Porto
Quinto do Noval
AV.Diogo Leite, 256
4400-111 Vila Nova de Gaia, Portugal
www.quintadonoval.com *page 302*

Ramos Pinto
Tawny Porto
Portugal
Av. Ramos Pinto,
400 - Vila Nova de Gaia, Portugal
www.ramospinto.pt *page 218*

Salamandre Wine Cellars
Late Harvest Viognier
Arroyo Seco
108 Don Carlos Drive
Aptos, California 95003
www.salamandrewine.com *page 296*

Truchard Vineyards
Late Harvest Roussanne
Carneros, Napa Valley
3234 Old Sonoma Road
Napa, California 94559
www.truchardvineyards.com *page 228*

Warre's 10 Year Premium
Tawny Port
Portugal
Symington Family Estates
Travessa Barão de Forrester 86
Apartado 26
4431-901 Vila Noa de Gaia, Portugal
www.warre.com *page 242*

Wellington Vineyards
Old Vine Port
Sonoma Valley
11600 Dunbar Road
Glen Ellen, California 95442
www.wellingtonvineyards.com *page 234*

Yalumba
Antique Tawny Port
Australia
Eden Valley Road
Angaston SA 5353 Australia *page 132 , 290*

index

Page numbers in *italics* refer to captions.

the girl & the fig
110 West Spain Street
Sonoma, California 95476
707-938-3634
www.thegirlandthefig.com

Country Food with a French Passion
Open daily for Lunch and Dinner
Plats du Jour Menus
Friday - Saturday late night Brasserie menu
Sunday Brunch
Unique Rhône-Alone Wine List, Wine Flights,
Garden Patio Dining, Full Bar featuring Aperitifs,
House Cocktails, and Local Beer.
Salon du Fromage; Cheese Sampling, Retail Cheese,
and FIGfood products made by the girl & the fig.
Reservations Suggested.

the fig cafe & winebar
13690 Arnold Drive
Glen Ellen, California 95442
707-938-2130
www.thefigcafe.com

Country French Home Cooking
Open nightly for Dinner
Weekend Brunch
Wine & Beer Only, Complimentary Wine Corkage Always
No Reservations
Private Parties, To Go Orders

ESTATE
400 West Spain Street
Sonoma, California 95476
707-933-3663
www.estate-sonoma.com

Country Food with an Italian Accent
Open nightly for Dinner
Family Dinner Menus Nightly
Sunday Bubbles & Brunch
Garden Patio Dining Full Bar featuring Aperitivos,
Specialty House Cocktails, Grappa Bar
Local and Italian Wines
Complimentary Wine Corkage Tuesday through Thursday
Private Dining Room, Private Parties
Reservations Suggested

the girl & the fig CATERS!
21800 Schellville Road
Suite C
Sonoma, California 95476
707-933-3667
www.figcaters.com

the girl & the fig CATERS! provides food and service
for weddings, full service catered lunches and dinners,
hors d'ouevres parties and receptions, picnic lunches
and Sunday Brunches.

FIGfood
21800 Schellville Road
Suite C
Sonoma, California 95476
866-420-3447 ext. 7
www.thegirlandthefig.com

Delicious condiments for easy entertaining. Perfect pairings for
cheese, charcuterie and salumi. Available wholesale and retail.